The Folklore
of Radnorshire

The Folklore of Radnorshire

by
Roy Palmer

Logaston Press

LOGASTON PRESS
Little Logaston Woonton Almeley
Herefordshire HR3 6QH

First published by Logaston Press 2001
Reprinted 2007
Copyright © Roy Palmer 2001

ISBN 978 1873827 17 8

Set in Times by Logaston Press
and printed in Great Britain by
Antony Rowe, Chippenham, Wiltshire

to the memory of my parents,
George and Gwen Palmer,
and my parents-in-law, Jim and Mabel Madin

If you do not like legends, keep out of Radnorshire, for here you can hardly avoid them. *County Handbook*, nd (?1950s)

The numerous traditions and tales, which in the past have been the poetry that brightened the grey lives of the uneducated poor of Radnorshire, will be treasured by their more enlightened descendants to while away their lesisure hours, to point some morals and to adorn their literature.
D.E. Owen (1911)

Contents

Acknowledgements

I am indebted to a wide range of writers, including the indefatigable W.H. Howse, as can be seen from my bibliography, and a number of them—Dr Owen Davies, Anthony Edwards, George Lewis, Mona Morgan and Keith Parker—have provided further assistance in addition to their published work. I am very grateful for help from Dr Brian Davies and Rev. Richard Hart, and I should also like to thank Peter Barnes, Nigelle de Bar Baskerville, Douglas Brooks, Rev. Alan Charters, Mrs Jean Christopher, Dr Mary-Ann Constantine, Dr Rhiannon Davies, Mr Robert M. Deakins, Rev. R.W.D. Fenn, Bob Jenkins, Douglas Jones, Tegwyn Jones, Dr Phyllis Kinney, Rev. Andrew Loat, Lyn Lloyd, Roger Pye, Mike Reynolds, Mrs S. Reynolds, Geoff Ridyard, Jeremy Sandford, Dr Hugh Shields and Philip Weaver.

My greatest debt is to my wife, Pat, who has accompanied me on many expeditions to Radnorshire, taken photographs, and inscribed music examples.

I should also like to thank the staffs of these bodies: Herefordshire Libraries, Gloucestershire Libraries, Lambeth Palace Library, Llandrindod Wells Library, National Library of Wales, Powys County Council, Powys Radnor Federation of Women's Institutes, Powys County Archives, Radnorshire Society, Royal Commission on the Ancient & Historical Monuments of Wales, Telford Library, University of Wales Library, Lampeter.

For permission to reproduce illustrations I thank the Ashmolean Museum, Oxford: 105 (upper); Hereford City Library: 33, 35, 54, 123; Pat Palmer: x (upper and lower), 4, 7, 10, 19, 22, 23, 51, 53, 59, 78, 80, 85, 87, 94, 103, 105 (lower), 106, 111, 113, 114, 124, 125, 128, 129, 130, 131 (upper), 132 (upper and lower), 133, 136, 137, 139, 142, 146, 152, 165, 166, 188, 197, 199, 201, 202, 204, 205, 222, 235 (all taken in 1999 or 2000); Powys County Archives: 81, 93, 160; and Roger Pye: 183.

Introduction

Although Radnor—'red hill' in Old English—was first recorded in one of Offa's charters in 774, the county came into existence only as a result of Henry VIII's Act of Union which joined Wales to England in 1536. Almost four and a half centuries later Radnorshire lost its autonomy to Powys, newly-created albeit with an ancient name, in the reorganisation of local government which came into effect in 1974. The former county retained some powers as a district council, but even these were lost in 1996 when Powys became a unitary authority. Some signs marking Radnorshire's ancient boundaries remain, but they will not be replaced when they fall into disrepair. The Brecon and Radnor constituency still sends an MP to Westminster and an assembly member to Cardiff.

The old county was small, covering some 500 square miles only, and it never completely lived down the seventeenth-century jibe:

> In Radnorshire is neither knight nor peer,
> Nor park with deer, nor gentleman with five hundred a year,
> Except Sir William Fowler of Abbey Cwm Hir.

Of its four towns—Knighton, Presteigne, Rhayader and Llandrindod Wells—the last and largest can boast a population of only 5,000. The whole county mustered just 23,630 people at the 1991 census, exceeding the figure of a century earlier by merely 3,500.

Small, perhaps, but also beautiful. A.G. Bradley called it 'a delightful Arcady', and George Bernard Shaw remarked that 'No man ought to be in the government of this land who does not spend three months every year in country such as this'. Beautiful, perhaps, but not arcadian. Radnorshire's past has often been bloody and bitter; its present suffers from shortage of work, low wages and lack of public transport.

As for the people, Lipscomb, who passed this way in 1799, wrote that 'every day [they] gave us fresh proofs of the generosity of their disposi-

The wording on Jonathan Williams's grave at Eyton,
near the south porch of the church

tions and the unaffected politeness of which we had so often heard'. Such opinions were not universal, though. The vicar of New Radnor, Dean Merewether, described his parishioners in 1845 as 'smock-frocks, hobnails and insolent persons'. I have to say that in our travels in the county my wife and I have met the Lipscomb rather than the Merewether pattern. One landowner, hearing that we lived in Gloucestershire, said 'Oh, the flat country'. Had he not heard, we thought, of the Cotswolds? but then reflected that the Cotswolds would be hard pressed to rival Radnor Forest.

Radnorshire inspires strong feelings of affection and loyalty, not least among those interested in tradition. 'It is possible that Radnorshire is the richest mine of folklore in England and Wales', commented H.J. Massingham in 1949. He, like all who have written on the county from the nineteenth century onwards, is indebted to Jonathan Williams's pioneering history. Williams,

Plaque to Francis Kilvert at Clyro

born in 1754, the second son of a Rhayader tradesman, took a degree at Oxford, then combined the curateship at Eyton, Herefordshire, with the post of first headmaster at Leominster Grammar School. His work on Radnorshire, inspired by Theophilus Jones's *History of the County of Brecknock*, was completed by about 1815 but remained unpublished in his lifetime—he died in 1829. It appeared in instalments in the periodical, *Archaeologia Cambrensis*, between 1855 and 1858, before coming out in book form in 1859. Its re-issue, fittingly, at Rhayader in 2000 is a measure of the perennial interest it commands.

Less than 40 years after the death of Jonathan Williams another clergyman came to Radnorshire. Francis Kilvert officiated at Clyro from 1865 until 1872 and at St Harmon from 1876-7. During the late 1860s he began to compile a book on the folklore of Radnorshire. His manuscript does not survive, but an article drawing on it was written by his wife's niece, Essex Smith (later Hope) and published in the *Occult Review* in 1921, 17 years before Kilvert's more celebrated diary began to appear.

William Plomer's three-volume selection (1938-40) was drawn from a typed transcript (later destroyed) of the surviving manuscript diaries. On the evidence of one of these later published in its entirety, Plomer chose only half its contents. In the 1960s the writer, Jeremy Sandford, made a radio programme on Kilvert, after which he received a congratulatory letter from Mrs Hope, then living in Hove, Sussex, and an invitation to call on her. In due course he did so, and over the tea cups Mrs Hope handed him a leather-bound A5 notebook with pages covered with spidery writing in brown ink and said: 'I'd like you to have this. It's one of only three that are left'. With a sense of 'exhilaration and shock', Sandford realised that this was one of the original Kilvert diaries. The volume eventually went to the National Library of Wales, which published a full transcript in 1982.

Habent sua fata libelli (books have their own destinies). As appears from my list of acknowledgements, they have been indispensable to my attempt to write on Radnorshire folklore. I have also deeply appreciated conversations and correspondence with past and present residents in the county which have contributed greatly to my knowledge (if I may amend David Cannadine's formula) of 'the unending dialogue between the living and the dead that is the essence of folklore'.

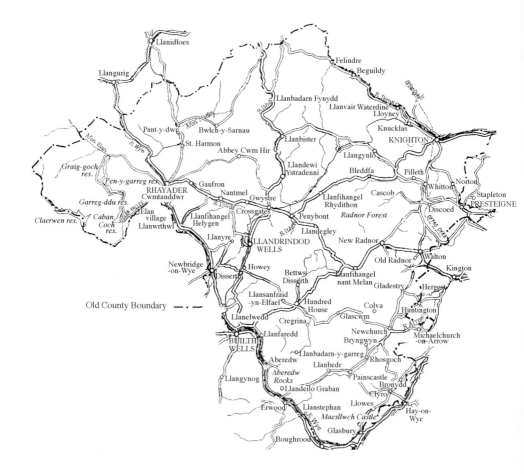

Radnorshire

CHAPTER 1

Landscape

'Oh, Aberedw, Aberedw' wrote Francis Kilvert with anguished longing in 1875, a decade after 'the day never to be forgotten when I walked over the hills from Clyro to Builth and first saw the Rocks of Aberedw, the day I first saw Painscastle and the ruined church of Llanbedr, and the morning sun shining like silver upon Llanbychllyn'. As well as being acutely aware of the beauties of Radnorshire's landscape Kilvert was also interested in the stories attached to it. This chapter explores some of the tales and traditions associated with rivers and streams, lakes and wells, standing stones and circles, hills and mounds.

Rivers and Streams

Several rivers rise in Radnorshire, including the Lugg, the Ithon and the Teme, the last of which marks the boundary with Shropshire. To the west 'the often wand'ring Wye' serves as 'the famous bound/'Twixt the *Brecknockian* earth, and the *Radnorian* ground'. So said Michael Drayton, whose long topographical poem, *Polyolbion* (1612-22), mentions woodnymphs urging the Wye onward from the Radnor bank. It also lists some of the Wye's feeders:

> First, *Clarwen* cometh in
> With Clarwy: which to them their consort *Eland* win
> To aid their goodly *Wye*; which *Ithon* gets again.
> She *Dulas* draws along: and in her wat'ry train
> *Clowedock* hath recourse, and *Comran*; which she brings
> Unto their wandering flood from the *Radnorian* Springs:
> As *Edwy* attends, and *Matchwy* forward heaves
> Her Mistress.

1

Aberedw Rocks, by Thomas Jones, from the 1905 edition of
J. Williams, A General History of the County of Radnor

There are inaccuracies. For example, the Elan receives the Claerwen before it joins the Wye. Yet the litany of names is just as lively now as when Drayton wrote. Dylan Thomas put more than one of them into the mouth of Rev. Eli Jenkins in *Under Milk Wood*: 'Edw, Eden, Aled, all ... Claerwen, Cleddau, Dulais, Daw'. Many of the names were recorded very early: the Teme in 757-75; the Wye (as Gwy) in *c*.800; the Lugg in *c*.1000. The Elan and the Ithon appeared in writing in the twelfth century. Teme probably means dark river and Lugg, bright, from the Welsh, *llug*. The latter characteristic is shared by the Arrow, from *arian*, silver. The Edw, Elan and Ithon are, respectively, flying, leaping and talking river; the Clwedog, humming stream. The Wye, whose name, essentially, means just water, is celebrated for its beauty as well as feared for its power. 'A rather wicked river' is how a Mrs Butler of Glasbury put it to H.J. Massingham, perhaps reflecting the Wye's reputation for wanting at least one human victim a year. She also had a version of a charming story shared by people in several counties washed by the Wye:

> Mother Plynlimon had three daughters, Rheidol, Severn and Wye,
> and bade them all to make the best of their way to the sea. Rheidol

The old bridge at Rhayader from a postcard

obeyed to the letter and fetched up in the sea by the shortest and directest route [near Aberystwyth]. Severn thought more of her own importance and, preening and giving herself Narcissus airs of grandeur took much longer to reach her destination. But Wye became so enamoured with the loveliness of the country through which she passed that she kept pausing and looking round and wandering about to fill her being with so much beauty. And so, though she set out from the same place and arrived at the same journey's end, she travelled twice as far as Severn and took twice as long to get there.

The rapids on the Wye at Rhayader which supplied its Welsh name of Rhaeadr Gwy (Wye waterfall) are now greatly diminished, thanks to road-works in the eighteenth century and waterworks (see below) in the twentieth. However, the cataract called Water-break-its-neck on the Black Brook near Llanfihangel Nant Melan remains spectacular. Its 70-foot, stream-fed plunge, already 'much admired by travellers' when B.H. Malkin wrote his book, *The Scenery, Antiquities, and Biography of South Wales* (1804), still attracts many visitors. Signs of new age style offerings appear here from time to time, for reasons which remain obscure.

Water-break-its-neck in Radnor Forest

A rather less accessible but no less spectacular waterfall is at Craig-Pwll-Du (Black pool crag) a short distance up the River Bachawy from its confluence with the Wye. Malkin had this to say about it: 'The story is, that one of the ancient princes had a castle here, where he kept his prisoners; and that he gratified the magnanimous propensities of his nature, by hurling them, in rotation, from the top of the rock into the dark pool below'. Three-quarters of a century later, Kilvert heard a variation on the tale from a local molecatcher: 'Here stood the tower of a Welsh robber chieftain, who ravaged the country and carried off captives to his strong-hold; if they were not ransomed, he hurled them from the top of the crag into the Black Pool far below'.

The story seems to have faded from local memory, though one of the pool's victims is remembered, a man acting as lookout for a gang of salmon poachers who fell in and drowned. Kilvert's molecatcher said he had been present at an attempt to test the belief that the pool was bottomless: 'A hundred-pound weight was tied to the knotted bellropes of Trewerne church and lowered down, but even this length of rope could not reach the bottom'. In fact, there is no Trewern Church, though Trewern Hill rises close to Craig-Pwll-Du; but bellropes could have been borrowed from Llandeilo Graban or Llanstephan. However, when members of the Woolhope Club visited the pool in 1867 one of their number claimed that he had found it to be just 9 feet deep.

4

Apart from such matters, Kilvert was greatly impressed by the grandeur of the scene:

> Through a narrow rift in huge black rocks burst a tumultuous mass of snowy foam that plunged forty feet into the black boiling pool below, with a thunderous roar that made the cliffs tremble. Rising sheer from the water's edge, the cliffs stood up black and towering round the pool, while the rocks reeked and dripped continually with the spray.

Lakes and Pools

Perhaps the most famous lakes in Radnorshire are man-made. The construction of dams on the River Elan above Rhayader, completed in 1904, established the reservoirs of Caban coch (Red hut), Carreg ddu (Black rock), Craig goch (Red crag) and Pen y garreg (Top of the rock). A further huge dam followed on the River Claerwen, built between 1946 and 1952.

These reservoirs are now a tourist attraction but the drowning of fields, farms and houses caused much sadness and some anger. People, especially those displaced, carried to the end of their lives a mental picture of the lost parts of two valleys. Beneath the water of Caban coch are two sandstone blocks which once stood by the Elan and were known as the Devil's Clogs. They acquired their name when a local man bet the devil that he could not jump, before cock-crow and with a great stone in the heel of each boot, across the valley from Y Foel to Craig Cnwch (The Hill to Hillock Crag). When he tried to win the wager the devil left his leap too late. The cock crowed while he was still in flight, and the stones crashed to the ground. There they remained to mark the incident until they were lost beneath the rising waters.

Another sinister landmark could be seen close to where the Pen y garreg dam now stands. Beside a footbridge over the Elan the prints of a human foot and a cloven hoof were incised three inches deep in a rock. Many were afraid to cross the bridge. Bolder spirits did so, but even they were reluctant to glance back lest they saw the devil. Near the same place before the bridge was erected, a notorious sheep stealer called Shoni Fechan made an epic leap over the Elan to escape from a party of men in hot pursuit.

Shoni is not commemorated in the new visitors' centre, but Shelley is. The poet spent the summer of 1812 in the mansion of Nantgwillt, which later served as the model for Nant Escob in Francis Brett Young's novel,

The House under the Water. Shelley's pastimes of riding the turbulent Elan on a plank, sometimes with a protesting cat as passenger, and of launching on the river miniature paper boats with five pound notes as sails stayed in local memory for a hundred years. Cwmelan House where he stayed in 1811 and whence he eloped with Harriet Westbrook was still known as 'Shelley's House' when the waters of Caban coch engulfed it in 1904.

Other Radnorshire lakes have more ancient histories. Gerald of Wales relates that on the night of 1 December 1135 when the English king, Henry I, died in Normandy two pools near the Wye, one artificial and the other natural, both suddenly burst their banks. Water from the first quickly flowed away but the second pool 're-formed itself, with all its fish and whatever else lived in it, in a certain valley not more than two miles away'. Henllyn (Old lake), lying between Llandeilo and Llanbedr, may be where the mysterious flow started, and Llanbwchllyn (Buck grove lake) where it finished. The latter, at nine or ten acres in extent, is the biggest natural lake in the county.

Cwm Elan before it was turned into a reservoir,
as drawn by R. Eustace Tickell in 1893 and published in his book
The Vale of Nantgwilt *(1894)*

Richard Williams of Clyro told Kilvert this story of chieftains he called 'Normandy Kings':

> One of them lived at Cefn y Blaen, one at Llanshifr, another at Great Gwernfydden. The one who lived at Painscastle was a giant. This giant carried off to Painscastle 'screaming and noising' Miss Phillips of the Screen Farm near Erwood whom he found disporting herself with her lover Arthur on or at Bychllyn Pool. Arthur sent for help to Old Radnor Castle and Cefn y Blaen. At Cefn y Blaen there were then 40 men each 7 feet high. The giant on the other hand sent for succour to Court Evan Gwynne where there was an 'army', also to Hay Castle and Lord Clifford of Clifford Castle. While these hostile forces were converging upon Painscastle, a woman in the castle favoured the girl's escape and dressed her in man's clothes to this end. Arthur watching for her outside and not knowing of the disguise, seeing what he thought was a man and one of his enemies coming out of the castle shot his lover dead with an arrow. Arthur then furious stormed the castle with a battle axe: took it and killed the giant. Next day the opposing parties arrived at the Rhos Goch, there was a fearful battle near Rhyd Llydan and the Painscastle party was defeated with great slaughter by the forces from Old Radnor and Cefn y Blaen.

The Claerwen Dam

A different version of the affair was related in 1923 by M.L. Dawson:

> Tradition records that a beautiful girl (daughter of one of the descendants of the old native reguli [petty kings, chieftains]) residing at Yscryn (now Skreen in the neighbourhood of Llandilo [*sic*] Graban) was disporting herself with her female attendants on the lake of Bwchllyn, some two miles from Painscastle. They were observed by de Braose [of Painscastle] and his followers returning from hunting. Enamoured of her beauty, he caused the whole party to be taken forcibly to the castle, where they were detained. Her relatives sought her in vain, though suspicion turned to the Norman lords and the castle was watched. After a short time the lady contrived to place at night a locket or token of her house over a lighted candle in an upper window of the castle.
>
> This was at last observed by her friends, and the suspicion of her incarceration confirmed. Petition was at once made to Prince Rhys, then [in 1196] besieging Radnor, to come and rescue his fair relative and dependent. He promised compliance as soon as he had demolished Radnor, and this done, he marched at once on Painscastle. The de Braose feigned ignorance of his mission, but at night, the signal being repeated, Prince Rhys announced his determination to attack the castle if the lady was not at once restored.
>
> His request was unnoticed, and a strong contingent coming to the assistance of the garrison from a dependency of the castle, Court Evan Gwynne, de Braose marched out and gave battle to his assailants in the plain below. A sanguinary engagement ensued, and the waters of Bachawy were turned red with blood. The crimson stream floated far down the Wye, keeping its separate course and colour unmingled with the waters of that river, and conveying the tidings of the battle to the inhabitants of the valleys. Victory, however, rewarded the gallantry of Prince Rhys. The fair prisoner was discovered and released, and the castle much despoiled.

So strong was the hold of the story that it came also to be applied to or confused with events of the 1280s when Rhys ap Maredudd, formerly allied with England, rose in revolt. He captured a stronghold—Painscastle, then called Castle Maud (see chapter 8)—and left there his English wife of two years' standing, Ada de Hastings. While Rhys was away fighting elsewhere the castle was besieged then captured. Before it fell the lady escaped with the garrison and was re-united with her husband.

The name of Llyn Cawr (Giant's Lake) near the top of Aberedw Hill is explained by a local story. A giant called Rhys Goch lived nearby in a castle—the place is still known as Pencastell—overlooking a great lake. His fairy mother had her own castle about a mile away at Llanrech or Lwyn y wrach (Fairy grove), where a frequent visitor was Edwy, a young chieftain who came rowing across the lake in his coracle to pay court to the fairy's daughter, Meilwn. For some reason, Rhys Goch favoured another of his sister's admirers, Rhys Ddu; the two of them picked a fight with Edwy and killed him. Aware in a flash of what had happened, the fairy caused the earth to open, fill with water and drown the murderers: hence Llyn Cawr and, close by, Askal Pool. Three prominent mounds rose at her command to commemorate the tragedy, and so that they could be joined for ever she turned the two lovers into water spirits—and the Meilwn still flows into the Edwy, near Hendre Bridge.

Llyn Gwyn, a few miles south-east of Rhayader, is reputedly called after Gwyn ap Nudd, warrior, hunter and ruler of Annwn (the underworld) in the time of King Arthur. Like others in the remote hills of Radnorshire, this lake was thought to be a haunt of the fairies. In the 1940s Robert Gibbings heard of 'an exceptionally beautiful maiden inhabiting the water', and W.H. Howse wrote that 'The natives shun it [the lake] at night'. A different kind of fear concerns the lake's reputed bottomlessness. One man, unwittingly carried by his horse over the frozen surface during a blinding snowstorm, is said to have dropped dead with terror on learning where he had been.

Tradition says that a now-lost town stood on one side of the lake. Carp in the water are claimed to be descendants of fish introduced by the monks of Abbey Cwm Hir. Alternatively, when St Patrick, on his way to a meeting with St David, rested with his followers on the adjacent common, Rhosfa (Little moor), he was for some reason insulted by local people, so promptly turned them into fish and consigned them to the lake. Many believed at least that Patrick had been there, and in early Christian times the lake became a place of pilgrimage. Yet another tale concerns the trout of Llyn Gwyn. When the monasteries were dissolved by Henry VIII, one of the monks of Strata Florida (of which Abbey Cwm Hir was a dependency), was so incensed that he travelled to the lake and prayed that from then on every trout caught should protest by croaking. The place soon became known as the lake of the croaking trout, and people would eat no fish caught there.

High in the uplands, Radnorshire is dotted with small peaty tarns called mawn pools, from the Welsh for peat. Doctor's Pool on Glangwye Farm between Boughrood and Glasbury is said to be where a doctor on horse-back drowned after fording the Wye, though neither horse nor rider was ever found. The explanation as to why St Michael's Pool near Llangynllo is so called is not clear; perhaps, like St Teilo's Pool near Llandeilo, it was used for baptisms. Gaer (Camp) Pool in the hills above Llanddewi Ystradenni derives its name from the three ancient camps or hill-forts nearby.

Llyn Heilyn or Hilyn, a short distance from the Fforest Inn, has lugubrious associations to this day for people living nearby. John Lloyd, known as Silver John, a noted bonesetter and animal healer, drove himself in his gambo to the Michaelmas Fair at Builth. When he failed to return to his home in the Harley Valley relatives and friends organised searches, which proved fruitless.

A few months later Radnor's Candlemas Fair was held on the ice of the frozen Llyn Heilyn. (In warmer seasons its one mile circumference served as a horse-racing circuit.) Fires were lit round the edge. People drank hot cider and ate cakes. Among the many skaters was the Fforest Inn land-lord's daughter. She slipped and fell, face down. Through the thick ice she saw the remains of Silver John.

He had presumably been murdered for the silver buttons and buckles which rewarded him for his healing work (see chapter 4). No one was ever brought to justice for the crime, but a chilling local verse put the blame on New Radnor men:

Llyn Heilyn

LANDSCAPE

Silver John is dead and gone,
So they came home a-singing;
Radnor boys pulled out his eyes
And set the bells a-ringing.

At one time, to recite this in the hearing of a New Radnor man was asking for trouble, and at the markets in Builth anyone from Radnorshire might be taunted with it. As for Silver John, when the ice melted on Llyn Heilyn his body was taken home for burial. He lies above Niblett's Quarry on the slopes of Great Greigiau in a grave above which the grass always grows green; but his spirit haunts Llyn Heilyn. Well into the twentieth century, children who would not go to sleep were warned that Silver John would come and take them away.

Springs and Wells

Writing in 1947, William Hatfield described Craig-y-don, a wooded outcrop just outside Knucklas, and an associated custom:

> It consists of a huge, stupendous rock containing a very capacious chasm, and watered by a clear and murmuring stream coming from the hill above. Hither the young people of Knighton were wont, till of late years, to resort on Sunday evenings, to drink the water of this pellucid spring, sweetened with sugar, and to hold social and friendly converse with each other. This custom undoubtedly originated in the veneration anciently paid to the occupier of this rock, whose name was Donna, a sainted recluse. He lived in the seventh century; the chasm in the rock was his bed; the spring supplied his beverage; and the roots that grew nigh and spontaneously were his food.

Hatfield added, somewhat incongruously, that when he was a boy the rock was known as the Devil's Chair. He also mentioned the local tradition that an underground passage led from there beneath the River Teme to Skyborry, a hamlet on the Shropshire side.

The notion of teenagers gathering to sup sweetened water is very hard to accept, but in his *History of Radnorshire*, published in 1859 but written some 40 years earlier, Jonathan Williams gives two more instances. The custom continued at Llanfihangel Rhydithon at the annual wake, when after drinking the water young people 'conclude the day with the dance,

11

and other innocent amusements'. At Rhayader 'heretofore'—and therefore, no longer—the same 'salutary beverage' had been drunk on Sunday evenings in spring and summer at St Mary's Well (Ffynnon Fair).

Even when these gatherings ended, a belief persisted that the well could bring young couples good luck, so they would make a point of including it in their walks. Within recent memory some believed they could find relief from anxiety or a problem by uttering at the well the (fairly meaningless) words: 'Frimpanfroo,/Frimpanfroo,/Sali bwli la/Iri a'. In addition, the water was considered good for health in general and eyes in particular. Francis Jones in his book, *The Holy Wells of Wales* (1954), commented: 'I have had the pleasure of speaking to many people who were bathed in that well as children'. It is no longer there, but was at the spot on the Llangurig road by Wye View Cottages where water still seeps from shaly rock.

Rhayader babies were also bathed in what was thought to be exceptionally pure water in a particular stream, which they might also be given to drink. This was the Bwgi, which flowed through North and West Streets (until it was culverted in 1877) and served as the town's water supply. It featured in the saying: '*Adarn Bwgi, glanha ynghymry*' (Drinking Bwgi [makes] the fairest Welsh children); and also in the couplet:

> The fairest children Wales can have
> Are those that dip in Bwgi's wave.

In addition, local people said that 'He who dips his feet in the Bwgi will come back again'.

Another St Mary's Well is situated close to the north side of the tower of Pilleth Church. J.A. Bradney described it in 1923 as 'formerly in great repute as beneficial to the eyes', but people still go there, if not for the medicinal, then for the spiritual help it is thought to give. By contrast, the appeal of Jacket's Well, less than half a mile from the centre of Knighton, seems to have faded. The name may be a corruption of the Welsh, *iachâd* (healing)—the water, renowned for its extreme coldness, was considered good for sprains and rheumatism—but the well was earlier known as St Edward's. Knighton Church is the only one in Wales dedicated to this Saxon king killed at Corfe in 978.

Two possible origins, one saintly and one secular, were claimed for a spring to the west of Llanbadarn Fynydd, near the hamlet of Llaethdy.

Some called it Ffynnon Dewi (David's Well). and in 1986 a local resident offered this explanation to Bryan Lawrence:

> It appears that St David was on an itinerary through Wales and when reaching the Llaithddu area he felt tired and thirsty. Seeing a cottage at the side of the road he enquired of the occupier, Edward of Snailshorn (a *Ty un nos* [a one night—that is, a squatter's—house] near the road by Fforddlas) where he could have a drink. Edward directed him to the well where David refreshed himself and after doing so he blessed the well.

A different school of thought called the spring Ffynnon Dafydd y Gof (Well of David the Smith), after the man credited with its discovery. Either way, the water, described by Jonathan Williams as 'strongly impregnated with sulphur and ... extremely efficacious in all cutaneous and scorbutic afflictions', was famous for miles around. Within living memory crowds came from all the nearby villages on Sunday evenings, together with visitors from Knighton, Llandrindod Wells, New Radnor, Rhayader, and parts of Herefordshire. They may not have been impressed when mangy dogs were bathed in the water, as indeed happened. Dog owners also travelled long distances to a sulphur spring on Temple Bar Farm at St Harmon whose water as well as curing the mange had the reputation of being something of a panacea for both dogs and humans.

Ffynnon Gynidr, about $1^{1}/_{2}$ miles north-east of Glasbury, took its name from St Cynidr, who was born close by. Converts were probably baptised there; and, as with a number of wells, the belief could have arisen that the water brought not only spiritual salvation but physical benefit. For centuries pilgrims visited the well but by the 1940s it was considered good only for making wishes. Until much more recently nonconformist sects conducted open-air baptisms at, for example, the spring in Parson's Dingle at Vron Farm, Beguildy, and in a pool on the Llaethdy stream in the hamlet of the same name. However, they do not seem to have generated the same odour of sanctity as Ffynnon Gynidr.

A different psychology again was at work at Disserth's Well of St Cewydd. Cewydd, who lived in the sixth century, spent a long time in the cave at Aberedw later associated with Llewelyn (see chapter 8). A thousand years after the saint's time a belief persisted that the first woman who dressed the well with mistletoe after midnight on New Year's Eve could then draw a pitcher of water known as the crop or cream of the well. This had the property, Edward Lhuyd noted when he went to Disserth in the 1690s, of beautifying those who washed in it. According to D.E. Owen, vicar of nearby Llanelwedd from 1900 to 1911, the custom by then had 'long ceased' though it was remembered by the older generation.

Certain wells seem to have been used solely for their medicinal value, with no added belief system. Many, in addition to some of those already mentioned, catered for skin problems through their sulphur content. These include springs in the parishes of Glascwm (at Blaen Edw), Llananno (Ffynnon Newydd, or New Well), Llanbadarn Fawr (near the Alpine Bridge on the River Ithon), Llanbister and Llandegley (near the River Cymaron).

Others were sought for their help with eye problems such as styes, soreness or irritation at Pen-lan and Tir y Mynach, both near Clyro, and at Presteigne and Llandrindod. The Eye Well at Llandrindod, now in Rock Park near the chalybeate spring, was used, according to tradition, as far back as Roman times. Some users followed the precise ritual which a Mrs Arthur Webb described to Francis Jones:

> 1. The visitor started to walk to the well taking a certain number of paces. 2. He uttered an incantation [unfortunately forgotten] in a low voice. 3. He then dipped the fingers of his right hand in the well and applied the water to one eye. 4. He then did the same to the other eye with the other hand. 5. It was forbidden to wipe the eyes after this bathing, and if they smarted and produced tears this was to the good.

From do-it-yourself treatment some wells moved to a more commercial basis. Blaen Edw today can be reached only by footpath or farm track, yet in the late eighteenth century the combined farm and inn there boasted 'a commodious bath and waters not inferior to those of Harrowgate' (in Yorkshire), at least according to an advertisement in the *Hereford Journal* of 27 June 1798.

Llandegley now shows barely a trace of its past as a spa, reputed for treating, among other ailments, St Tecla's disease or the falling sickness. However, its sulphurous and chalybeate springs were well frequented in the eighteenth century and fell out of favour only by the middle of the nineteenth. On his way from Gloucester to Aberystwyth in 1837, Thomas Turner stopped at Llandegley and remarked: 'We found at this secluded spot a comfortable and very neat inn, which was chiefly occupied by a party of ladies, who were sojourning here for the benefit of the waters'.

Turner went on to Llandrindod Wells, just a few miles away. Although the Romans probably did take the waters there, the first recorded instance was not until 1696 when members of the Vaughan family travelled from Herefordshire for the purpose. By the mid-eighteenth century there were many visitors who stayed in farmhouses dotted round the great common which stretched four miles from Llanbadarn Bridge to Howey.

In 1748 an anonymous contributor sent a 78-line poem entitled 'Nature's Pharmacopoeium' to the *Gentleman's Magazine*, which begins:

> Let *England* boast *Bath's* crowded Springs,
> *Llandrindod* happier *Cambria* sings,
> A greater, tho' a modern name,
> By merit rising into fame;
> Tho' recent from the womb of time,
> Mature at once in earliest prime;
> No infant state restrained the pow'r
> Conceiving in its natal hour,
> Pregnant of health! - the lovely child
> Was born, reviving nature smil'd.

The writer goes on to celebrate the beauties of the landscape, to recommend the pastimes of riding, fishing, hunting and eating, and to praise the

Old Pump Room and Hotel at Llandrindod, 1850

profusion of religious services. The town's growing reputation did attract a less highminded element, including rowdies and gamblers. Young women came both to take the cure and to seek a husband. Fathers whose daughters seemed to be slow in marrying would tell them that it was time for a visit to the wells.

By the early nineteenth century Jonathan Williams could describe Llandrindod as 'the Montpelier of Radnorshire, preserving the health of its inhabitants to a great age, and speedily restoring invalids who resort thither for the benefit of the waters to a gladsome state of convalescence'. A high Victorian heyday followed, after the arrival of, the railway in 1866.

The original group of springs, Ffynnon-llwyn-y-gog (Cuckoo grove spring), is said to have been discovered or re-discovered in 1736 by a Mrs Jenkins, then a farm tenant on land where the Pump House—now part of Powys County Council headquarters buildings—was later erected. More springs, including a chalybeate, are in what is now called Rock Park but which was originally known as Cwm-y-gof (Blacksmith's dingle). Among them are represented the different kinds of water of which the 1748 poet wrote:

> Three streams a diff'rent aid bestow,
> As sulphur, salts, and min'rals flow,
> Uniting all that med'cine claims,
> And answ'ring Nature's various aims.

Spa Road, Llandrindod Wells, from a postcard dated 1904

LANDSCAPE

A different account of the origin of Llandrindod's wells was published by an anonymous English contributor to the *Cambrian Quarterly Magazine* in 1829. It is fanciful—one wonders whether the publication date of 1 April had any bearing—and also lengthy, so I offer this paraphrase:

An earl's son called Pengrych (Curlyhead) is out fishing when he meets an old woman. She tells him to look into a pool, and he sees the vision of a beautiful young woman. 'This is my daughter', says the old woman, and then disappears. Pengrych haunts the pool, hoping to see the vision again. One day he meets the old woman once more and she tells him that her daughter was imprisoned five hundred years earlier after being chosen as a sacrificial victim: 'I saw the white-robed priests lead her in procession; I saw the crown of oak upon her brow; I saw the glittering knife; and then I heard the crash, the roar, the shrieks of despair, and the howlings of agony. I woke from my trance, and there was silence and desolation. There was none of the assembled crowd; the very stones of the temple were broken and dispersed; all save the altar where they laid my child'.

The woman is drawn back every third night to the stone circle, where she sees her daughter dancing. Pengrych asks how he can free her. The old woman says he must approach the circle from the east and seize the girl when she next appears. They will be pursued by three figures but he will deal with each in turn by means of an object in the bag which she gives him. He later looks in the bag and finds a yellow lump, a piece of rock salt and a small bar of iron.

Pengrych keeps watch and in due course sees figures whose shapes change from grotesque to beautiful as they dance inside the circle. Among them is the girl he seeks. When a black cloud begins to descend she is led by three green-cloaked figures to a stone on the eastern side of the circle and made to lie down on it. At this point, Pengrych dashes forward, takes the girl by the hand, and runs away with her. The three give chase.

The first to draw near to the fugitives is a hideous dwarf. Pengrych feels in the bag and takes out one of the objects, which happens to be the salt. He throws it at the dwarf, who melts into the ground. The second pursuer, a revolting hobgoblin, is liquified in a similar way by the second object, the lump of sulphur. The third challenge is from a hirsute figure, but when Pengrych feels in the bag for his third item, the iron, it is no longer there. As the monster grasps at him he draws his dagger, and at the touch of the metal the monster melts away like his two companions.

Freed from her thralldom, the young woman marries Pengrych. When he becomes ill she draws on instinctive knowledge and makes him drink from one of the three pools, ill-tasting though it is, to recover his health. The news spreads, and visitors come to take the waters of Llandrindod, advised by Pengrych's lady who becomes renowned as a cunning woman (*gwraig hyspys*) or healer.

Standing Stones
The stone circle from which Pengrych made his bold rescue inspired the naming of Llandrindod's Temple Street and Gardens. Unfortunately, this is a fake, or a joke. As long ago 1867 a member of the Woolhope Club wrote in its journal: 'A Druidical circle! no such thing! It is simply an enduring emblem of practical fun, made with the stones which formerly marked the road across the common'.

On the other hand, genuine stones elsewhere have disappeared, leaving behind only the name of fields such as Hoarstone Piece at Presteigne or Tir-y-maen at Llanwelwedd. Some are known to have been deliberately destroyed, for example the monolith near the Mount at Hundred House reported by Alfred Watkins as 'now inexplicably blown into several pieces by a quarryman's charge'.

The *meini llwyd* (grey stones) often inspired awe and even fear. As late as 1949 W.H. Howse could write: 'Even today there are farmers who prefer to leave the hay uncut which grows around such stones, and some people avoid them at night as they would a graveyard'. A misshapen erratic by the roadside at Pen-y-fforest, a mile west of Clyro, was shunned at night until early last century because of the belief that it sheltered 'a spirit that used to ride behind anyone on horseback who passed there after sunset'. The stone, which still exists, gives the rough impression of a human figure buried almost to the shoulders in the ground.

Just to the north of Clyro, in 1870 Kilvert visited the great stone on Crossfoot Farm and wrote in his diary:

> I suppose no one will ever know what the grey silent mysterious witness means, or why it was sent there. Perhaps it could tell some strange wild tales and many generations have flowed and ebbed round it. There is something very solemn about these great solitary stones which stand about the country, monuments of some one or some thing, but the memory has perished and the history is forgotten.

LANDSCAPE

*Standing stone
at Crossfoot Farm, Clyro*

Those more superstitious than Kilvert talked of the druids or the devil. The tumbled white stones scattered in profusion on the Carneddau Hills above Llanelwedd were popularly believed to have been carried there in druidic times. The Stanner Rocks, west of Kington, only just inside the Radnorshire boundary, are still known as the Devil's Garden. They are, incidentally, the only place in the whole of Britain where the Radnor lily grows. A cairn some 2½ miles south of Abbey Cwm Hir is called the Devil's Apronful. Two large stones on Tan-y-cefn Farm at Nantmel go by the name of the Devil's Clogs, though they seem to lack the story behind their namesakes in the Elan Valley (page 5).

A stone with deep indentations claimed to be the marks of fingers is said to have been hurled by the devil from Craig-y-don at Beguildy Church but to have fallen short between two farms—Bryndraenog and Pentycaragle. The same stone is thought to mark the midway point of a tunnel linking the two farms. Once the Pentycaragle farmer hitched a team of horses to the stone with the intention of moving it; he immediately desisted when thunder rolled and lightning flashed. Some local people currently believe that the stone is diminishing in size.

A sudden thunderstorm coming out of a clear sky caused activity to be abandoned on another occasion, some time in the nineteenth century, when lead miners began to dig for giants' bones near a commemorative stone inscribed:

19

Mae tribedd tribedrog
Ar Llanerch dirion feillionog
Lle claddwyd y tri Chawr mawr
O Sir Frecheiniog
Owen, Milfyd, a Madog.

The vicar of Cwmdauddwr, T. Thornley Jones, freely translated this in 1951 as: 'Three graves there are in this pleasant, clover-covered spot, burying place of the three great giants of Breconshire, Owen, Milfydn, and Madog'. Local tradition adds that the three were brothers who lived at Llanerchycawr, a farmhouse on the Claerwen. While tending sheep two of them quarrelled and fought each other till they lay exhausted. The third brother found them and was so enraged that he killed them both and then himself. According to Jonathan Williams, who knew the area well, the stone stood at Abernant-y-beddau (Mouth of the stream of the graves). The place where the stream joined the Claerwen is now beneath the reservoir.

In the same parish, that of Cwmdauddwr, on the high slopes of Penrhiwwen some $2^{1}/_{2}$ miles north-west of Rhayader, there is stone called Carreg Bica, which bears the crude imprint of a cross. Einion Clud—so called after Fforest Clud (high), the old Welsh name for Radnor Forest—was lord of Elfael, brother of Cadwaladon the founder of Abbey Cwm Hir, and son-in-

Carreg Bica

law of Rhys ap Gruffydd, Prince of South Wales. At Christmas in 1176 Rhys gave a great feast at Cardigan Castle, followed by an eisteddfod and a jousting tournament from which Einion emerged as the victor. However, as he travelled home to his castle at Boughrood Einion was waylaid and killed by Flemings and Normans at the lonely place now marked by Carreg Bica. To punish the crime Rhys seized land from the Mortimers and built a castle at Rhayader. Einion's name is still borne by a number of local landmarks, including Gaereinion, a hill one mile north-east of Llanelwedd, and also a house in the Edw Valley, Hendre Einion, which as the name implies might have been his winter quarters.

A more humble memorial is the three-foot high stone on a hill above Llanbwchllyn which stands over Twm Tobacco's grave. Who was Twm Tobacco? Kilvert tried to find out, and failed. Shirley Toulson in her book on Welsh drovers' roads (1977) reported that John Hunt of Llandrindod 'believes that this Tom may not have been a brigand, despite his burial place [at a crossing of tracks], but a packman, who would have been popular if he carried tobacco ... In that case 'the grave' may mark the place where he was murdered for his wares and money, or where he may have met his death from exhaustion'.

In 1995 a correspondence in the *Brecon and Radnor Express* advanced further theories: Twm was a seller of contraband tobacco killed for his takings, one of the Daughters of Rebecca (see chapter 8) shot by soldiers and buried on the spot, a pipe-making shepherd who died in a fight with another shepherd after a dispute, a *ty un nos* dweller buried on his little patch to save the expense of a pauper's funeral. These suggestions, plausible or otherwise, do not solve the mystery.

According to tradition, the well known Four Stones at Walton also stand over graves, those of four kings slain in a great battle which raged nearby. 'If you stamp on the ground between them it sounds hollow', wrote Alfred Watkins in 1925. 'Fifty years ago', he added, 'I was told at the Crown at

Marker at Twm Tobacco's Grave in 1990

21

The Four Stones at Walton

Walton, "They do say how when the Four Stones hear the sound of Old Radnor bells they go down to Hindwell Pool to drink"'. A great boulder stood in a field called Cartre Faelog, opposite the site of Capel Maelog on Gors Farm at Cefn-llys. This, too, local people told T.P. Davies, 'goes to the brook to drink when the cock crows'. Such stories about stones are widespread; they hinge on the word, *when*.

The Six Stones are near the northern boundary of Bryngwyn, and a stone cross 1¹⁄₂ miles to the south-west of them used to be visited when the parish bounds were beaten. Unlike most stone circles, which are usually depleted, the six are nearer to twelve in number. By contrast, only one remains — embedded in a yew tree — of those which surrounded what became the churchyard at Llanfihangel Nant Melan. Two circles near St Harmon are greatly reduced: of fourteen monoliths only two remain in Cwm y Saeson (Englishmen's valley) a mile east of the River Dulas; and a group of five on Hendre-rhiw Farm is down to a single massive block 7¹⁄₂ feet tall by 4 wide and 2¹⁄₂ deep. The name Cwm y Saeson may allude to the Mortimers' ownership of this remote valley which was at the north-western extremity of the tract of land they granted to the monks of Abbey Cwm Hir in 1200. One of the Fowlers, who later owned Abbey Cwm Hir, is commemorated in the massive so-called chair and horseblock by the stone circle and cairn some 4 miles roughly west of Llanbadarn Fynydd.

The Fedw Circle

With a circumference of 237 feet the Fedw Circle was once the biggest in Wales. It is on private land near the Fforest Inn, by the A481. In 1860 there were 37 stones but about 20 years later the farmer broke up some and took away others—and this was a monument erected probably in the fifth century BC by a Celtic people, the Brythons. Its purpose remains obscure. Druidical rites have been suggested, and such ceremonies as the lighting of Beltane fires (on 1 May). There were no burials here, nor are there signs of habitation.

My wife and I visited in January 2000, thanks to the farmer's kindness in giving us permission to go on his land, though he remarked: 'There's not much to see, mind'. There was a nip in the air and frost in the ground, and wisps of white mist clung to the great bowl of hillsides in which the circle stands. Was it fancy, or did we feel a thrill of kinship with the simple people who came here 25 centuries ago?

Hills and Mounds
The Radnorshire uplands, according to H.J. Massingham are 'good theatre'. They certainly provide dramatic views, such as that from the Carneddau to the Wye Valley, 1,300 feet below; and even smaller moors and hills have their grandeur.

To the south and east their names are predominantly English, and idio-syncratic to boot: Black Mixen, Smatcher, Squilver, Whimble. Some, like Great Rhos (moor), mix Welsh and English. Further west there is a profu-sion of Welsh terms for different shapes and sizes of eminence: *allt* (cliff, height), *banc* (bank, hill, mound), *beili* (bailey, mound), *bryn* (hill), *bwlch* (gap, pass, notch), *carn* or *carnedd* (cairn), *cefn* (ridge), *crug* (hillock, mound), *cnwc* (hillock), *esgair* (ridge), *fron* (breast), *gwar* (ridge), *moel* (bare hill), *mynd/mynydd* (mountain), *rhiw* (hill), *tomen* (mound).

Bryn Sadwrn near Disserth is called after the oddly-named Saturnius, a saint and missionary who came to Wales in the fifth century with St Cadfan. Cefn Ceidio, half a mile east of Rhayader, bears the name of a sixth century saint, the nephew of St Cynllo. Archaeologists have found bones there, though not necessarily Ceidio's. More bones, excavated in a tumulus by the church at Llansanffraid Cwmdauddwr, were claimed as those of St Ffraid (Bride or Bridget), who may have been fictional but if she existed at all, died in about 525. However, a silver coin found during the dig was brought back from Palestine by Crusaders not earlier than the eleventh century.

Nearer to that time was Hywel ap Madog, the last native-born chieftain of Maelienydd, who died violently at Bridgnorth in 1212. For some reason he is commemorated in the name of a mountain near St Harmon, Moel Hywel.

The hills are covered with burial mounds and cairns dating from the Bronze Age onwards. D.E. Owen claimed that there were 30 tumuli within half a mile of his church at Llanelwedd. Some of these, he believed, were the resting places of men killed in battles between Welsh and Normans, but local people preferred to call them Druids' Graves.

Others thought of stranger creatures. A meadow with two tumps on Hindwell Farm at Old Radnor is called Monster Field. There is a Giant's Grave at Glascwm, watched over by fairies, and at Llanddewi Ystradenni Tomen Beddugre has the reputation of being the burial place of a long-dead giant. The alternative spelling of Bedd-y-gre, the last word an abbre-viation of *greorion*, translates as grave of the equerry, though this merely poses another question.

Even excavations could deepen mystery rather than disperse it. One can see how the discovery of a burnt burial and a great empty stone chest after an eighteenth century dig on Camlo Hill, again at Llanddewi, could give rise to speculations which turned into stories. At Nantmel the explanation emerged for Gwar-y-beddau (Ridge of the graves) that three brothers fought each other there and died. Perhaps the tale travelled from Abernant-y-beddau.

Merely giving names to barrows could help to allay the enigma or potential threat they concealed. J.A. Pugh wrote of six of them at St Harmon in 1934, of which one had been removed, another almost levelled and the rest 'much reduced': 'In my boyhood, our inhabitants gave the following names to these mounds: Crugyn Waen Marteg, Crugyn Pantydŵr, Crugyn Beilicoch, Crugyn Llawrllan, Crugyn Coedleision, and Crugyn'. These mean Marteg Moor Hillock, Pantydŵr Hillock (after a neighbouring hamlet), Red Mound Hillock, Village Moor Hillock, Sounding Wood Hillock and (simply) Hillock.

Perhaps because of its hilly nature Radnorshire has few of the traditions widespread elsewhere of mysterious underground passages. One already mentioned (page 11) claimed to run beneath the Teme. Another, presumably as an escape route, was said to run to the Wye from Clyro Castle. The nearby Clyro Court had its own secret underground exit to the valley below. Another tunnel was thought to link Llanerch Fraith Farm with Abbey Cwm Hir. A century ago the discovery of the mouth of an underground passage in the castle grounds at Builth revived the old belief that this led beneath the Wye to Llanelwedd Hall. In January 2000 a hole in the ground which suddenly appeared near Builth's war memorial prompted speculation that the tunnel might have passed that way.

Travellers above ground sheltered in rough wayside shanties known as Coldharbours, which are reflected as a field name common in England but not in Wales. However, it occurs in three Radnorshire parishes: Llanbister, west of Moelfre Hill; Llangynllo, on Bailey Hill; Llanyre (as Caer Harbor), on Little Cilgu Farm.

Many wayfarers now pass through 12 to 13 miles of Radnorshire as they follow the Offa's Dyke Path. This opened from Chepstow to Prestatyn in 1971 after a ceremony at Knighton. The original dyke, a ditched earth bank of which only some stretches remain, is in places 60 feet wide and averages 6 feet in height, though near Knighton it can rise to 20 feet. Offa, king of Saxon Mercia, who died in 796, wished to mark his boundary with the Welsh, and no doubt to impress them with his power.

The modern path goes within 1 1/2 miles of Rhosgoch (Red moor, heath), which for Kilvert was 'a place of magic and marvel'. Old people told him that a great battle was fought there which caused the brook to run red for three days at the western end of the common, and so gave it its name. In addition, since they had seen carved oak beams dug out of the peat, they declared the Rhos to be the site of a long lost city, the biggest between there and London. Perhaps this was an echo of the ancient Celtic belief in an enchanted other-world, lost from sight.

CHAPTER 2

Land Work

Radnorshire farming life and traditions received a great deal of attention as a result of Bruce Chatwin's novel, *On the Black Hill*, published in 1982 and adapted as a film five years later. Drawn to Radnorshire by the memory of childhood holidays there, Chatwin returned to do research for his book by walking the hills, talking to local people and reading old issues of the *Hereford Times* kept in the library at Hereford.

On the Black Hill is nevertheless a work of fiction, which it is interesting to compare with accounts of life written by those who grew up on Radnorshire farms, such as Elizabeth Clarke, Mona Morgan and George Lewis, the last two published after Chatwin's death. People still remember the yearly hirings at which farm workers, male and female, made 12-month agreements to work for employers who sealed the bargain with 'earnest' money which could then be spent on the fun of the fair.

Working wisdom was passed on by example and precept in tightly-knit communities united not only by unremitting toil but also by mutual obligation. The great events of the farming year—sheep shearing, haytime and harvest were communal occasions when neighbours gathered for exhausting work redeemed by the pleasures of eating, drinking and socialising.

Through this rather static and parochial world came the drovers and their herds of black cattle who traversed Radnorshire by various routes during the course of their journey of up to 200 miles from west Wales to south-east England. The passage of perhaps 30,000 cattle a year through the county brought benefits to innkeepers, farmers (who provided grazing) and craftsmen such as smiths. When the great cattle drives were superseded by railway travel drovers continued with sheep, then with merely local movements of stock, but the landscape is dotted with reminders of their presence.

Hiring

Farm workers were formerly engaged on what would now be called one-year contracts, starting in May after spring sowing and before sheep-shearing and hay-making (with the exception of so-called summer engagements which ran until Michaelmas). Hiring fairs were held for the purpose. 'To these fairs', wrote Wirt Sikes in 1881, 'troop men and maidens in vast numbers, on fun and profit both intent. To them also troop the farmers, in search of the human toilers on their farms for the coming year'. In Radnorshire such fairs took place at Presteigne (9 May), New Radnor and Rhayader (12), Penybont (13-14), Franksbridge (16), Newbridge (17) and Knighton (17-18). Some workers preferred to go further afield to Builth (9), Kington (11) or Hay (17). Kilvert noted at Clyro in 1871:

> The great May Hiring Fair at Hay, and squadrons of horses came charging and battalions of foot tramping along the dusty roads to the town, more boys and girls than usual. All day long the village has been very quiet, empty, most of the village folk being away at the fair. Now at 8 p.m. the roads are thronged with people pouring home again ...

At the fair men and women would stand in the street waiting to be sized up and approached by a farmer. According to Rev. Albert Jordan of Llanbadarn Fawr, maids wore a white or check apron, men a white linen smock-frock (or if they could not afford one, a short white linen coat known as a slip). Once they were hired they removed the distinctive garment. They were given a small sum as 'earnest' money, and only if this were returned within a set space of time could they go back on the bargain they had struck. For much of the nineteenth century men and women absconding from service could be punished by between one and three months' imprisonment. The Workmen's and Employers' Act of 1875 changed the penalty to fines of up to £1, with costs.

In the early 1980s Charles Kightly interviewed several Radnorshire people who had hired themselves at fairs. Edith Watkins, daughter of a shepherd at Cwmgilla, near Knighton, left school at the age of 14 in March 1914 and went to the local May Fair two months later. When some people she did not like asked whether she was looking for work, she replied: 'I don't know as I'm in a hurry just yet'; but when Mrs Deakins of Cwm Fawr, in Llanfair Waterdine parish, of whom she approved, made the same approach, she replied in the affirmative. They agreed on a wage of £5 and 'all found':

> And I said I wanted a holiday before I came - we generally had a week's holiday when we hired. 'Well', she said, 'I'll come and collect you after that. And to make sure you come to me, I'll give you two shillings'. That was earnest-money, they called it; and then she came and collected me later, in a horse and trap, and away we went. It was right up at Bettws-y-Crwyn, a little farm called Cwm House, and there I stayed for several years.

The Clock Tower, Knighton, 1903, from a postcard

Elizabeth Clarke (born 1910) remembered the May Fair at Rhayader, where 'young men in search of fresh work stood in bunches on the pavements, wearing buttonholes of flowers - a survival of the knot of wool or whipcord previously worn as the badge of their trade - until they had made terms with a new master, who then gave them half-a-crown as earnest money'. At Knighton men, sporting a bit of wheat straw in their caps, stood round the clock as farmers appraised their physique: 'The old farmer'd say, "Dust ee want a job, boy? How much be you asking?" And you'd say, "Twenty-six pound a year"; and he'd say, "It's too much, I'll give you twenty-two". And you'd bargain with him, just like selling cattle, really'.

Deals would often be struck over a pint in the Red Lion.

Some men might agree to work for several farmers, and spend several lots of earnest money on beer, with no intention of honouring any of the bargains. However, it was accepted that an earnest of half a crown was binding, at least to the extent of a month's work, followed by a further month after giving notice. On the other hand, a farmer dissatisfied with a man he had engaged could dismiss him after a week.

The wage of £26 a year mentioned would have been for a labourer who had board and lodging provided. He was expected to work from six in the morning until eight at night (less late in winter), with breaks for breakfast, bait, dinner and tea. Except for bait, consisting of bread, cheese and a pint of cider, which was taken outside, the other meals, depending on the establishment, would be eaten alone in the back kitchen, or in rather more state with the farmer and his wife and the maid. Fat bacon, turnips and potatoes featured strongly in the diet. The claim that Wyeside farms guaranteed to serve salmon not more than twice a week seems to be completely mythical: hired hands considered themselves lucky if ever they fed on salmon.

Earlier, at the end of the eighteenth century century single men living in were paid between £7 and £9 a year; married men living out had a shilling a day and a cottage. By the early 1860s wages for the latter were much the same, at 6s. to 7s. a week, but those for the former had risen to between £8 and £10 a year. Female servants in farms received between £3 and £5 yearly. Thanks to campaigns in the 1870s—Joseph Arch of the National Agricultural Labourers' Union spoke in Presteigne in 1874 and other union speakers addressed meetings elsewhere—weekly wages had risen to between 9s. and 10s., while those living in received between £18 and £20 a year, and even up to £25 for the most skilled and experienced. Domestic servants expected up to £10.

Hiring fairs were popular with farm workers. They provided a brief opportunity for pleasure, combined with the chance to seek better wages and conditions. In addition, those working on isolated farms might have a rare chance to meet a future wife or husband. Wirt Sikes described a typical scene:

> Having stood waiting in the market-place till they have found masters who will pay them for the coming year the small wages they demand, and so laid out for themselves twelve months of good hard work, Sion and Mairi feel like celebrating their success. So when the shades of evening fall, the serious work of the day being done, the merriment waxes furious. ... Torches light up the scene;

drums beat; hawkers and Cheap Johns bawl; Punch and Judy add
their squeaking to the din; and any Mairi or Catti whose waist is not
encircled by the arm of a Twm or Sion, is a reproach to the traditions of her race.

Others took a less liberal view. In June 1854, W.T.K. Davies of Croft
Castle in Herefordshire, addressing the Farmers' Club at Knighton on 'The
Condition of the Agricultural Labourer', made these remarks:

Go to what are called the May mop fairs; can a worse system exist,
can anything be done more likely to increase immorality? Bringing
together numbers of men and women like horses at a fair to be
hired, walking them out to see if they are strongly built and look
likely to do a good day's work for a bad day's pay, and leaving them
together to spend half the night in ale-houses, cider-shops, and other
debaucheries:- from these days many an unfortunate girl (every
Magistrate knows) date their first start on an evil course, which
eventually leads them to starvation and ruin.

At the speaker's suggestion the meeting passed a resolution urging
farmers to raise wages, improve housing, give allotments and to replace
cider allowances with money payments—but these things remained pious
hopes. Increasingly, though, the May Fairs concentrated on pleasure rather
than hiring. The institution of labour exchanges from 1909, and the intro-
duction of newspaper advertising for workers provided other avenues for
recruitment. Hiring was discontinued at Franksbridge by 1901 and at
Penybont by 1914, but lingered until 1947 at Knighton and Rhayader.
Mona Morgan remembers the May Fair at Hay, which she associates with
the thrill of the occasion, combined with its 'acrid smell of stale beer, horse
manure and urine'. She claims that a farmer would urge a good man to stay
with him, and offer a small wage rise as an inducement, but 'for the lazy
and incompetent it was time to pack the tin trunk and seek labour elsewhere'. She concedes, though, that even a good man sometimes preferred
a change of scene. 'On Fair morning', she writes,

men and maids were paid their yearly wages, minus some small
advances that had been requested during the year; they had little to
pack: their only decent suit would be worn. Wagoners, shepherds
and cowherds wore marks of distinction to advertise their skills. At
one time the maids wore aprons to the Fair, returning them when

31

they were hired. It was not uncommon on Fair Day to see a young lad, leaving home for the first time, standing self-consciously on the pavement beside his tin trunk, waiting to be hired. Lost and bewildered, he no doubt considered what the future held for him, what kind of a place his new home would be, how he would be treated.

With the hiring fairs the living in system largely ended too, though itinerant casual labourers—also remembered by Mona Morgan—came for spells of work and slept on hay in barns, with a pail to use as chamber pot.

Clothes worn throughout the day served as nightwear. A change of underwear was carried in a small bundle on a stick over the shoulder. Their laundry was done in their spare time and hung to dry in their sleeping-quarters. When they left, a strong smell of corduroy, twist-tobacco and cider permeated the barn for days.

One of the roadsters, as they were called, known as Radnor Tom, came several times, and was eventually promoted to having his meals in the Morgans' kitchen, where he distinguished himself by licking the top of the sauce bottle after using it. One day, having fallen ill, he left never to return.

Weather and Wisdom

Those working the land scrutinised the skies very carefully for weather signs. Near New Radnor there was a saying:

> When Whimble wears his cloudy cap,
> Let Radnor boys beware of that.

At St. Harmon heavy falls of snow were thought to be indicated when sheep moved from the slopes of Moel Hywel to the deep dingle of Lleuast Bica. Sheep in general instinctively seek sheltered ground when bad weather threatens. In the county a hard winter was predicted by the rhyme:

> If the sun shines on Christmas Day,
> Saddle your horse and go to buy hay.

Similar uneasiness at Christmas sunshine lay in the belief that it portended some sort of damage by fire during the ensuing year. Bad weather was forecast when birds sang before Candlemas Day (2 February) because they

*Standing stone at Kinnerton with the
Whimble in the background*

would then cry before May. Another belief was that if the wind blew on Candlemas Eve it would come from the same quarter until May Eve.

The timing of activity required great care. Planting seed only with a waxing moon was considered desirable; pig killing, too, so that the bacon would swell in the boiling rather than shrink, as it would if the killing had been done beneath a waning moon. When eggs were set to hatch under turkeys, geese and other poultry they were timed so that the chicks would emerge as the moon waxed, and so be stronger.

To cure 'foul foot' in cattle the first sod on which the animal placed the affected limb in the morning was cut out and hung on the nearest blackthorn hedge. As the turf withered, so it was thought, the swelling would disappear. To see the first black slug of the year on the hard road, as opposed to earth or grass, signified a bad season to come. Unlucky actions included transplanting parsley and destroying a swallows' nest. A variant from Llanbadarn Fawr on the well-known cuckoo rhyme runs:

> The cuckoo comes in April,
> She sings her song in May.
> In June she finishes her time,
> In July she prepares to fly.
> Come August, go she must.

The yearly pattern of life and work on farms followed a similarly inexorable pattern.

From Sheep to Suit

Once, it was said, you could drive a flock of sheep to Felindre in the morning and collect a worsted suit made from their wool in the evening. The life cycle of a sheep began in March or April, when the gales sweeping across the uplands were known as 'lamb winds'. Hill farm children vied in guessing who would have the first lamb of the new season. Ewes would have been brought down for lambing, but as soon as the new arrivals were strong enough the whole flock would go back on the hills. Some six weeks later the lambs would be rounded up to be marked.

The next major chore, before the June or July shearing, was washing the sheep, which was done in pools and streams. To make up for long hours in cold water men would be given hot gruel made of oatmeal, currants, spices and sugar, boiled in home-brewed beer and laced with gin. Plentiful fare was also supplied for the sheep shearing, when as many as 30 or more men would band together to go round the farms in their locality. Each farm had its own traditional day. For example, Rhiwnant in the Claerwen Valley stuck to the Wednesday before the last Friday in June.

At daybreak on the set day (or perhaps on the previous evening), shepherds and dogs combed the hills for the flock. The shearers, each equipped

*The Shearing, as drawn by R. Eustace Tickell in 1893
and published in his book* The Vale of Nantgwilt

Woman knitting outside a cottage at Knighton (?late nineteenth century)

with his own shears, worked till midday when they had a substantial meal which the women of the farm would have been preparing since early morning. Usually it consisted of meat and gravy with potatoes and bread, followed by plum duff and custard or rice pudding An hour later work resumed for the rest of the day, save for a break for tea. Shearers slaked their thirst with cider, and might even down shears in a good natured mock strike if supplies faltered. One parson, Rev. Thomas Walters of Aberedw (incumbent 1953-9) was well known for turning up at shearings where, as one of his successors, Rev. Alan Charters, writes: 'He drank many a pint of cider ... before weaving an uncertain way back to the rectory to sleep it off'.

The host farmer orchestrated proceedings, making sure that no shearer ever lacked a sheep. In turn, he and his sons would act as shearers on other farms in obedience to the unwritten rule that help received from neighbours had to be returned in full and fair measure.

There is a fine description of a shearing day in Elizabeth Clarke's book, *The Valley*, relating to the years after the First World War. After another war, in 1945, Sid Wright watched very similar scenes at Cerrig Cyplau and Rhiwnant, two farms in the Claerwen Valley:

The whole business is wonderfully organised; each person knows his or her job, and does it with a smile. Benches are placed around the inside of a barn on which the shearers place the sheep while, with hand shears, they remove the wool, and there the men remain all day, except when it is eating time. The sheep are carried to them and carried from them, when shorn, by the 'carriers'. Young boys distribute the cords to tie the sheep's legs. When they have been shorn, the sheep are carried out, still tied, and put to lie outside in rows, so that they can be easily examined for cuts and be doctored if necessary and then pitch-marked. This means they are marked with an iron dipped in boiling pitch which bears the initials of the owner. ... One very important feature of shearing day is the selection of the sale ewes and wethers, which is done by looking at their teeth.

Lambs were sold in June or July, ewes and wethers in September or October. When Rev. Daniel Parry-Jones held his first harvest festival at Llanfihangel Rhydithon (in 1927) it was, to use his own words, 'a disaster' in that he expected the church to be packed but the attendance was little more than usual. A few days later he asked a churchwarden, a farmer, what had happened: "'Well", he said, "you put it on the same day as the great annual sheep sale at Knighton". I said, "Why didn't you tell me then?" His reply was: "You didn't ask me"'. Parry-Jones deduced from this that Radnorshire people mind their own business and keep their mouths shut. The sheep fair at Knighton was on 1 October, with animals from outlying parishes leaving their farms as early as 2 or 3 a.m. in order to be there on time.

For a few weeks after lambs had been sold cheese was made from the ewes' milk—at Llaethdy, for example (the name of which means milk-house or dairy). Fleeces went from the same place to a man at Newtown who paid partly in money and partly in the form of an 18-gallon barrel of beer. Leominster also provided a ready market for wool. Weavers and mills in Radnorshire and Montgomeryshire also bought wool which they wove into the cloth which made blankets, bed quilts, and the Radnorshire Grey Coat, renowned for being warm and hardwearing. Llanidloes produced the broad-striped flannel shirts which were almost a uniform for farm labourers. Mills also bought wool from wool gatherers, parties of women who gleaned wisps of wool from furze, heather and thorn to earn a small supplement to their household income.

Haytime and Harvest

Writing of the 1860s, W. Watkins remarked that hay was mown with a scythe, a good man managing one or two acres a day, depending on conditions. The same tool was used for oats and barley but not wheat, for which a hook (sickle) was preferred. A man 'reaped with a hook in the right hand, using the left to collect the sheaf against the left leg and lift it. The boy or woman who bound them, took the sheaf, and tied it with a band of straw taken from the previous one. It was then ready for stooking'.

In time the scythe replaced the sickle, even with wheat. Mona Morgan remembers that at harvest

> The reapers moved in a slanting line, keeping the same distance apart. Before the long, rhythmic sweeps of the scythe the standing corn fell with a ripping, rasping sound. ... Women were enlisted to bind the sheaves and set them up in stooks to dry and ripen in the sun.

As with shearing, harvesting was a communal activity accompanied by hearty socialising. Watkins again:

> The 'reap' was looked forward to with pleasure by the young folk. The custom was, to arrange that the reaping took place on a different day at each farm, so that everyone helped each other and finished the task on one day. The occasion was a sort of social gathering in which the young and old joined, and special preparation was made for feeding the extra number. After supper a little merri-

Reaping with sickles, from W.H. Pyne's Microcosm *(1824)*

*Midday meal during harvesting, Llwynpenfaen Farm,
Llandeilo Graban, 1935*

Harvesting near Knighton, early 1950s

ment was often indulged in, in the way of a sing-song and a drop of home-brewed ale before separating.

Beer or cider was also provided for the reapers as they worked. William Barrett, who moved from Lingen to Knucklas in 1890 when he was 14, wrote:

> It was the custom in haying and harvest time for us boys to carry from the farm house the beer for the workmen. Every man had his costrel and cider or beer horn. We put a pole through the handles and walked single file with them on our shoulders. The 'Maister' did not stint the supply and the two servant girls always filled them up no matter how many trips we made.

Young Barrett was nonplussed by the behaviour of one man who declined beer and drank water from the stream which ran through the fields. His mother explained later: 'Oh, he has been to Knighton and joined the Blue Ribbon Army' — the teetotal movement.

Some farmers preferred cider to beer. Travelling cider makers broke up the apples with a 'chawling mill', also known as a 'scratter', and then pressed juice from the fragments in a portable press. Few Radnorshire farms now produce their own cider but Ralph's cider is still made by traditional methods at Old Badland Farm between New Radnor and Kinnerton, a welcome survivor of old times.

After harvest some of the bigger farms killed a goose or two and served a special supper to all the workmen and helpers. This Harvest Home,

Gleaners, from W.H. Pyne's Microcosm *(1824)*

The Harvesters at Supper, from the book by David Davies (1897)

followed by an impromptu concert, seems to have been last held at Lower House Farm, Boughrood. The Victorian innovation of a harvest festival service in church substituted a solemn and decorous ceremony for the uproarious feasting, drinking and singing of earlier days.

Another post-harvest custom, that of gleaning in the fields after harvest, which went back to biblical times, is now also gone, ended by the combine's efficiency. It did enjoy a revival during the Second World War when the old binders left enough for people to collect to feed their chickens.

Following the Black Ox
From the Middle Ages until the railways took over in the nineteenth century herds of up to 200 black cattle from west Wales were driven to markets and fairs in Leicester, Northampton, London, and even Kent. Drovers and their dogs (often corgis) urged on the cattle for up to 16 miles a day at an average speed of two miles per hour. Using ancient trackways, crossing rivers by ford or ferry, they followed several routes through

Radnorshire, their passage still indicated by field or farm names including the words *ych* (ox), *bustach* (bullock), *gefail* (smithy), *gof* (smith) and *rhiw* (drover's road, but also farm driftway or slope). Halfpenny Field recalls the fee of $^1/_2$d. per beast which drovers paid for an overnight stop with good grazing for their charges. Drover's Meadow on Cefn-y-Blaen Farm at Clyro must have served this purpose.

Farmers are said to have planted three Scots pines to advertise to drovers that they were willing to provide accommodation for man and grazing for beast. Pedolfa, a field near Rhayader of which the name means shoeing place, is where shoes known as cues (from the Welsh, *ciw*) were fitted to animals. Each required eight cues, shaped like commas, two to a foot because of the cloven hooves. Until the mid-20th century a forge could be seen at Cregrina where cues were made and fitted, next to the Black Lion Inn (itself closed in 1906). Penrhiwlais, another shoeing shop and drovers' inn, still exists in ruined form on Glan-edw Farm at Rhulen.

Like Penrhiwlais, many of the inns which accommodated drovers—who expected to pay 4d. a night in summers, 6d. in winter—have now disappeared or been converted to other uses. The curiously-named Tabor Wye, a triangular field on the north side of Aberedw Hill, is particularly

Drover, by W.H. Pyne, from Costume of Great Britain *(1808)*

Cider House Farm

verdant to this day because of generations of cattle pastured there by drovers so long ago. Close by is the site of a drovers' inn.

At Glascwm the Drover's Arms is no more, though a pub of the same name flourishes at Howey. The Black Ox (*Yr Eidion Du*) at Painscastle is also gone. Another Black Ox Inn which stood in a field called Cold Brook on Penrhoel Farm at Clyro had disappeared before Kilvert's time. The derelict Cider House Farm (up for sale in 2000), a mile south of Dolfor on the B4355 from Knighton to Newtown, formerly catered for drovers travelling the ancient ridgeway which crosses Kerry Hill. Such customers expected a jolly evening with singing and dancing to the strains of a fiddle. As a further attraction fights for small purses were sometimes organised between local men and drovers in transit.

West to east routes through Radnorshire included Rhayader-Penybont-Fforest Inn-New Radnor-Stanner-Kington. Some of the smaller herds from Tregaron and Lampeter passed through Cregrina, Glascwm, Colva and Huntington to Kington, and then went on via Leominster, Bromyard, Worcester, Stratford-on-Avon and Banbury towards London. The last drove of mountain ewes from Tregaron followed this route in 1900 (through Gladestry rather than Huntington) on the way to Harrow-on-the-Hill.

A drover's diary of some years earlier shows a variant itinerary from Abergwesyn across the county through Newbridge, Llandrindod and New Radnor. The 9,000 black cattle which passed through Kington each year were greatly outnumbered by those following the main route from Llandovery to Erwood on the Wye. Erwood is a corruption of the Welsh, *y rhyd* (the ford), and cattle did ford the river there when it was safe to do so. Otherwise they used a flat-bottomed box-like ferry run by Twm Bach, after whom the local Boat Inn was known as Caban Twm Bach (though the landlord told Fransis Payne in 1958 that this was a mistake for Cafn Twm Bach — Twm Bach's Ferry). Twm is reputed to have habitually prayed for rain so that the river's level could rise and oblige drovers to pay for his ferry. Once he was carrying cattle across the Wye in spate. Terrified by the raging river, the animals crowded together on one side and capsized the ferry. Two drovers saved themselves by grasping the tails of animals which swam to the bank, but Twm Bach and his son were both drowned as they tried to salvage their boat.

Barring such accidents, droves went on from Erwood to Painscastle, where the Black Ox — one of six inns — offered both a field for grazing and a smithy for shoeing. The next stage ended at the Rhydspence Inn — known 'till recently', wrote Robert Gibbings in 1942, 'as the Cattle Inn' — where re-shoeing was also available. With dogs barking, cattle lowing, and drovers shouting, the drove then went on to Willersley, Hereford, Ledbury (where drovers favoured the now genteel Feathers), Little Malvern, Welland, Upton-on-Severn (where they forded the Severn), over Bredon Hill to Broadway's Lygon Arms, and eventually to Barnet or Smithfield, so ending a journey of some 200 miles.

Drovers had to be tough because of the rigours of the journey and responsible because of the value of their charges and the proceeds of their sale which they took back to Wales on foot. At 3s. a day they received well above the pay of an agricultural labourer, and in addition they earned a bonus of 6s. on arrival. One of their number, Evan Davies, served twice as High Sheriff of Radnorshire. When many were put out of work by the advent of railways they worked as grooms or drivers in circuses. Others took to driving sheep, a practice which continued well into the twentieth century. Some found work driving small numbers of cattle and sheep to and from local markets and fairs. One such, called Cider Billy, died in Knighton Workhouse in 1903, aged 101. George Lewis remembers 'droviers', as he terms them, as late as the 1950s.

The Rhydspence Inn, by just a few yards on the English side of the
border, up for sale at half a million pounds in early 2001. Its two bars
were part of a forge which made cues for cattle (seep.41). Top drovers
paid 6d. a night to sleep in the inn, while hired hands occupied the half-
penny field over the road, where they were supplied with cider.
One landlady is said to have witched drovers' cattle, rooting them to the
spot until all bills were paid

Now they, too, have gone, but as one turns a corner on a winding
Radnorshire road and encounters cattle or sheep being driven from farm to
field the drovers of old might well come to mind. The tracks they followed
have been admirably traced by Shirley Toulson in her book, *The Drovers'*
Roads of Wales (1977), which in addition to careful sketch-maps has
evocative photographs by Fay Godwin. It lacks only the drovers' cries of
'Haip-trw-ho' or 'Ho tarw', which we shall never hear again.

The Drover's Farewell

When I set out a-droving
My Father said, You're mad,
Why leave the farm, why come to harm
And go for a droving lad?

LAND WORK

But I saw the wide world beckon
Beyond the roads I knew,
And beyond the tower of Brecon
Fresh fields and pastures new.

Haip-trw-ho, haip-trw-ho!
And a-droving we will go.
Upon my sturdy pony
My saddle I did throw,
I whistled to my corgi-dog
And off we both did go,
I bad a young man's longing
For new cities and new sins
So I set out a-droving
And that's how life begins.

Haip-trw-ho, haip-trw-ho!
And a-droving we will go.

Once past the Bwlch, they told me,
No Welshman ever comes back,
But my homeland could not hold me
And I took the droving track.
To taverns called The Feathers,
Welsh Harp and Prince of Wales
I rode through Etigland's weathers
And drank deep of England's ales.

Haip-trw-ho, haip-trw-ho!
And a-droving we will go.

Great herds I drove to market
From many an upland farm,
I stored up many a sovereign
And I never came to harm.
I stood my round, I stood my ground,
Drank deep of many a glass,
And many a broad-beamed Saxon wench
I pleasured in the grass.

Haip-trw-ho, haip-trw-ho!
And a-droving we will go.

THE FOLKLORE OF RADNORSHIRE

But now the railway's coming,
I see a cloud of steam,
I hear the rails a-humining,
I hear the whistle scream,
Its message to the drover
Is carried loud and clear,
It says, Your days are over
And the cattle trucks are here.

Haip-trw-ho, haip-trw-ho!
And a-droving we will go.

I'm setting sail tomorrow
At the rising of the sun
And I'm going off to Texas,
Though they say I'll need a gun,
And I'll drive the Yankee long horns
Through lands that once were Spain's
As I drove the small Black cattle
Through our green and narrow lanes.

Haip-trw-ho, haip-trw-ho!
And a-droving we will go.

Harri Webb (1920-95)

CHAPTER 3

Word for Word

Once, the words spoken in Radnorshire, at least by the common people, were Welsh. Then the dominant—and later more or less exclusive—language became English. In a recent article, David Crystal, honorary professor of linguistics at the University of Wales, Bangor, suggested that when one culture assimilates another a language passes through three stages:

> The first is immense pressure on the people to speak the dominant language. The second stage is a period of bilingualism: people become increasingly efficient in their second language, while still retaining competence in their old. Then, often quickly, bilingualism starts to decline, with the old language giving way to the new. This leads to the third stage, in which the younger generation increasingly finds its old language less relevant. This is often accompanied by a feeling of shame about using the old language, on the part of the parents as well as the children.

In 1901 half the people of Wales spoke Welsh; a century later the proportion is a fifth. Powys as a whole is on a par with this figure, thanks to Breconshire and Montgomeryshire, but under a tenth of Radnorshire people speak Welsh. A hopeful sign for the language may be that a quarter of those aged between 5 and 15 speak it, thus reversing Crystal's third stage. In 1995 Powys set up a Welsh Language Board, and adopted the principle that in the conduct of public business and the administration of justice the Welsh and English languages would have equal treatment.

Though the Welsh language suffered eclipse in Radnorshire it left a lasting legacy of farm, field and place names. In addition it made an enduring mark on the county's English dialect, which also has its own rich vocabulary and characteristic expressions. According to one commentator, A.G. Bradley, who knew the area well, 'Radnorshire English is extraordinarily good'. To this statement, made in 1903, he added, some 25 years later: 'the Radnor vernacular is just about the best rustic English in Britain'.

Between them, the two languages demonstrate a marvellous affinity with the landscape and a precious ability to feel at home in it.

Welsh into English

Writing on Llanfaredd, where by 1843 'few if any of the inhabitants could speak Welsh', Roger Williams produced this graphic passage:

> The invasion of a language is like that of an army taking possession of the slain, and the best part of the country, clearing everything in front of them, and causing the defending army to retreat if it is weaker than the attacking force. The last resting place of the defeated army as a rule is in the mountain fastnesses, and so it is with language.

Remarks by different travellers in Radnorshire illustrate how the Welsh language was faring. During a journey from Knighton to Llandrindod in 1743 a Shropshire solicitor met only Welsh speakers, most of them barefoot. When he visited Disserth and Aberedw for the wakes (see also chapter 7), he remarked that almost everyone spoke Welsh.

Half a century later George Lipscomb noted at Rhayader, with some surprise: 'Mr Evans who keeps the Red Lion is a well informed man, and a good humoured Welsh girl, with no knowledge of English, was the only attendant, but possessed genuine politeness'. However, Benjamin Heath Malkin, who travelled in the county more widely than Lipscomb just a few years later, observed that it was 'uncommon to meet a peasant who understands Welsh'—though he did not say how he determined this. He then modified the generalisation to except Rhayader and neighbourhood, 'where the few scattered people speak nothing else' but Welsh, and went on:

> Nay, in the south-east part of the county, about Clyrow, Paine's Castle, and other places in that neighbourhood, ... the Welsh language is still understood, and all are able to speak it, though they decidedly affect the English. About Presteign, no natives understand Welsh, but it is partially known to all or most in the places five or six miles to the westward.

D.E. Owen described in 1911 his conversation with a Radnorshire woman aged 93, who would have been born in 1818 or thereabouts. She told him that her grandparents could speak English but preferred Welsh, and that her parents could speak Welsh but preferred English. One could infer that she herself spoke only English. If so, the three generations would have followed exactly David Crystal's three stages.

Elizabeth Clarke, author of that delightful book, *The Valley*, tells how her grandmother, feeling low, remarked 'I have no *hwyl*'. Clarke adds: 'and though our grandmother was the last of the family to be truly Welsh-speaking, we knew enough to understand the variations of meaning in a word associated with the old Welsh preachers, beside which "rapture" is a toneless imitation'. She does not say whether the reference is to her paternal or maternal grandmother; if it is the latter, this was Hetty Price (born 1874) who published her memories of Cwmdauddwr (see below). Clarke affectionately describes a shepherd called Emrys who 'when he came direct from the hafod, talked, in exact translation from the Welsh. There was a need for food on him, he said ... He would have two eggs after boiling and a cupful of tea'. After 'a meal of food' in the kitchen at Gwynant he complained of a plan to cut down some sheltering trees because: 'the wind will be full the house, all'.

The congregations of some churches and chapels strongly resisted the encroachment of English. In 1742 Glascwm parishioners petitioned the bishop of St David's to remove their vicar, Walter Meyric, because 'he could not officiate in the tongue understanded of the people'. When Meyric left, three years later, a 'thorough Welshman', Cambele Davies, followed.

The move ran counter to the advancing tide of English exemplified by Aberedw, where in 1743 all spoke Welsh but where by 1820, as shown in the churchwardens' visitation returns, Welsh had ceased to be used in services. Jonathan Williams wrote with some warmth of a similar change at Llanbadarn Fynydd:

> About a century ago the Welsh language was generally spoken in this parish, and even used in the Divine Service of the church; and though many old people continue to speak, and more to understand, the tongue of their forefathers yet, to the present race of young people in general, it is become unintelligible and obscure.

Nevertheless, islands of Welsh remained. During his stay at Nantgwyllt in 1812 Shelley—somewhat bizarrely, perhaps, for a self-proclaimed atheist—went to a service and wrote afterwards to his friend, Thomas Hogg: 'I have been to church today: they preach partly in Welsh, which sounds most singularly'. Not far from Nantgwyllt was a baptist chapel recalled by Hetty Price. She and her sister as children went to the church Sunday school in the afternoon and the chapel service in the evening:

> How my sister and I used to love the evenings there! The preacher generally spoke in Welsh, but he had the regular Welsh 'hwyl', and if we did not understand all he said it melted our young hearts, and so did the singing of the grand, old Welsh hymns. Oh! the memories of it all. It is too sad to think about.

When the chapel was submerged in the rising water of the Elan reservoir its services moved to a room in the Elan Valley Hotel and continued there until 1914. 'The Cwmdauddwr Hills were the last stronghold of the Welsh language in Radnorshire', wrote T.P. Vaughan Prichard, introducing Hetty Price's reminiscences. Nearby Rhayader must have been a close second. The 1891 census shows Welsh still spoken by one or more members of the majority of households; and in the last decade of the 19th century as much Welsh as English could be heard there on market days.

Four miles away, at St Harmon, Welsh also lingered. Although weekly services in the language ended at the church in 1835 they continued once a month for the next 30 years. At the three nonconformist chapels services lasted respectively until 1860 (baptist), 1870 (wesleyan) and 1876 (calvinistic methodist).

Fortunately, these 'last ditchers', to use Rev. Parry-Jones's term, proved after all to be not the last users of Welsh in Radnorshire. According to census returns the county's speakers increased by 3% during the ten years ending in 1991. In Gladestry, Rhayader and Llandrindod over 11% of residents speak Welsh. Hetty Price, if she chose her place and time carefully would again be able to attend services and sing hymns in Welsh. The unnamed woman whom the vicar of Glascwm described to Kilvert would not now lack for conversation since well over 30 people in the parish now speak Welsh:

> Mr Marsden told me that only 4 years ago died the last old woman who could speak her native Radnorshire Welsh, her northern tongue

which she had learnt as a child from her mother and grandmother, never having lived out of her own parish. No one else in the parish could talk Welsh to her except Mr Marsden and her great delight was when he would read to her from a Welsh book.

Placenames

On its formation in 1536 Radnorshire borrowed the name of the existing settlements of Radnor (meaning red bank). Old Radnor is first recorded in a charter of King Offa (774); New Radnor dates from roughly 200 years later. The county's Welsh name, Maesyfed, may derive from the plain of Hyfaidd on which New Radnor was established. Jonathan Williams devotes several pages to alternative theories which exemplify the heated and sometimes inconclusive debate which the etymology of placenames can arouse.

Knighton may take its name from *cnwc-din* (fort on the spur) or *Chenistetune*, recorded in the *Domesday Book* and meaning knight's town. The Welsh *Trefyclo* or *Trefyclawdd* (Dyke town) first appeared in 840, only 50 years or so after the feature to which it refers, Offa's Dyke. There can be no confusion because it is the only town on the dyke.

A fanciful and tongue-in-cheek etymology puts forward the notion that as Saxons pursued Welsh raiders westward they found traces of their quarry near Knighton at a place which they gratefully dubbed Heartsease. A few miles further on they stopped as night came on: hence, Knighton. Next day, over the hill, they lurked in hope of surprising the raiders, and baptised Lurkenhope.

Apart from Knighton, several other Radnorshire towns and villages have alternative Welsh and English names. Presteigne, first recorded in

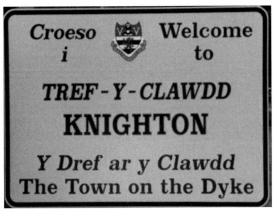

1252 as *Presthemede* (Household of priests), supplanted *Llanandras*. Harpton literally translates as *Tre'rdelyn*, but there is some confusion because its original name apparently meant not harp town but filth town. Another theory involves a kind of riddle for sifting salts known as a *hearpe*.

Both Gladestry (locally pronounced Glade-stry) and its Welsh opposite number, *Llanfair Llwythyfnwg*, date from the 13th century. The former may mean Glad's tree; the latter, Mary's church of the tribe of Dyfnog. Glasbury (locally pronounced Glazebury) seems to be a hybrid of Welsh — *clas*, meaning monastic community — and Old English — *burh*, meaning fort or enclosure. Since the 16th century the Welsh name has been *Y Clas-ar-Wy* but according to a different story Glasbury is called after Gwladys, the saintly daughter of Brychan.

Interchanges between Welsh and English have occurred in several names. *Pont newydd ar Wy*, recorded in 1679, appeared only three years later as Newbridge-on-Wye, a straight translation. On the other hand, Newchurch, recorded in 1497, took some 70 years to acquire the Welsh guise of *Llannewydd*.

Cascob scarcely looks English but its second syllable is a version of the word, *hope*, meaning valley, which is also found in Burlingjobb and Evenjobb. The first syllable is a form of the personal name, *Casca*. A completely different etymology has been suggested — *Cae-yr-esgob*, meaning bishop's field — but this has no support in early records, of which the first is Domesday, which gives *Cascope*.

Certain names become readily comprehensible as soon as garbled or incorrect spelling is rectified. For example, Monaughty (locally pronounced Munawtee) is *Mynachdy*, Monastery; Clyro, *Claer wy*, clear water, though modern Welsh convention prefers the spelling *Cleirwy*. Not that the etymology is entirely clear: since the place was first recorded (in 1232) as *Ruyll*. This could have been *yr heol* (the road), a reference to the Roman thoroughfare which ran nearby; or *rhwyl* (court or palace).

Many of the 'Llan' names in the county are considered in chapter 6. These include the first element of Llandeilo Graban. The second, no doubt intended to distinguish this church of Teilo from others, means corn marigold, which grew locally. It is worth adding that in Radnorshire when 'llan' appears in the name of a feature of the landscape it may well be a modification of the Welsh *llwyn* (grove), *nant* (stream) or *glan* (bank).

The names of Radnorshire's villages and hamlets, not to speak of rivers and hills (for which, see chapter 1), are full of interest and character. They are carefully explained in Richard Morgan's invaluable book, *A Study of Radnorshire Place-Names* (1998).

Farm and Field

As the Welsh language ebbed westward it left behind many a *beili* (enclosure, yard), *gilfach* (sheltered place), *hafod* (summer dwelling) and *hendre* (winter homestead). Large numbers of farms still have Welsh names, albeit sometimes with irregular spellings. Dolewynner Farm at Llanyre is *Dol-llwyn-hir* — 'Tall tree meadow'. Neuad-Glan Gwy at Llandewi Fach translates as 'Wyebank Hall'. Llanbister has a Rhosegree Farm (*rhos grug* means 'heather moor') and there is a Bryndreinog ('Thornyhill') Farm at Beguildy. At Llandeilo Graban the name of Pen isa'r Plwyf Farm indicates that it is at the top of the lower part of the parish.

Although Gladestry is right on the border with Herefordshire, Kathleen Biggerton-Evans pointed out that farms there retained Welsh names such as Pentwyn, Llanhowell, Llan-y-felin, Cwm, Wern, Gwerndyfnant, Hengoed and Llanerch-y-frain. She went on to say that these were 'intermixed with pure English names such as Stone House, Burnt House, Court, Rabber, Foyce, Wood'. Yet at least two of these are anglicisations of Welsh words: Foyce, from *ffos*, ditch; and Rabber, from *yr aber*, the confluence.

Another farm to be Englished, purely phonetically, was Ar-hyd-y-fro (meaning 'Along the vale') at Michaelchurch-on-Arrow, which became Redborough. Of course, there are plenty of straightforward English names, too, such as Wyecliff (Clyro), Wolfpits (Harpton), Paradise (Presteigne) and Stannage (Llanhyre). The unusual name of Nimble Spent at Llanbadarn Fawr is said to come from the spend-thrift habits of a former owner who soon had to sell up. A local rhymester added it to a list of other farms:

Looking north in Gladestry with Yewtree Bank in the background

Clyro.

The usual etymology of this name, viz. "Clear Wy, that is clear water," appears to the author of this work objectionable on these two grounds: 1. The adjective is placed before the substantive of the word, a collocation militating against the grammatical idiom of the Welsh language. 2. Because clearness is a quality not confined to the character of the waters of Clyro in particular, but is common to all the springs in this county. The derivation, then, of this name must be sought in another source, affording a signification descriptive of the peculiar site of this parish, and indicative of the reason why it has been so denominated. This desideratum will be obtained by restoring the original & ancient orthography of the name, viz. Clidderwy, as it is written in all old records & manuscripts. Now, the signification of Clidderwy is the "Wye flowing on a bed or stratum of Clay," and Clyro is the first parish in this county in which the river Wye flows on a stratum of clay: the whole extent of its course, from its source on Plinlimmon hill, in the county of .... to this place in the county of Radnor, being upon a bed either of gravel, or of rock, or of both intermixed. Immense rocks, having deep holes, some of which, called Salmon holes, are from 30 to 40 feet deep, compose for the most part its bottom & its sides. It is in the parish of Clyro, that it begins to lose this characteristic feature, and to assume a more tranquil current, as well as a softer place for repose. From a careful inspection of the banks of this rambling river, it appears very evident, that the old course of the Wye, which is yearly shifting, and consequently the Romans justly characterised its current by the epithet "Vaga", has in this undergone a great change. In former times it certainly ran close to the foundation of the mansion of Clyro court and apparently, to the centre of Clyro ruins, pointing as it were to a subterraneous passage: from which

Page from the manuscript of the History of Radnorshire *by Jonathan Williams, dealing with Clyro*

Nimble Spent, Poor Man's Tent,
Cobbler's Hall, Butcher's Stall,
New House, and the Holly
Are all perched upon Rhoslowddy.

The last word means 'bright black moor'.

As with farms, so with fields and other features of the landscape such as woods and valleys, Welsh names remain widespread. Over and over again words recur such as *bryn* (hillside), *cae* (field), *coed* (wood), *cwm* (dingle), *dol* (meadow), *ffin* (boundary), *ffrwd*, (stream), *llwyn* (tree, grove), *nant* (stream, valley), *rhos* (moor, bog), *rhyd* (ford), *tir* (land), and *twyn* (hillside). On the farm where Mona Morgan grew up at Newchurch were 'Cae Milw - the field through which the Milw brook ran; Cae blaidd - the wolf's pasture; Cae drain - the thorn field; Dol-garn - the rocky pasture; and two fields called the Panneys (Pannau) - the fields of hollows'.

Similar names can be widely documented, thanks to the information from surveys of 16 parishes carried out by the Radnorshire Society in the 1930s, and of the whole county some 30 years later by members of the Women's Institute. The W.I. initiative, inspired by Mrs J.A.P. Thomas of Felindre, resulted in eight invaluable typescript volumes which are now kept in the public library at Llandrindod Wells.

Field names often reflect a gradual slippage from standard Welsh to garbled but still recognisable forms of the language. Pencaenewydd (Llanbedr), Blaen y cwm (Glascwm) and Y ddol cam (Disserth) are perfectly correct, and mean respectively 'New field top', 'Valley head' and 'Crooked meadow'. One could provide a thousand more examples.

Others require a little more thought. Cae rhyn doy cwm (Aberedw) should be *Cae rhwng dau gwm*—'Field between two dingles'; Eskirwndwm (Llanbadarn Fynydd) requires to be amended to *Esgairgwndwm*—'Ridge of never-ploughed land'; Worlodd dan y fordd (Llanstephan), with a change of the first word to *gweirlglodd*, becomes 'Field below the road'.

Some names are open to more than one interpretation. At Llanfihangel Helygen, Cae cobbin could indicate the presence of either a sprite (*coblin*) or a woodpecker (*coblyn-y-coed*). Cwm twrch at Aberedw probably owes its name to the wild boar (*twrch*), but another possibility could be turf or peat (*tywarch*). Cae'r delyn at Cefn-llys may signify a harp-shaped field, but one wonders whether at some time the instrument was played there.

A great many fields took their names from some now-forgotten person or story. Fortunately, certain tales remain. Cae Shon at Bwlch Gwyn Farm, St Harmon, bears the name of the man who reputedly cut its three acres with a scythe in a single day. Fields involved in much bloodier encounters are described in chapter 8.

More normal stints than Shon's are recalled in fields named One, Two and Three Days' Math (Glascwm), Eight (Bryngwyn) and even Nine Days' Math (Pilleth), recording standard mowing times. Disserth has both a Four Days' Math and a Gwaith-Gwr-Mawr, work a big man would have been expected to do in a day. Gwaith-Gwr-Bach in other parishes indicated rather less, as did Gwaith-Din-Bach. A somewhat complex variant at Llanbadarn Fynydd, mixing Welsh and English, was Cae dean and gwarthuluch Bach, meaning 'Man field at back of house by little lake'.

English field names range from the prosaic to the exotic. Slang (narrow strip), plock (small field) and orls (field with alders) occur in large numbers of parishes. Hopyard appears at both Aberedw and Knighton, though the crop is no longer grown. Peat field (Llannano and elsewhere) marks a fuel no longer dug. Distant or isolated holdings bear names such as Newfoundland (Llanbister), America (New Radnor), Canada (Llanddewi Fach) and Quebec (Llanbedr). Poor or difficult soil inspired Starvy Rascal (Aberedw), Starvecrow (Clyro), Starvation (Llowes), Famish Goose (Llanbedr) and Break Bones (Llananno). On the other hand, friendly and fertile fields produced Paradise (Knighton), Jacob's Bosom (Presteigne) and Heartsease (Clyro).

Glimpses of local history are provided by the Shinmey (Llanbadarn Fawr), where shindy or bandy—an early form of hockey—was played; the Turbary (Brandy Hall Farm, Knighton) and Turbary Piece (Beacon Lodge Farm, Beguildy), where the poor once had the right to dig peat—the word derives from *turba*, mediaeval Latin for turf; Hangman's Dingle (Witterleys Farm, Beguildy), claimed to be the last place where prisoners from Presteigne Gaol were hanged; Timballs (Pentrusco Farm, Heyope), where a man called Tim allegedly found a cannon ball.

A spring in Parson's Field (Vron Farm, Beguildy) served for baptisms, while Gospel Field (St Harmon) and possibly Hymns Piece (Lea Farm, New Radnor) were connected with the beating of bounds (see chapter 6). More workaday activities are reflected in Cae pandy (Fulling mill field, St Harmon), Clogger's Field (Llanelwedd) and Oven Close (Beguildy), where people collected the gorse which they used to heat ovens. One would like to know the story behind Jack the Liar's Wood, at Pilleth, but it is likely to remain obscure.

As the name implies, Pound Meadow (Caepandy Farm, Llanstephan, and also elsewhere) was used for penning stray animals until they were collected by their owners. The Welsh, *y ffald*, with the same meaning, is also found in numerous parishes, including Llanfaredd. In Clarks Field (Larch View Farm, Llandegley) horses were temporarily kept after being bought at Penybont Fair. Perhaps the name derives from a clerk or clerks who booked them in and out.

Victory Field (Cwm-hely Farm, Llanbedr) is probably where a squatter's house once stood. Such a dwelling, built in a single night sufficiently for a fire to be lit and smoke to emerge from a chimney, was known in Welsh as a *ty un nos*. Hafan Farm at Nantmel was originally called the Victory for the same reason. Morning Surprise, another triumphant name, existed at Llanbadarn Fawr, where it was built in a night on Clwedog Common by David Morgan (who died in 1884).

Squatting of this kind had customary but not legal support. However, when the new owner of the manors of Iscoed, Uwchcoed, Rhysslyn and Neithon evicted a squatter early in the 19th century a combative Presteigne lawyer, Cecil Parsons, took up the case, presumably on the grounds that enough time had passed for tenure to have become secure. Though he lost at the assizes he won on appeal at the Court of Common Pleas in 1835. There were huge celebrations as evicted squatters returned home. Church bells rang, fireworks exploded. Parsons, hailed as the cottagers' champion, was the guest of honour at a triumphant dinner at the Radnorshire Arms in Presteigne.

Radnorshire English

The county's English speech has a long pedigree, with some of the field names, as well as general terms such as 'to taber' (knock lightly) and 'to oss' (try), going back perhaps to Anglo-Saxon times. Not surprisingly, certain Welsh words remained in circulation until well within living memory. Mona Morgan recalls that her grandmother used *cornel* (corner), *cwt* (sty), *dowlod* (hay loft, from *taflod*), *gwern* (swamp), *gwdihw* (owl) and *poon* (to beat, from *pwnio*). She also used terms closely based on Welsh such as 'a hurry', meaning a short time, and 'albease', in a leisurely manner.

In 1934 J.A. Pugh noted over 50 Welsh words and expressions, not counting field and farm names, which were still used at St Harmon. These included *achifi* (an exclamation of astonishment), farming words like *bwbach* (scarecrow) and *caib* (mattock), children's expressions such as *Dafydd y gwlaw* (the rain), *Morus y gwynt* (the wind) and *chwyl i gogan* (magic wheel, a plaything made from a cotton reel), and terms for the creatures of the countryside such as *piogen* (magpie), *wincyn* (chaffinch), *wnt* (mole), *yscall* (adder) and *pilc* (small trout), from which the English pilchard, incidentally, is derived. It would be interesting to see how many, if any, of these words would still be recognised in St Harmon but until very recently in the Radnor Forest *mochyn* (little pig), *tarw* (bull) and *bach* (as a term of endearment) were everyday currency.

Expressions deriving from Welsh included 'Thank you for my good place', said when expressing gratitude for hospitality, and a direct translation of 'Diolch am fy lle da'. 'Full the house of people' was another. Mr Peter Barnes of Llanddewi Ystradenni, who in the 1960s gathered a considerable collection of terms and expressions which he kindly passed to me, wrote:

> Another curiosity was that it was never afternoon. Morning went on till 'middle day', after which it was evening. A man might say 'Not a bad evening' at 3 pm. Then as it turned to dusk it was 'the edge of night'. Another thing was that a man might be described as 'keeping a noise', which was, of course, the opposite of keeping quiet.

As in Wales as a whole, many Radnorshire families bore the same surnames, and were distinguished by the names of their house, business, farm or village: John the Wern, James the Shop, Lewis the Mill, Evans the Molecatcher, Powel Nantmel. Nicknames, too, were widespread. W.H. Howse in *Radnorshire* quotes for men, the Old Duke of York, Curly Jack, Black Tom, Old Anne's Tom, Nutty, Nosey, Happy Jack, Dandy, Ned the Rose, Apple O, Billy my Dear; and for women, Boxing Poll, Sally-rue-the-day, Trouncy Nancy.

The Radnorshire dialect has fascinated a whole series of observers. Kilvert supplied a list to a friend, A.L. Mayhew, who published it in *Notes & Queries*. Items included frame (skeleton), to the height of music (very much), load (skin eruption), Noah's Ark (the Great Bear) and pungar-licking (worried). In addition, as Frederick Grice has pointed out, Kilvert 'spices his prose' with local words, 'using them, in general, unselfconsciously, as if they were part and parcel of his everyday vocabulary'.

Examples include glat (gap in hedge), to cratch (eat heartily), mawn (peat), soul bell (funeral bell) and steen (earthenware vessel). A number of terms concern flora and fauna, such as askal or asgal (newt), hardy-straw (shrew), wittan (mountain ash), pembolade (tadpole), kiss-at-the-garden-gate (woodruff or pansy) and bloody man's fingers (foxgloves). The last term features in Geoffrey Grigson's book, *The Englishman's Flora*, together with other Radnorshire names such as crowfoot (bluebell), red bird's eye (red campion), shoemaker's heels (Good King Henry), spotted Mary (lungwort) and white bird's eye (greater stitchwort).

W.H. Howse wrote a great deal on the subject of dialect in a series of contributions to the *Transactions of the Radnorshire Society*. He also published glossaries in both *Radnor Old and New* and *Radnorshire*. On the occasion of the Royal Welsh Show at Llanelwedd in 1988 the Radnor Women's Institute produced a pamphlet listing dialect words, together

with an audiocassette recorded by Emlyn Pugh and Peter Barnes. Unfortunately, no copy of the cassette seems to have survived but Mr Barnes has described its contents. His lists, supplemented from a variety of other sources (for example, a manuscript of unknown provenance in the Radnorshire Society's archives, and information from Mike Reynolds of Lanfihangel Rhydithon), have provided the basis for the glossary at the end of this chapter.

The richness of vocabulary is matched by a wealth of sayings and expressions. Favoured similes include simple as a chicken, lively as a maggot, as hard as a

A signpost illustrating the jumble of Welsh and English placenames in Radnorshire

toad (meaning fit), strong as a buck and wild as a hawk. Among figurative sayings are to play the smoke (cause havoc), listen to the oonts (be dead), and enough to sicken a snipe. 'Don't fill up your fancy' warns the person addressed not to expect too much.

These expressions come from the notebook of Kilvert's friend, Edith Burnham Thomas:

> They that do wear a hole in the middle of their shoe, they'll never want bread.
> He who takes what isn't hisn, when he's cotched is sent to prison.
> Plant and prune in the increase of the moon.
> It's the early crow as eats the late un's breakfast.
> Many fish can go down the stream but it takes a strong one to come back.
> I must speak well of the bridge as do carry me over.
> Whatever is young learnt is never old forgot.

Such speech well illustrates the strength of local vernacular. One hopes that the power and pleasure of expressions such as these will continue to thrive, as they indeed do in three concluding formulations noted by Peter Barnes: No more use than a side pocket to a toad. Stick to 'em all the while, like Jesse agin the cat. I hopes the crows never peck your taters.

Glossary

acting a tale — telling a story
adlands — headlands
afeard — frightened
afore — before
aim — as in 'He didn't know no aim what he was doing'
all — as in 'They ate the buns all'
anunt, anunst — up against, close to
arm — help, offer an arm to assist
askel — adder (Welsh, *yscall*), lizard

bad ways — infected, as in 'He cut his hand and it went bad ways'
bakkus — kitchen
bannut — walnut
beethy — rancid, bad; also soft, spongy
big sorted — bumptious, conceited
bing — passageway in cowhouse for feeding

biscake — biscuit

bistee? — are you?

bitaweddy — monotonous, tedious, as in 'It's a bitaweddy road from
    Penybont to Rhayader'

blow — shot, as in 'fire a blow'

bodge — stuff bushes in hole in hedge

boiling jumping — on a fast boil

bolus — temporary improvement

boonting — knocking by calf at its mother as it suckles

boosey — manger

boughten — not homebaked

breach — many, as in 'a breach of folks'

brivet — to pry, or sort out

brown Sheila — proverbial expression, as in 'off like a brown Sheila' (that is,
    quickly)

bullygullion — bullhead (small fish)

butty — mate, friend

cade — bottle-fed, as in 'cade lamb'

caedrws — shut the door (Welsh, *cau drws*)

cag — tear, as in 'I've cagged my coat on the barbed wire'

chats — kindling, fire wood

clemmed — famished, starved

coddlement — mixture of medicines

colly — dirty

come — affected, as in 'I don't know what come to him'

cop — two furrows leaning together

cornel — corner (Welsh)

couse — worry, as in 'His dog was cousing your sheep'

cowfer — coffer, chest

cratch — feed rack (for cattle or sheep); also used as verb, to eat heartily

crod — small boy

crowsty — unpleasant, bad-tempered

cutch — mound in which potatoes stored; hare's form; to lie down; to
    cuddle

dandy — conceited fellow, clever Dick

Davy Lowcher — small, worthless fish

donst — beat, as in 'I'll donst thee'

doubles — as 'in his doubles', doubled up with laughter

doubt — without doubt, as in 'He's gone, I doubt'

dowlod — hay loft (Welsh, *taflod*)

dullness — rubbish, as in 'a pack of dullness'

dunna — do not, as in 'You munna say dunna, that inna right; / You
    shouldna say shunna, that inna polite'
dunning — failing, as in 'That awld yow (old ewe) be dunning'
dyern — eager, determined
dytch — ditch (showing local pronunciation)

ean, yean — give birth to
edge of night — gloaming
elder — udder
evening — after noon
every one, every other — alternately

faring — doing well, as in 'He's faring'
fastenment — latch of gate or door
feg — rough grass
fettle — condition (noun); repair (verb)
figairiment — predicament
fitchet, fitchuk — polecat
fled — flew, as in 'The bird fled out'
flens — fleas
form — make up, as in 'Form my mind'
forret — early, forward
foul — ugly, as in 'a foul man'
fretchet — irritable, bad-tempered, upset
frum — early (in crops)
full his hide — in good condition
fyern, feurn — bracken

gambrel — notched stick or bar used to hang up a carcase
glat — gap in hedge
glemmy — sultry
gorby — half-wit
gornal — half-mad person
grub — worm
gull, gully — gosling
gwathel — weeds, rubbish (Welsh, *gwaddod*, dregs)
gyeland — bump, as in 'The wheel went over the gyeland'

had him a good un — caught him out
hard — angry
hard as a toad — fit, in robust health
hauve — haft
heady — brainy

heathering — long sticks used to top a laid hedge

heed — credibility, as in 'There's no heed to him' (You can't believe a
    word he says)

heft — large number, as in 'I have any heft of those'

hesper, hespel — worry, as in 'I won't be hespelled by him any longer'

hevers — hogweed (Welsh, *efwr*)

hisht — hush

hognel, ognel — awkward, pig-headed

hogo — bad smell

hoit — beckon

honer — top dog

hool — dig, as in 'hool a hole'

hoot — shout

housing time — winter period when cattle brought indoors

huckin — period of work, shift

indisgestion — indigestion

inna — isn't

jag — small load

jern, jeurn, journ — energetic, keen

kank — fit of bad temper, as in 'in a bit of a kank'

kayle — fade, die, as in 'He was almost kayling off'

kex — wild parsnips or wild parsley

kiddling — dribbling

killsheep — dog that worries sheep, as in 'a killsheep dog'

kilt — female salmon in close season

kimet — silly or dull person

knocking in — courting

kweek — squeeze

lamp — beats as in 'I'll lamp him'

lease — glean

linno — flexible, supple

lump, lumper — young boy; lout

mawn — peat (Welsh)

meg — worry, henpeck

mex — clean out cowshed

miawkin — scarecrow

middleday — noon

minching — nibbling

63

mixen — dung heap
moither — ramble in speech
moithered — confused
moocher — self-setting potato
mopple — maple
mould — soil
Mr Bugger — mock-ceremonious form of address
muce — hole in hedge
mun — man
munna — musn't
munt, muntin — mountain pony
murren — strong smell
mutch, mitch — play truant
mye — hay; or to tread down

nesh, neesh, nish — tender, delicate
next to next — one after the other
nid — wooden wedge
nineter — caution
nip — notch, as in 'You've nipped the axe'
niscal — small, smallest in litter
noggin — one or two-quart can
noise — in 'keeping a noise' (making a noise)
not centre — daft
nut — small, as in 'That calf is a nut'

ongo — going, in working order
orl — alder
oolent — owl
oona — won't
oont, wunt, wnt — mole
oonty tump — molehill
oot ee? — will you?
orts — leftovers
oss — try, as in 'The dog would not oss to work'
oxet — hogshead

partly — almost, as in 'I was partly there'
pentice — blacksmith's shop
pergy — perky, saucy, obstinate
piece — field, as in 'tumpy piece'
piert, peart — lively, in good health

pikel — pitchfork
pilk — minnow (Welsh, *pilc*)
pincens — pinchers (pliers)
pishty — small dog
pivish — miserable
plock, pleck — paddock, small field
poon, pun, pund — hit, beat (Welsh, *pwnio*)
poother — muddle about at a job
prill — stream

quab — bog
qualm — sudden turn of illness
queek — squeeze
quell — kill, as in 'That goose will quell the gullies' (goslings)
quench — taste, appetite, as in 'He's lost his quench for it'
quist — wood pigeon

rack — footpath
raip, hraip — whetstone
ratch — rocky soil
reasty — bad, rancid
reen — open furrow between two cops (q.v.)
reynolds — fox
rimily — rumpled, untidy
ross — moor (Welsh, *rhos*)

sally — willow (Welsh, *helyg*)
scallion gate — lych gate
sclem — thief, cat that steals or begs food all the time
scoot — piece, patch, corner, as in 'He's plough a good scoot this morning'
scud — passing shower
scutch — rubbish from land, as in 'They're burning scutch'
shade — shelter (even in winter), as in 'Get in the shade out of the wind'
shape — as in 'There's no shape to him' (He's not doing well)
shunna — shouldn't
sidelant — steep
skilt — always gadding about
skinning — slyly peering
slaunch — slop, spill
slike — sleek, shiny
snag — ledge, as in 'a snag of rock'
sniving — teeming, as in ' a field sniving with rabbits'

solar, sollar — ceiling, upper floor of outhouse
some bit — a little, slightly
soon — early, as in 'soon tea' or 'You're soon'
sore — sad, bad, as in 'a sore nuisance'
soundly — heavy, severe, as in 'I hit the car soundly a bang'
spleenish — spiteful
squang, squerny — hare (Welsh, *ysgfarnog*)
squat — block to stop wheel moving on cart etc.
squomble — work awkwardly
starved — cold
steel — stale; handle of broom etc.
steen, stean — earthenware pitcher (Welsh, *y stên*)
stelch — post in cowhouse to which cow is tied
suck — gutter behind cows in cowhouse
sucker — foal
surry, zurry — familiar form of address; exclamation
swinge — singe

t — sometimes added to words, as in 'gallont' and 'boilt'
tally — as in 'living tally', co-habiting without being married
tare — eager, troublesome (Welsh, *taer*)
theave — female lamb
think — used interrogatively, as in 'Will he go, think?'
three half year old — describes animal $1^{1}/2$ years old
tiddling — lamb fed by hand
tollent, tollat — hay loft (Welsh, *taflod*)
torrel — useless person
trim — scold
trowse — brushwood to fill gap in hedge
tush — pull along, drag
twarly — mischievous, troublesome

urchin — hedgehog

warmship — warmth
welter — fine specimen, as in 'That's a welter'
whanders — pieces (as in 'Break to whanders')
wozzle — twist about
wunst — once

yarp — talk in stupid way
yow — ewe

CHAPTER 4

Life Cycles

The Llandegley churchwardens complained in 1694 that 'we have ... no doctor of physick, midwife, nor chirurgeon'. At least for the first and last of these, the same could have been said for most parishes, not only then but long afterwards. Even when doctors became available they were often unaffordable. Some were generous to needy patients, 'never sending a bill if it would mean hardship to pay it': so wrote Minna A. Barron of Dr Debenham and his nephew and son-in-law, 'Young' Dr Debenham, who were 'much loved' in late Victorian Presteigne; but she adds that another doctor who insisted that all his bills were paid before he left the town was burnt in effigy on Guy Fawkes Night.

The poor were long used to treating themselves by the waters of medicinal or magical springs (see chapter 1) or the virtues of healing herbs. Where family wisdom failed people might apply to local practitioners such as charmers and conjurers, who provided treatment and help for both humans and animals, though they sometimes descended into quackery. Bonesetters employed practical techniques, some of which are still used by the chiropractors of today.

The climactic events of birth, marriage and death were subject to a good deal of belief and ceremony. The zest with which women practised divination to discover the identity of their future husband underlines the importance attached to marriage. If present trends continue fewer than half cohabiting couples will be married by the year 2011, yet local newspapers in Radnorshire seem to show that marriage remains popular as week by week the time-honoured pictures of newlyweds appear, with brides more often than not clad in white.

The fragility of health and the dangers of death dogged the minds of communities in which life was hard and precarious. People tiptoed past hazards of ill-luck and illness, and went in fear of harbingers of death. When death came, they reacted with dignity and a deep desire to honour their departed friends and relations.

Self-help and desperate remedies

Until well into the twentieth century home-made herbal remedies were widely used—and are now being re-discovered. For example, extracts from sage, long considered a wisdom-enhancing plant, are currently being given to Alzheimer sufferers to reduce memory loss. Children suffering with worms were given to drink an infusion made by pouring boiling water on leaves of rue (*Ruta graveolens*). Because of its reputed capacity to cure drunkards of their addiction, rosemary (*Rosmarinus officinalis*) was dropped in infusion into casks of beer. Stonecrop—variety unspecified, but probably *Sedum telephium*—was fed to animals for its diuretic effects and applied to humans to rid them of shingles and to heal wounds. Expectant mothers were given fortifying strawberry or raspberry tea. Yet another infusion, of broom and burdock, was thought to be good for the bladder.

Rue

Both Mrs Mills (born in 1895 at Llaethdy) and Mrs With Watkins (born in 1900 near Knighton) remembered the use of sennygreen (or houseleek, *Sempervivum tectorum*), whose fleshy leaves, squashed and mixed with lard, helped to treat cuts and sores in man or beast.

Comfrey (*Symphytum officinale*), boiled into a mush, spread on a bruised, sprained or even fractured limb, and held in place by bandages, justified its other name of knitbone or grow-together-plant. An old farm remedy for a cough was to drink the liquor which ran off from chopped onions placed between layers of brown paper. For a dry cough a hazel nut sized quantity of a mixture of two teaspoonfuls of honey with white pepper was taken. Fairground boxers used to put on dirty wounds either an onion poultice or honey (now well known for its germicidal properties).

In the Marteg Valley in the 1940s Robert Gibbings heard that elder-flower wine was 'The best thing in the world for inflammation - they calls it pneumonia now ... Drink it as fast as you can; 'tis better than any doctor'. In the Elan Valley Elizabeth Clarke's family made not only wine from the elderflowers but lotion for soreness and ointment for chilblains. In addi-tion, she writes in *The Valley*, 'A basin of goose oil was kept in the bread oven between bakings, ready for aches and sprains, bronchitis, whooping cough - anything suggesting relief with a rubbing'. When one of the farm boys was plagued with warts, she continues 'Grandmother cured him with instructions to dip his hands in the blacksmith's cooling tank when he took a pony to be shod and not to dry them'.

Elder flower and berries

Another blacksmith at Chapel Lawn, near Knighton, made warts disappear simply by marking them with indelible pencil. His success with a child's crop of warts which its own father, a doctor, could not cure, is remembered at Knighton, where a wart charmer still practises.

George Lewis, in conversa-tion in 2000, recalled that a blacksmith would tie a horse hair round a wart, 'while uttering certain words', in order to make it disappear. Other strategies were to rub the wart with a black snail, impale the snail on a thorn and throw it over one's shoulder without looking back; to cut a potato in two and throw away one half while retaining the other: as the latter dried, so would the wart diminish.

Other well-tried expedients involved making notches on a stick, one for each wart; or making up a parcel containing as many small stones as there were warts. Stick or parcel was dropped at a crossroads, and whoever picked it up would receive the warts. Alternatively, warts were rubbed with elderberry leaves picked at night. When these were burned, the warts disappeared.

The cakes known as marshmallows were once made from the roots of the plant of the same name (*Althaea officinalis*) which, according to Nicholas Culpepper's famous herbal of 1653, could be used in various forms to treat 'Belly, Stone, Reins, Kidneys, Bladder, Coughs, Shortness of Breath,

Marsh Mallow,
the roots of which were used
to make marshmallow cakes

Wheezing, Excoriation of the Guts, Ruptures, Cramp, Convulsions, the King's Evil, Kernels, Chincough, Wounds, Bruises, Falls, Blows, Muscles, Morphew, Sun-burning'. More particularly, in Radnorshire a marsh mallow poultice served as an infallible cure for a poisoned arm or foot, though a poultice of cow manure might also be tried.

One of the diseases listed by Culpepper, the king's evil—so called because of a belief that a royal touch would cure it—was a form of tuberculosis of the bones and lymphatic glands, also called scrofula. Many sovereigns solemnly touched for it, some with apparent success, though the practice was discontinued early in the eighteenth century by George I. For a hundred years after that a lengthy proclamation dated 1683 remained on display in Disserth Church:

Whereas by the grace and blessing of God, the Kings and Queens of this realm, by and for many years past, have had the happiness, by their sacred touch, and invocation of the name of God, to cure those who are afflicted with the disease called the King's evil; and His Majesty [Charles II] in no less measure than any of his royal predecessors, having had success therein, and in his most gracious and pious disposition being as ready and willing to relieve the distresses and necessities of his good subjects; yet in his princely wisdom, foreseeing that in this (as in all other things) order is to be observed, and fit times are necessary to be appointed for the performance of this great work of charity, his Majesty was therefore this day pleased to declare in Council his royal will and pleasure to be that (in regard heretofore the usual time for presenting such persons for this purpose have been prefixed by his royal predecessors) from henceforth be from the Feast of All Saints, commonly called All Hallowtide [1 November] to Christmas, and from Christmas until the first of March, and then to cease till Passion Week, on account of the temperature of the season, and in respect of contagion which may happen to his Majesty's sacred person.

The document goes on to stipulate that candidates for the touch must only present themselves at the appointed times, and must carry churchwardens' certificates confirming their parish and also that they have not previously attended. The last condition seems to imply deficiencies in the therapeutic powers of the 'sacred person'—the king. A different kind of touch—that of a man who had eaten eagle's flesh was thought in parts of Radnorshire until the early twentieth century to cure shingles. The ability was believed to persist in both the son and the grandson of the qualified man.

Only slightly less bizarre is the idea that some of the sap bubbling from burning green ash could be poured into the ear as a remedy for earache. Kilvert noted something similar in 1870:

Old James Jones was breaking stones below Pentwyn. He told me how he had once cured his deafness for a time by pouring hot eel oil into his ear, and again by sticking into his ear an 'ellern' (elder) twig, and wearing it there night and day. The effect of the eel oil at first was, he said, to make his head and brains feel full of crawling creatures.

The River Wye and Llanelwedd Rocks, near Builth Wells, from a postcard

Adder skins were thought to help in treating rheumatism, when made into bands to encircle the afflicted limb, and also blood poisoning when applied at the point of injury. W.H. Howse mentions (1949) the case of a girl with a piece of needle broken off in her hand: 'After hospital treatment had failed to dislodge the needle, an adder skin was applied to the hand and the broken piece (so my informant said) was easily extracted'.

A stone — dropped from heaven, according to tradition, on a clear day — at Welfield House, Llanelwedd, was firmly believed to cure rabies contracted after the bite of a mad dog: scrapings from it were mixed with milk and drunk. The remedy was sought by people from all parts of mid-Wales and Herefordshire until the 1870s when, wrote D.E. Owen, 'the pilgrimages to Welfield ceased, not because people abated their belief in the healing qualities of the stone, but because the measures taken by the Board of Agriculture practically exterminated mad dogs'.

Asthma was treated by putting a bible for three nights running under the sufferer's pillow. W.C. Maddox reports from the late 1930s the case of a boy on a remote hill farm who pulled through pneumonia by the 'unflagging attention' of a doctor who was disgusted to find that the boy's parents attributed his recovery to the pig's trotters they had placed at the foot of his bed.

Charmers, Conjurers and Bonesetters
Though of different kinds, both charmers and conjurers were unofficial medical and veterinary practitioners. Charmers treated minor injuries and

common ailments such as shingles, snake-bites, toothache, thorn-pricks and warts. Their methods included charms (verbal formulae, oral, printed or hand-written), objects with curative properties, and healing touch. By tradition they accepted neither thanks nor payment for their services. However, as early as Henry VIII's time Lewis ap Morgan—recorded as rector at Aberedw in 1535—found himself imprisoned in Radnor Castle on charges that 'he daily frequentith him selfe for lucre or money to charme for horses, beastes and other catall that be syke [sick], and makith writynges to set over the dores where the same beastes shall entre into for their soccour at nighte, for the which the Kynges subgiettes daily resort to him xx myles compase thereaboutes'. Furthermore, ran the accusation, 'he maketh writynges for younge children that cryeth in their sleape to hange about their neckes'.

Five hundred years later, according to commissioners sent to enquire into the state of education in Radnorshire (in 1846-7), people still 'commonly resorted' to charmers when they were ill. A charmer called Stokes was still alive as an old man at Llangynllo in 1875. At Gladestry a Mr Bufton and a Mrs Wanklin who cured lameness in horses and rupture and toothache in humans were remembered well into the twentieth century.

Griffin Lloyd, a small farmer from upper Glascwmig at Glascwm, who died between 1905 and 1910, had a considerable reputation as a charmer. A friend of W.H. Howse's, still alive in 1951, went to Lloyd to seek a cure for his daughter's acute toothache:

> He first asked for an assurance of my friend's belief in his ability to effect a cure. Having satisfied himself on this, he moved his lips in silence for a moment or two, and then told my friend that when he returned home he would find his daughter cured of her toothache. And so it was! The toothace went, I was told, about the time the charmer was casting his spell. No money was paid, - my friend said this would break the spell. Doubtless a gift was made later on.

A charm against toothache obtained by D.E. Owen, presumably in Llanelwedd, runs as follows:

> And Jesus saw Peter sitting by the wayside crying and he said, 'What aileth thee, Peter?' and Peter answered, 'Oh Lord I have the toothache'. And Jesus said, 'be thou healed' and the toothache left him that very hour.

A piece of paper bearing these words would have been carried in the sufferer's pocket.

The sardonic joke in one such document, trustingly worn round the neck in a bag, is revealed by the Northamptonshire doctor, John Cotta, in his book, *A Short Discovery of the Unobserved Dangers of Several Sorts of Ignorant and Unconsiderable Practices in Physicke* (1612). It proved to contain the words 'Diabolus effodiate tibi oculos, impleat foramina stercoribus', which may sound impressive but means 'May the devil tear out your eyes (and) fill the holes with excrements'.

A Radnorshire cure for a nose-bleed cosnsisted of tying a length of four-ply red wool round the sufferer's little finger. Red wool was also bound round pigs' tails and fastened to babies' cots to ward off elf shot, an affliction, according to a belief going back at least to Anglo-Saxon times, caused by the tiny darts fired by elves. The colour red was thought obnoxious to evil spirits.

Within living memory a charmer called Stephens, who lived at Cwm Gwyn in the upper reaches of the River Teme, enjoyed a reputation for the ability to stem bleeding. One day as he walked homewards from Knighton past Lloyney some people were killing a pig. One of them turned round, recognised him, and tauntingly enquired 'Can you and your charm stop this bleeding?' Stephens grinned, said nothing, and walked on. The flow of blood from the pig did stop, much to the consternation of those involved, and one of them had to walk back to the charmer's house to plead with him to take the charm off.

Owen, writing in 1911, observed that 'Radnorshire has never been without its noted conjuror'. Like charmers, conjurers—sometimes called wizards or white witches, cunning men or women, wise men or women— practised healing but in addition offered a range of other services including astrology, fortune-telling, the detection of lost or stolen property and protection against witchcraft. Unlike charmers, they required payment, and often inspired fear.

A conjurer from Llansanffraid-yn-Elfael was drawn to the attention of John Wesley after he had preached there in 1746:

> As soon as we came out of church a poor woman met us, whom Satan had bound in an uncommon manner for many years. She followed us to the house, weeping and rejoicing and praising God. The odd account which she gave of herself was this (concerning

which let everyone judge as he pleases). That seven years since she affronted one of her neighbours who thereupon went to Francis Morgan (a man famous in those parts) and gave him 14s. to do his worst to her; and that the next night, as soon as she was in bed, there was a sudden storm of thunder, lightning, and rain, and in the midst of which she felt all her flesh shudder, and knew that the devil was close to her; that at the same time a horse she had in the stable below, which used to be as quiet as a lamb, leaped to and fro and tore in such a manner that she was forced to rise and turn him out; that a tree which grew at the end of the house was torn up by the roots; that from henceforth she had no rest day or night, being not only in fear and horror of mind, but in the utmost torment of body, feeling as if her flesh was tearing off with burning pincers; that till this day she had never had any respite or ease; but now she knew God had delivered her, and she believed he would still deliver her body and soul, and bruise Satan under her feet.

People's belief in the power of conjurers remained just as strong in the nineteenth century. William Harris of Cwrtycadno—taking advantage of the similarity of his name to that of the well respected Harries family of conjurers from the same Carmarthenshire village—travelled from town to town, including Llanidloes and Rhayader, distributing handbills in which he claimed to be a doctor and herbalist capable of curing everything from sore eyes to lunacy and of removing curses and spells. He was in fact a quack. Harris, aged 66, and described as 'well known throughout the Principality', was charged in February 1867 at Rhayader magistrates' court with obtaining money by false pretences and acting as a professional medical man without being duly qualified. Edwin Jones, who had come from America to live with his uncle at Boughrood, told the court he had come across a handbill in which Harris described himself as a medical doctor and herbalist. At a consultation in Llanidloes Harris informed Jones that he had a bad heart and lungs, an elbow out of joint, and cancer in one leg, and that he had been witched by a woman in America. He offered to cure him for £6 and handed over a piece of paper, to be worn round the neck in a small bag which was on no account to be dropped on the ground. The paper was later found to bear these words:

The fourth is Maynom, one of the powers who hath the ability of superficient administration and protection, that is at one and the same time to be present with many. His presence must be sought by humility and prayer; the fifth good genius is Gaomum, an angel of celestial brightness, who hath the peculiar ability of rendering his pupil invisible to any evil spirit whatsoever.

Another witness, a Builth carpenter called Samuel Phillips, testified he had gone to Harris with a leg injury which his doctor said needed an operation. Harris told him that he had been witched by his next-door neighbour and provided a formula which his (Harris's) daughter copied out of a large book on to a piece of paper and his wife sewed into a small calico bag. In addition, Harris supplied £5 worth of medicines and pills; and when Phillips failed to pay in full Harris said he was 'the master of hell and the devils' and would see him in hell.

The magistrates referred the case to the assizes at Presteigne, where a jury found Harris guilty, but recommended mercy. Harris claimed to have become blind in prison whilst awaiting trial. The gaol surgeon, one Dr Philpot, confirmed the condition, which he said, somewhat bizarrely, could have been caused by damp. The judge passed sentence of 'only' three months imprisonment, 'but taking his condition into consideration it would be without hard labour'. Harris made no further appearance in recorded history.

Unlike him, genuine conjurers—though one has to admit that they, too, relied on, not to say imposed on the credulity of the ignorant—remained in their own town or village, where people sought them out. The name of Jones the Conjurer of Llangurig was known throughout Radnorshire in the 1870s, and many visited him. One of his clients, due for trial in the magistrates' court at Knighton, engaged him to cast a spell on the prosecution witnesses. Jones duly attended, but the effectiveness or otherwise of his intervention has unfortunately gone unrecorded. A further anecdote about Jones is given by Howse in his book, *Radnorshire*:

> An old man told me that he once went to Jones the Conjurer for a charm to take away his toothache. The conjurer covered a piece of paper with writing and, after folding it up, handed it to my friend with the injunction that it was to be held to his face for half-an-hour and then put into a hole in the wall and never looked at again. The cure worked, - such are the miracles of faith.

Another conjurer called Evan Meredith still practised at Llandeilo Graban in the early years of the twentieth century. He cured bleeding, toothache and other ailments, and also traced stolen sheep. Because of his reputed knowledge of witchcraft people took care not to offend him. His niece, 'Taffy' Prothero, writing in 1985 contended that the role of conjurers was 'entirely benevolent', and that Meredith said:

> the secret had been passed to him as a young man. When he told his father, a strict Baptist, he met with strong disapproval and was told to have nothing to do with it, to leave it entirely alone. But the young man thought 'I have been given this and I can do much good with it, I ought not just to let it lie idle'. So the news got around that the mantle had fallen on him. Farmers came to see him. They would describe the symptoms of their ailing beast with particulars of any visible signs such as swellings or stiffness. The conjuror would listen attentively. The farmer would go back home and the beast would recover.

Elizabeth Clarke, too, emphasised the benevolent intentions of conjurers, though she was well aware of the magical side to their activities, and even mentioned their magic books. She relates how when his scythe was stolen, her grandfather, suspecting a certain person but having no proof, went to see the most famous conjurer of the day (could this have been Jones of Llangurig?) who lived within an easy ride. At the end of the consultation the conjurer said: 'If you will give me a drop of your blood I will set the mark of a scythe on the thief's face that he will carry to the end of his life'. Grandsir declined, since he did not wish his neighbour to be so branded. The thief was left unpunished but years later the stolen scythe came to light on his land, buried under some peat.

Clarke's grandfather went to the conjurer on another occasion when the butter would not come and no doubt he feared that some malign influence was at work. He was given an envelope and told to keep it in the dairy, without ever allowing it to be opened. Clarke's grandmother evidently did look inside because she said that the paper carried diagrams of half moons and stars.

Until the late 1930s Radnorshire people were among those who visited Jonathan Griffiths at Pantybeny Farm near Llanidloes to ask for help with sick cattle and sheep and lost or stolen property. Usually they would take a taxi from Llanidloes or a car from a particular garage. In either case the driver would sound his horn at the top of a hill on the Plylimon road to give warning of his approach to the farm in the hollow below. Griffiths would wait in one room as visitors were shown into another. While he listened through the door his wife, saying that he had been delayed, would engage the visitors in conversation for up to 20 minutes in order to elicit information from them. When Griffiths emerged his knowledge of their affairs would make a profound impression.

The link between conjurers and witchcraft is considered in the next chapter. Their role has now long receded into the past, even though one of their functions, fortune-telling, has a wide following in the popular press. A Conjurer's Pitch is still to be found at Knighton; and a field at Presteigne, Conjurer's Plock, recalls Edward Morgan, a conjurer who lived at Rodd Hurst and is buried in the churchyard.

Where both charmers and conjurers employed psychology and suggestion, not to speak of sharp practice, bonesetters were—and are—reliant on practical techniques. In Radnorshire the Lloyds were an important family of bonesetters. John Lloyd, who lived in the Harley Valley in the eighteenth century, manipulated joints, used splints to set broken bones, and applied herbal poultices. Like charmers, he would take no money for his services, but he would accept gifts. Because of his fondness for silver he was given such things as coat and waistcoat buttons, shoe buckles, a snuff box and a walking stick top in the precious metal, and this earned him the nickname of Silver John. It also caused him to be murdered and robbed as he came home from Builth Fair (see chapter 1).

Hugh Lloyd's tomb at Michaelchurch

A later member of the same family, Hugh Lloyd of Baynham Hall near Newchurch, is buried at Michaelchurch-on-Arrow. He died in 1856 at the age of 86, so he could well have remembered Silver John. His imposing tomb, which attests considerable prosperity, is now marked by a self-set hawthorn tree. It bears this inscription:

> A talent rare by him possessed
> T'adjust the bones of the distressed;
> When ever called he ne'er refus'd
> But cheerfully his talent used.
> But now he lies beneath this tomb
> Till Jesus comes to adjust His Own.

The Lloyds no longer live at Baynham Hall, but several later bonesetters — the Bywaters of Knucklas and Llangynllo, Mrs James of Leintwardine and Mrs Drew of Lyonshall, both in Herefordshire — are said to be related to them. Mona Morgan (born 1916) tells how her older sister received treatment:

> One night Mu hurt her foot ... For days it remained swollen and painful, so brother took her in the trap to Mrs Drew, the bonesetter, who lived some eight miles away. Mrs Drew came from a long line of bonesetters who had lived in the area for many years. Generations of folks from far and near had sought relief from the family and few had left disappointed. Chatting to Mu, Mrs Drew gently took the injured foot, felt it all over, then suddenly gave it a sharp wrench; there was a click, a gasp from Mu, and the pain was gone.

Until the late 1950s, Tim Bywater, whose mother was a Lloyd — and the gift was thought to pass down the family — practised as a bonesetter at Knighton, where he held a kind of surgery in the Horse and Jockey public house. He boasted that he could pull a bull's hip back in — a tremendous feat of skill and strength. He took no payment for his ministrations but would accept a gift, preferably of whisky. One farmer, invited to choose between a doctor of 40 years' experience and the bonesetter, said 'Bywater every bloody time'.

Bywater himself died in about 1970, leaving a son who had become a vet and a daughter, a physiotherapist. The family's Lloyd's Oil is remem-

The Horse and Jockey, Knighton, where Tim Bywater 'practised'

bered as being on sale in chemists' shops, in competition, perhaps, with Massey's Oil or The Radnorshire Remedy, an embrocation for everything from rheumatism to whooping cough, as well as all external injuries.

Births and Baptisms

In the early days of Christianity baptisms were conducted in springs and streams; for example, in the Teme near Rydycwm at Knucklas after missionary camp meetings held near Brookhouse Chapel at Beguildy, at St Teilo's Pool near Llandeilo Graban, at Parson's Dingle, Beguildy, in a pool on the stream at Llaethdy, in the Elan near the Baptist Chapel and probably also at Ffynon Gynidr near Glasbury and in St Michael's Pool near Llangynllo. Only later were church fonts used. Llanbister is perhaps the only church in Radnorshire which re-introduced (in 1908) the practice of baptising by total immersion, albeit within the building. However, the purpose-built baptistry (still there) was used only four times in the whole of the twentieth century.

The move was made in response to the strong influence in the Ithon Valley of the Baptists who practised total immersion, though not of infants. When Mona Morgan's mother was baptised, ice fringed the water; when her sister was similarly immersed in the River Arrow below Newchurch School, 'the shock of the icy water made her gasp for breath'. 'My turn came a couple of years later at Gladestry', writes Mrs Morgan. 'I well remember wearing a pale green slip under my white dress for the occasion

A river baptism at Howey, 1927

and being embarrassed to find the colour showing through the white dress as I came up out of the water'.

Such ceremonies were taken very seriously indeed. A long remembered cautionary tale concerns one Griffith ap Bedw Du of Pilleth, who in 1574 'upon a proud stomach' caused his newly-born son to be christened in wine instead of water. The action, deemed to be impious, resulted in a decline in the family's fortunes—or so local people firmly believed. This Griffith is likely to have been related to John Dee, for whom, see chapter 5.

Surnames of course pass from father to son, but by long standing practice in Radnorshire, eroded only in the last few decades, a first son always received the same first name as his father.

Courtship and Marriage

John Byng, viscount Torrington, bitterly complained of the behaviour of the three Davies sisters who were staying in the same boarding house as him at Llandrindod in 1789. He concluded, judging from the high spirits and tomboyishness, that they had come to the wells less for their health than in hope of finding husbands. Writing some 150 years later, T.P. Davies commented: 'It is extraordinary how this reputation of the Wells has persisted down to the present time. Even today the father of too many unmarried daughters in Wales will say in a half joking manner that he will be obliged to take them to the *Ffynonau*' (*sic*).

A courting couple on Llandrindod Lake,
as depicted on a postcard of 1912

Llandrindod's lake seems to have been a popular haunt of what used to be called courting couples. Lovers' Leap to the south-west of Rock Park seems to have no firm history, but one suggestion is that a young man picking flowers for his sweetheart fell 30 feet into the River Ithon, which was in spate at the time. Either in the hope of effecting a rescue or simply giving way to despair, the grief-stricken woman plunged in after him and both were drowned. An alternative story is that the couple jumped in when parents rejected their plan to marry.

The motivation of at least the groom seems very clear in a match mentioned with heavy irony in the *Hereford Times* for 5 January 1775:

> Saturday last was married at Clyrow, in the county of Radnor, Mr Eynon Beynon, an eminent Methodist Preacher in that neighbour-hood, aged *eighty-seven*, to an agreeable young lady of *nineteen*, with a *handsome fortune*. - The motives to this union are not easily to be accounted for, as the above gentleman has ever been remarkably severe in preaching against covetousness, worldly desire, &c. &c.

Lower down the social scale premarital sexual relations were common. One woman claimed that she would not marry a man until 'her knew what a could go'. Another method of checking was the practice described by Ronald Frankenberg as current until the mid-twentieth century at Llanfihangel-yng-Ngwynfa:

A young man, after the male 'peer group' gathering had broken up, went to the house of the girl of his choice and attracted her attention by tapping on the window. If she liked him, she would invite him into the house (her parents by this time sleeping). At first, she would entertain him to light refreshments in the kitchen, and sometimes later, if the affair went well, to courting in bed. This interesting custom ... [is] known as 'bundling' ... its secrecy makes possible trial and error, and it ensures a choice of partner to the girl and boy concerned at the same time as giving the community and the parents some control over who marries whom.

Now I have no evidence of bundling in Radnorshire, but Llanfihangel-yng-Ngwynfa is only 20 miles away in Montgomeryshire, and it would be surprising if the practice had not been common to both counties or at least parts of them.

In Kilvert's day Llanhallant Eve (Hallowe'en, 31 October) had considerable importance for those inclined to marry. A girl who could count the spots on a ladybird's back on that day would know how many years would pass before she became a bride. On the same occasion a Llanhallant Cake baked in tongs over the fire had nine ingredients: floury water, spice, currants, balm (yeast), salt, pepper, mustard, and either a grain of wheat or a bean. Each unmarried member of the household broke off a piece of the finished cake and the one finding the grain or the bean was sure to be lucky in love. Finally, on the same night, girls went out and sprinkled hempseed round the leek or onion bed in the belief that they would see behind them, raking in the seed, the image of their future husband. As they sowed they sang:

> Hempseed I sow,
> Hempseed I hoe.
> He that is my true love,
> Come after me and mow.

A chilling sequel to the ceremony 'came within Mr Kilvert's own knowledge' and was recounted by his niece, Mrs Essex Hope:

A servant girl at a country farm went out as usual on Llanhallant Eve to sow hempseed, and, suspecting that some trick might be played on her, said to her mistress: 'Don't send master out after me'. The mistress promised not to, and the girl went out, and began sowing the seed and singing the song. In a few minutes she became aware of the figure of her master raking the earth after her. She threw down the rest of the seed angrily, and ran in, crying out, 'Why did you send the master when you promised not to?' The mistress turned deadly pale and cried: 'He has never left the house! Oh, Gwenny! be kind to my poor children'. She died soon after, and the master married the girl before a year had passed.

A custom common to Radnorshire and other parts of Wales was the bidding, a pre-wedding, fund-raising entertainment to which the friends of both parties were invited—or bid. Anyone attending, and even giving apologies for not doing so, was duty bound to bring or send a contribution to the new household, ranging from a cow or a calf down to half a crown or even a shilling. 'In dresser-drawers of farms, among old receipts and certificates, invitations to Biddings were still to be found when I was a child', writes Elizabeth Clarke. 'Printed or hand-done on discolouring paper - the work presumably of a local scribe, judging by the fineness of the writing - they were delivered by anyone taking a pony in the right direction'. She concludes that 'in the old days couples used to set up home on the products of a bidding'.

Esylt Newbery moved to Presteigne from Llandrindod in 1883 when her father became headmaster of the grammar school and chaplain to Sir John Arkwright of Kinsham Court. The Newberys lived in the head-master's house near the church, and their neighbours included a disrep-utable family, the Partons. A new rector called on them and to his horror found the parents to be unmarried. 'To everyone's amazement', wrote Esylt Newbery, 'he bullied the couple into going across to the church one morning where he read the marriage service over them'.

Rev. John Price, the eccentric vicar of Llanbedr-Painscastle from 1859 until the 1870s, at one stage offered five shillings to each pair of vagrants living in sin who would agree to be married. 'As his sight was very weak', wrote T.P. Jones, 'several business-like couples let him marry them half a dozen times'. Since there was no vicarage, Price lived in three old bathing machines until they were accidentally burnt down. He then moved to a brick and slate henhouse. When Kilvert visited his colleague in 1872 he found him living in a little grey hut built of dry stone, roofed with thin and broken thatch, and standing in a little valley, Cwm Cello (Ceilio), at the foot of Llanbedr Hill. Inside, the horrified Kilvert noted: 'The squalor, the dirt, the dust, the foulness and wretchedness of the place were indescrib-

Llanbedr Church, where Parsons Price and Williams preached

able, almost inconceivable'. Vestiges of the house remain in Little Pencwm Field on Penbedw Farm, Llanbedr.

It so happens that one of Price's predecessors was another noted eccentric, Rev. Williams, otherwise known as Parson Button. W.E.T. Morgan published this account of him in 1914:

> For years he was vicar and schoolmaster combined. The school was held in the church, as it so often was in those days. He was a bachelor, and spent much of his time in the village alehouse. Often he set the children a task while he adjourned for refreshments. The consequence was that frequently the children got tired of waiting, and despairing of the return of the master deserted the school and made tracks for their respective homes. Sometimes it happened that they were confronted by the returning pedagogue, and sternly ordered to come back. Bidding one of their number to cut him a hazel twig, he drove them back to the church, and soundly trounced them for their disobedience.
>
> Once he was discovered by the children removing his possessions from one lodging to another, and carrying his bed on his back. This was too great a temptation, and so one of the more daring of the boys approached him from the rear, and giving the bed a good tug, down goes the bed, Parson Button and all. On another occasion, having partaken of his favourite beverage a little more freely, he was discovered asleep on the roadside not far from the castle,

wholly oblivious of all things mundane. This put it into the head of
one of the more ingenious and venturesome lads to summon his
companions together, and tie the hapless victim to the axletree of a
pair of old cart wheels, bowl him to the top of the ramparts and then
send him careering madly down the steep descent of the mound,
amidst the approving cheers of the interested spectators, but to the
imminent peril of the life of poor Parson Button.

When Kilvert asked Hannah Whitney of Clyro how she could describe
Parson Button both as a good churchman and a very drunken man she
replied that he was a capital preacher who used to remark to parishioners:
'My brethren, don't you do as I do, but you do as I say'. 'He was very
quarrelsome', Kilvert added, 'and frequently fought at Clyro at on his way
home from Hay. One night he got fighting at Clyro and was badly beaten
and mauled. The next Sunday he came to Llanbedr Church bruised black
and blue, with his head broken and swollen nose and two black eyes.
However, he faced his people and in his sermon glorified himself and his
prowess and gave a false account of the battle at Clyro in which he was
worsted, but in which he represented himself as victorious'.

Kilvert, who liked a good wedding, disapproved of register office ceremonies which he called 'gipsy "jump the broom"' marriages. The broom
wedding was not uncommon in Wales, where it was called *priodas ysgub*,
nor confined to gypsies. A couple considered themselves married after
jumping over a broom placed across the doorway of a house or inn—the
Plough at Knighton is one establishment where such ceremonies are
recorded. Despite Kilvert's view, register office weddings had greater legit-
imacy. One of these, between Catherine Price of the New Inn at Clyro and
a young Painscastle blacksmith called Davies, had a splendid reception. In
describing what he heard of it Kilvert was obviously longing to join in:

> The wedding feast was at the New Inn which is now shut up as an
> inn and abolished. As I passed the house I heard music and dancing.
> They were dancing in an upper room, unfurnished, tramp, tramp,
> tramp, to the jingling of a concertina. The stamping was tremen-
> dous. I thought they would have brought the floor down. They
> seemed to be jumping round and round. When I came back the
> dance seemed to have degenerated into a romp and the girls were
> squealing, as if they were being kissed or tickled and not against
> their will.

In his account of another wedding, seven years later, in 1878, Kilvert mentions several customary features:

> Friday, 26 April. To St Harmon's by 9.10 train to marry David Powell and Maggie Jones of Tylare. Mrs Jones of the Gates had made a triumphal arch of moss over the Churchyard gate and flowers were strewn in the bride's path. Maggie was surprised and delighted to see and be married by her old friend. Fog signals were laid on the line and the wedding party issued from the Church just as the noon train came down with the banging of crackers and guns and a great crowd at the station crossing gates. The wedding party and guests went to the Sun where I joined them for a minute to drink a glass of wine to the health of the bride and bridegroom.

Kilvert then joined the wedding dinner at Tylare and helped to carve before running to catch the 4.45 train and begin his journey back to Bredwardine.

A custom which lingered until at least the 1940s in parts of Radnorshire involved stretching a rope across the road or path after a wedding service. The groom paid a small sum to those holding the rope and then he and his bride, one last obstacle overcome, embarked on married life.

'When thee went a-courting', said a Radnorshire quaker to his son on his wedding day, 'I told thee to keep thy eyes open; now that thou art married, I tell thee to keep them half-shut'. The point seems to be empha-

The Sun Inn at St Harmon

sising the mutual tolerance needed to make a marriage work. Mishaps certainly attracted more attention than harmony. C.G. Portman quotes from an eighteenth-century notebook the sad story of a man from Clyro who married a catholic. On the day after the wedding she went to Hay 'secretly, in her wedding dress, and returned home greatly besmirched and bedraggled'. The purpose of her journey was to drink the water of a certain well—probably either the Swan Well or the Black Lion Well—because she thought that by so doing she would acquire the power to 'rule over him'. On the way to the well she fell into a brook. When the news leaked out it 'stayed on the tongue' for a long time. The husband became the butt of ribald jests, and the village rhymester 'made a stave' on the incident entitled 'Who will wear the breeches?'

A strong feeling existed that the community should intervene if marital discord went beyond certain limits. An instance of a wife's ill-treating her husband aroused particular indignation. Wirt Sikes wrote in 1881:

> There is an ancient custom called the *ceffyl pren*, or wooden horse, still occasionally encountered in Wales, whose purpose is the punishment of scolding wives. The virago is ridden in effigy thereon, and subjected to such indignities as being pelted with addled eggs. This has been called the Welsh lynch law, and its spirit still survives actively; but, instead of being evoked for the punishment of viragos its chief service nowadays is to serve the cause of morality in graver matters. Aggravated adultery, outraging the community and exciting deep and bitter indignation especially among the women, is extremely liable to be met with punishment of this sort.

One thinks of the treatment meted out at Llanbister in 1898 (see chapter 8) to those considered to be flagrantly flouting moral canons, though this was not *ceffyl pren* but Rebecca.

If all else failed when a marriage broke down, divorce—at least after the act of 1857—was theoretically possible though far out of reach financially except for the extremely well-to-do. However an unofficial (and illegal) form of divorce, known as wife selling, did exist, though many thought it degrading. Two instances have come to light in Radnorshire, both in Knighton, and both reported in the *Hereford Times*. On 1 March 1851 the paper, under the heading of 'Disgraceful Affair', stated that the town crier 'by the sound of his bell' had proclaimed 'the sale of a woman by public auction at the Town hall, ... being the property of a jockey'. No further details were given, though more were promised for the following week. The writer concluded 'Henceforth any of our Neighbours who may be in want of a wife will at once see that he can be supplied at Knighton market'. Nothing more appeared in succeeding issues of the newspaper.

Three years later, however, on 6 May 1854, a different case was reported under the heading of 'Scandalous Proceeding':

> On Saturday last [29 April] the town crier announced through the streets the public sale of the young wife of William Jones, which was to come off at the market-place on that evening. The sale did not, however, take place, the fair dame, as it was understood, having been disposed of privately. All parties concerned in these outrages on public decency ought to know that the sale of a wife is a misdemeanour.

One should perhaps add that many loving and long-lasting marriages in Radnorshire are attested by epitaphs given in chapter 6.

Bad Luck and Ill-omen

A large number of omissions (and of commissions) were—and in some cases still are—thought to bring bad luck or adverse consequences. Wearing green is unlucky, especially at a wedding, perhaps because the colour was associated with fairies. Refusing the offer of an overcoat signifies that one is too old or too proud. Failing to burn hair clippings may result in their being taken by birds to line nests, and this would produce headaches. Cutting down witty (mountain ash) is unlucky, perhaps because so doing removes protection against witches. Bringing may blossom into a house is a sign of death—and recent scientific research has established that a chemical present in the blossom is also produced when decomposition of the human body takes place. Bringing in hazel catkins (known as lambs' tails) or willow catkins (known as gullies) results respectively in a bad lambing season or upsetting sitting geese.

When a death occurs in a household especially of the master or mistress, the bees' attention should be attracted by tanging (tapping a metallic object) and then they should be told, lest they, too, die or leave. The carrion crow, raven and magpie have been birds of ill omen for centuries. One of them can spell trouble, but two mean good luck, 'possibly on the ground that two negatives make a positive', according to D.E. Owen. In an article published in 1911 Owen adds:

Most of the very oldest inhabitants of Radnorshire will tell you that they have heard the 'hell hounds' howling as they pursued the spirits of the departed on their way to heaven. When they give details it is abundantly clear that the night call of the curlew and the wild goose, high in the heaven on their spring migration, is what was generally supposed to be the howling of those hounds (Cŵn Annwn). More deaths take place in the spring of the year than at any other time, and these frequent events, synchronising with the noisy night-flight of goose and curlew, largely account for this weird belief.

The hell hounds were thought to portend a funeral, as were corpse candles—glimmering lights—seen on a path or road. Old Sam Handley of Aberedw saw one in November 1901, at the foot of his bed, and concluded that his death was near. Unfortunately, Tudor and Lloyd, who record this, do not say whether the omen proved to be accurate. George Lewis heard corpse candle stories from Crychel Rhos near Abbey Cwm Hir.

A small candle meant the cortege of a child, a bigger, that of an adult. Two coming from opposite directions and crossing signified two funerals would follow the same routes. W.B. Hamer tells this story in his book, *Radnorshire in History, Topography and Romance*, published in 1914:

> Late one night a farmer's wife saw one of those weird precursors of death hover up and down the river bank in front of the homestead. Calling her husband they both watched it for some time and then went to bed. A few weeks later a young woman from an adjoining parish called at this farmhouse while journeying to stay with friends who lived on the other side of the river. Her intention was to ford the river at the spot where the light was seen. The river being at that time in flood the farmer and his wife endeavoured to dissuade her from so doing. She declined to take their advice, and soon afterwards was observed walking up and down the river bank in the same manner as the candle had been seen. Next day her dead body was taken out of the river.

It would be interesting to know where this happened, but Hamer provides no identification.

The strange case of a presentiment related by W.E.T. Morgan concerns a family at Glasbury of father, mother and two daughters, one of whom was considered to be rather weak-minded. A ne'er-do-well young farmer in the parish courted her and persuaded her to marry him:

All was kept a strict secret between them, and it was arranged by him that the wedding was to take place in the parish church, near her home, at 12 o'clock one night, when she should come dressed in her best, wearing all the jewels she possessed, and as much money as she could lay her hands on. On the appointed night she went alone to the church, and waited in the porch.

Meanwhile, the curate of the parish, who lived not far off, had retired to bed with his wife, and fallen asleep. Just before midnight, he awoke suddenly, and exclaimed to his wife, 'O Betty, Betty, there's someone calling me at the church'. 'Nonsense, William', she replied, 'lie down and go to sleep'. And so they both went to sleep again. Soon, however, he was again roused by the same voice calling to him: 'Mr ---, Mr ---, come at once to the church'.

The good man immediately got up, dressed, and hurried to the church. On approaching the west door he distinctly heard the sound of a pickaxe in the churchyard, and at the same time a woman's voice calling from the porch: 'Why are you so late, Mr --- ? I've been waiting for you here a long time'. To this he replied, 'Why are you here, Miss --- ? What's the matter?' 'O, we're going to be married'. said she. To this he answered, 'Why, you can't be married at this time of night'. 'O, yes', she said, 'I'm going to be married to Tom --- '.

He then persuaded her to go with him home, and as they were passing that portion of the churchyard from whence he had previously heard the sound of digging they beheld a newly-cut grave, which had evidently been prepared for her by her pretended lover, who had ere this decamped, and was never seen in the neighbourhood again. The young lady returned to her home.

The curate's perception may have been akin to second sight, of which Elizabeth Clarke quotes the instance of a woman who heard trains running near Rhayader 25 years before the railway came, and dreamed of water lapping at the door of her cottage before the drowning of the Elan Valley was mooted. She also saw a hearse whose runaway horse tipped out a coffin which fell open to disclose her own body. Years later at her funeral the horses did bolt, flinging off both driver and coffin at a point in the road which in time disappeared beneath the water of the reservoir.

Death signs still featured in the superstitions noted in the early 1950s by Iona Opie from Radnorshire teenagers. They included seeing a falling star, blowing up a paper bag in the house and bursting it, and a white pigeon's landing on a chimney pot. One Knighton girl averred that deaths come in threes. Another girl believed that the last egg a hen lays is some-times very small and it should not be brought into the house because that would mean a death in the family. To make sure this does not happen any such egg should immediately be picked up and thrown over the left shoulder.

Deaths and Funerals

As well as being the time for divining future partners Llanhallantide could also provide news of deaths. A fairly general belief in Radnorshire was that those who listened at the church door at midnight would hear 'the saints within call out the names of those who were to die within the year'. At Clyro, listeners were required first to run nine times round the church, then go into the porch. They would hear a bell toll and then a voice in the church listing the names of the doomed. One man apparently repeated this procedure for many years until he heard his own name. Greatly distressed, he went home and died immediately.

Such signs and intimations, or merely the recognition of advancing years, might cause a person to make a will. Elizabeth Clarke mentions two customary ways of doing this, and says that for good measure her grand-mother took advantage of both. The first was simply to devise a will in consultation with vicar or minister, depending on whether a farm were church or chapel. ('Years ago', she writes, 'the old people established the creed of their house and a bride generally followed her husband's persua-sion'). A document in due form would then be drawn up and witnessed. One example from Cregrina, dated 13 October 1572, is as follows:

> Rees Hergest of parish Kerigryna, sick. Soul to God. Body to be buried in parish church aforesaid. Cathedral Church of St David's 4d. To poor men's box of Kerigryna 8d. To Catherine Hergest my daughter 4 marks and 12d upon Jevan Gwin ap John and 26s 4d upon Jevan ap Owen and 5 lambs. To daughter Jaine Hergest 20 lambs & 2 kine, 2 heifers of 1 year old. To daughter Margaret Hergest 22s upon Griffithe James clerk. To Ales Hergest my wife 2 kine, a black colt, & my bed and the pewter dishes. To son Edward Hergest 20 nobles upon Lleine Myrig 8 lambs. To son John Hergest £14.6.8 upon Rees ap Jevan Hir 20s upon Jevan Gifin ap John 8s 4d upon Moris ap Guillim do. & 6 lambs and my household stuff. Residue to son John Hergest, Exor.
> William Hergest and John ap Rees Goch overseers.

Witnesses: John ap Rees Goch, Jevan ap Owen & others.

Inventory

3 kine 40s

39 sheep   50s

1 horse 13s 4d

in corn 20s

in household stuff   20s

in debts   £15.10.0.

'Willing by word', the second kind of will making, was when 'with the family assembled, the testator declared how the property was to be distributed naming where each possession was to go'. In the case of any disputes every beneficiary had witnessed every intended legacy. 'Occasionally arguments flared up', Clarke adds. 'Quarrels might divide a family for a lifetime or more. But I never heard of anyone daring to go against the word of the dead'.

She goes on to describe, very movingly, her grandmother's last journey. Mourners, some 40 in number, gathered outside the house round the bier to sing the 'rising out' hymn to the tune *Aberystwyth*. Then relays of four men in Sunday-black and heavy boots carried the coffin through fields and streams, down tracks and lanes. In the chapel by every hymn book lay decorated cards in memory of the deceased. On them, 'grandmother's circlet of ivy leaves was identical with Grandsir's, twelve years before'. The production of these 'death cards', as they were called, lasted until the 1920s.

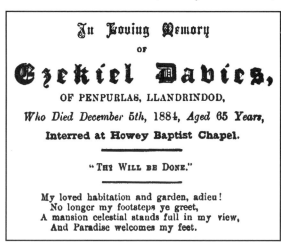

In Loving Memory

OF

Ezekiel Davies,

OF PENPUBLAS, LLANDRINDOD,

Who Died December 5th, 1884, *Aged* 65 *Years,*

Interred at Howey Baptist Chapel.

"Thy Will be Done."

My loved habitation and garden, adieu!
No longer my footsteps ye greet,
A mansion celestial stands full in my view,
And Paradise welcomes my feet.

A funeral card of 1884

Rev. Daniel Parry-Jones remarks on the custom which obtained throughout Wales 'to hold a short service of reading and prayer in the house before taking the body out, round which the neighbours gathered to sing a hymn before the procession moved off. All this was called "the rising of the funeral"'. Two other clergymen who served in Radnorshire, Rev. Albert A. Jordan of Llanbadarn Fawr and Rev. David Edmondes Owen of Llanelwedd, comment on the custom of giving cake and wine at the house before the funeral party left. Jordan's parishioners, he says, still (1926) held to the belief that every drop of wine consumed released the soul of the departed from some fraction of its burden of sin. This must surely have been the tail-end of the ancient practice of sin eating—the transference of the deceased's sins to others, when they ate and drank over the corpse—of which John Aubrey (1626-97) wrote: 'I believe this custome was heretofore used all over Wales'.

There was great anxiety to do the right thing at funerals, not merely by way of ostentation but so as to give full honour to the deceased. In the parish accounts for 1718 at Llangynllo the considerable sum of £3 12s 6d is recorded as having been spent on a single dependant, Elinor Griffiths: '£1 6 0 to the Bonesetter for her 3 0, to Mary Jones for tending her £1 10 0, for a shroud for her 6 0, for shrouding her 1 0, for ale for burying her 2 6, for bread cheese and butter 1 0, to the parson 1 0, to the Clark'. No coffin is in the list because the pauper's shrouded body would have been lifted from the communal coffin into the grave. A few years later coffins were being provided at Disserth, where the standard expenses for a pauper's funeral came to 16s 6d, comprising 6s for a coffin, 6s for six yards of shroud, 2s for shrouding and washing, 1s each for the parson and clerk and 6d for ale. It was customary to dress a female corpse in the deceased's best hood and cap, scarf, girdle, apron, hose and gaiters, and buckled shoes. Her purse would be put in the coffin. A male corpse would be accompanied by knife, sheath and fork, tobacco box and pocket tongs, and would wear hat, cravat, gloves, belt, breeches, hose and gaiters and buckled shoes.

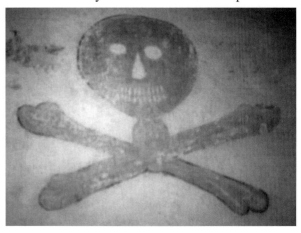

A fourteenth-century memento mori, *faded but still striking, on the north wall of the nave at Colva*

At the other end of the social scale funerals were naturally much more lavish. When Edward Gour of Bryngwyn was buried at Clyro in 1788 after dying in his 104th year his body travelled in a wagon followed by 20 men and 20 women, all kinsfolk, on horseback. W. Watkins, referring to funerals in the 1860s at Llanfihangel Rhydithon, says that each mourner was given a pair of black gloves, the women receiving in addition black handkerchiefs. Of her brother's funeral in 1922 Mona Morgan writes: 'As was the custom, the bearers had been provided with black gloves and armbands. Later, bereavement cards, in black-edged envelopes, were sent to relatives and friends'.

The longer the cortege, the greater was the feeling of satisfaction as doing honour to the dead. Until perhaps the early nineteenth century walking funerals were led by the parish clerk or sexton with a small bell, called a *bangu* (see also chapter 6). Mourners stopped at intervals for the bell to be rung and a psalm to be sung. A cortege always paused at a cross-roads which were considered to be uncanny places. Thanks to the firm (though legally unfounded) belief that to carry a corpse over private land created a right of way, a nominal payment of a penny or a halfpenny would be made to the owner in recognition that his property was being crossed with due leave only.

A burial custom which survived into the twentieth century at Rhayader and 'on the hills above Erwood' is claimed by some to date from prehistoric times. According to Owen, 'at a given place, generally near a bend of the road, between the house of mourning and the church, everyone in the funeral throws a stone on to one spot until quite a heap is formed'. Others speak of druidical survivals, adding that as each stone was thrown on to the cairn the person doing so said: *'Carn ar dy ben'* — 'A stone on thy head'.

Until the end of the 19th century as the mourners left the open grave at the end of the ceremony the sexton stood with spade held out to receive tips. The Welsh term is *arian-y-rhaw*, shovel money. Only gold and silver coins were acceptable. Unfortunately, if the total amount collected included an odd sixpence, this portended another imminent death. The sum contributed by the mourners would have been considered yet another measure of respect (or otherwise) for the dead. As a last echo of the custom after it had lapsed, the gravedigger would always be paid more than his due fee.

After the interment, at least in Elizabeth Clarke's experience, 'knots of men were already on their way to compensating for the day's hardship in making a night of it. As the evening wore on in the pubs in town, one by one they would break into music, not of massive choral hymns like *Cwm Rhondda* ... but the nostalgic tunes learnt at firesides - "Come home. Come home. Calling, oh sinner! come home"'.

A memorial service, known as the Month's End or the Month's Mind, was held for the deceased, usually in fact on the first or second Sunday after the burial (though originally a month afterwards). The commemoration, which dates back to pre-Reformation times, was still common practice with the Victorians but gradually fell out of use, though it lingered until the mid-twentieth century. Until the Month's End service had taken place members of the dead person's immediate family considered it unlucky to move house.

CHAPTER 5

Fears and Fancies

Except when disbelief is willingly suspended as a person reads a novel or watches a film, the supernatural commands little allegiance today. Yet until perhaps a century ago many country people held to the notion that fairies not only existed but possessed considerable powers for good and ill.

The devil, too, was still a force in the land. Various features of the landscape were attributed to his actions. The loathing he inspired, in North Wales at least, caused people to spit when they heard any of his various names mentioned. Rather more comfortingly, a number of tales circulated in Radnorshire in which the devil came second best in battles of wit with humans.

On the other hand, it did not pay to be too wise. The polymath, John Dee, who had strong links with Radnorshire, found himself imprisoned at one stage on suspicion of sorcery, and in 1583 during his absence abroad had his house at Mortlake, Surrey, pillaged by an angry mob, and his books burned. Alleged witches were both feared and hated in local communities; and until well into the twentieth century people took careful precautions against their perceived powers.

Of all supernatural phenomena a belief in ghosts seems to have lasted most vigorously in many people's minds. One explanation for sudden terror experienced in particular places, linked sometimes with the sight of various apparitions, has recently been advanced by Vic Tandy of Coventry University. He suggests that ultrasound at 18.9 Hz. can cause certain people to hyperventilate and their eyeballs to vibrate, thus producing feelings of profound unease combined with visual disturbances. He cannot yet explain why some are deeply affected by exposure to ultrasound while others seem immune; nor can he always trace the source of ultrasound, which is inaudible in the normal way—though in one case it came from an object as banal as a newly-installed extractor fan.

Belief or lack of it in these matters should not detract from the interest of stories on them from Radnorshire. If nothing else, they are enjoyable, intriguing, and sometimes chilling.

Fairies

Some Radnorshire people once believed that fairies were the souls of druids too good for hell but not good enough for heaven. They therefore lived under the earth or in lakes. (Mention of their association with Llyn Gwyn is made in chapter 1). Humans enticed into their territory or blundering into their company were required to remain for a year and a day.

The aged Hannah Whitney, brought up at 'the Bryngwyn', told Kilvert in the 1870s how as a child she sat by her grandfather's chair and heard old people talking of the girl from Llan Pica lured and eventually killed by fairies; of Thursday market-goers anxious to be home in good time 'lest they should be led astray by the Goblin Lantern'; and of boys wearing 'their hats the wrong way lest they should be enticed into the fairy rings and made to dance'. Decades later, W.H. Howse heard of the same protective reversing of hats in New Radnor.

Hannah also knew of an old man who slept in the trough at Rhosgoch Mill, where 'he used to hear fairies come in at night and dance to sweet fiddles on the mill floor'. The same man told the story of a woman from Llandeilo Graban called 'Llewelyn' who suspected that her two weakly little girls were really changelings—fairies substituted for her own children:

> One harvest time, to test this belief, she remarked in their hearing that she was going to cook a dinner for eight reapers and the family in an egg-shell. 'Well', cried one girl, off her guard, 'I have lived in the world for five-score years, and never heard the like of that'. 'And I', cried the other, 'have lived six-score years, neither did I'.

We are not told what happened next but presumably the fairies, having been unmasked, had to leave; we can only hope that the woman recovered her own children.

Just above Craig-pwll-du (see chapter 1) is a field, called Fairyland which takes its name from the classic tale that a ploughman one day heard a tiny fairy voice there crying 'My peel is broken'. (A peel is a flat wooden shovel used for putting bread into a hot oven). 'Bring it here and I'll mend it', called the man. He found the peel on the headland, repaired it and put it back. For several days grateful fairies left food and drink for him but when he stole a silver spoon from them the gifts abruptly ceased. Kilvert, who relates a different version of the same story, also mentions a fairies' garden and other haunts near Llanstephan.

Workmen digging at Painscastle in the nineteenth century uncovered a tessellated pavement. 'Unfortunately', wrote Mrs M.L. Lawson, 'local superstition pronounced it to be a "Fairies' pavement", and consequently it was covered up again lest the fairy folk should be offended, and take vengeance on those who had unwittingly invaded their realm'.

According to Kilvert, or rather the people with whom he conversed, the last place where fairies were seen in Radnorshire was the rocks at Blaen Cwm or Pen Cwm 'about a mile and a half above Llanbedr Church'. Yet W.B. Hamer, writing over 40 years later in 1914, recounted this tale from 'old Clifton', mole-catcher, rabbit-snarer, otter-hunter and story-teller, 'a welcome visitor at all farmhouses for miles around' Rhayader:

> The quality are ever scoffing at the fairy lights and the country's tales, but if you feel disposed to listen for a while I'll do something to shake your belief. ... I remember some years ago hearing a friend of mine in the upper part of this parish say that one night when he and his family were in bed he suddenly awoke with a feeling that something untoward was about to happen. Lying still, he was astounded to see a light enter the room where he lay. This was followed by about a dozen tiny men and women, some of the latter with small children in their arms. These little people began to dance about the room, which in the eyes of the awestruck farmer seemed to be larger than usual. After a while they ate bread and cheese, offering their unwilling host some of it. They smiled upon him but did not speak. He endeavoured to waken his wife, but she slept soundly the whole time. At length, feeling thoroughly alarmed, he called upon God to bless him, when he heard a whisper in Welsh bid him hold his peace. The revels, which began about midnight, continued for about four hours. The fairies then left his room for another, where he heard the dancing continue until cock-crow, when the visitors all departed.

Old Clifton also told of a personal encounter with the fairies. One dark night, lost in a great bog on his way home to Pencaemynydd, he appealed for help to the fairies. A series of lights appeared, indicating a particular direction. Despite fears of being led further astray, 'I took heart and ventured, and wherever I put my foot the place was as light as day, and I walked the swamp as safely as if I had been walking the road to Pont-ar-Elan'. On arriving safely in front of his house he made a bow and said 'Gentlemen and ladies, I'm humbly thankful for your civility, and I wish you now a merry night of it'. He heard a great roar of laughter, then the lights went out. With great difficulty, he made his way into the kitchen, then fainted. 'I shall never to the longest day I live forget that night, sir', he said.

As late as 1949 W.H. Howse could write of a quarryman he had known many years earlier 'who maintained that in going to his work on a dark winter morning he had been accosted by fairies'. The man was so evidently fearful that his employer permitted him to leave home at first light, even though this would have made him regularly late for work.

The Devil
To various sites associated with the devil, including his garden at Stanner Rocks (chapter 1), one could add the bridge he is supposed to have built 'about four miles from Pentre' (says W. Howells). Pentre, a hamlet near Cascob, is by several bridges over the River Lugg, but I have not been able to identify the devil's. Howells, writing in 1831, adds that 'the people, imagining that he had some mischief in his head when he built it, and thinking it unsafe to trust to his architectural remains, have thrown an arch over it'.

Suspicion of the devil's motives is justified by stories such as that of the young farmer presented with a harrow by a blacksmith newly arrived in Radnor Forest. He would see coming events for the next two years, said the blacksmith, if he stretched himself on his back beneath the harrow on Good Friday or one of the three 'spirit nights' — May Eve and Hallowe'en would have been two of these but the third is unclear. When the farmer did so he saw imps with fiery tongues. He tried to creep out from beneath the harrow, but felt himself held fast. The devil then appeared and offered to release the farmer if he could give him a coal-black dog. The man spent a day and a night in the predicament until an old woman came by. In response to his plea, she went to the village and begged a black pup from the publican. With it, the devil flew away high over Radnor Forest. The farmer missed his chance to see the future, but with great relief avoided entanglement with the devil-blacksmith. Rather more contempt for the devil is shown in a cycle of stories noted from several people in central Radnorshire by W.J.H. Watkins, and published in 1932. They concern one Davies Sirevan who personifies the perpetual joker triumphing in a battle of wits.

How Davies had his first deal with the devil

It was fair day, and Davies was left at home by his master to keep the crows off the newly-sown wheat. While he was doing this, a stranger came by, and asked him why he was not at the fair. When Davies gave the reasons the stranger offered to take his place for the day. Davies eagerly accepted his offer, and in a very short time arrived at the fair. Before long he was seen by his master, who angrily demanded why he was not at home watching the crows, Davies replied that a strange man had undertaken the job for him. Disbelieving this story, the master set off post-haste for home. When he got there, not a crow was on the wheat, but perched on the barn door was one big black crow. When the master came in sight, this big black crow cawed loudly, and left his perch. Thereupon a great black cloud of crows flew out of the barn. The big crow was the devil, and this was Davies's first deal with him.

How Davies puzzled the devil

The devil asked Davies to give him a task that was impossible. Davies asked him to carry water in a riddle. The devil tried, and failed. Davies then brought out a feather bed, and cut it open. As it was a windy day, the feathers blew all over the place. Davies now told the devil to put the feathers back into the bed, but the devil found it much too difficult a task, and had to admit that he was beaten.

How Davies and the devil had a mowing contest

On Davies's boasting what a good mower he was, the devil challenged him to a contest, the winner being the one who mowed a single swath most quickly. Davies dropped some old harrow tines along the devil's swath, so that his opponent continually notched his scythe, and had to stop to 'whittle-whattle' (sharpen). In the meantime Davies kept on mowing steadily, and won easily.

The devil chooses a poor alternative, twice over

Davies and the devil were setting potatoes, so Davies asked the devil which he would prefer: what grew below the ground, or what grew above. The devil thought things over very carefully, and decided to have what came above the ground. He therefore had the holm (haulm), while Davies had the potatoes.

When sowing wheat on another occasion, Davies offered the devil the same alternative. The devil thought he would be on the right side this time, so he chose what grew below the ground. Again he made a bad bargain, getting stubble while Davies had corn.

How Davies had the muck spread

Davies had a field of muck to spread, so the devil made a bargain with him. The instant the devil started to spread the muck, Davies was to race out of the field. Any part of him that was left inside the field by the time the spreading had finished was to be the devil's property. Davies got right by the hedge, and said that he was ready. Then there appeared at every heap a little black man, each with a flame on his head, and a dung-fork in his hand. In the twinkling of an eye the manure was spread, the little men making it fly through the air as thick as falling snow. The devil at once ran after Davies, but all he got was the tails of his coat as he jumped the fence.

Davies sets the devil to race with a hedgehog

Davies twitted the devil with the fact that he could not race as fast as a hedgehog. A contest was therefore arranged, and in order to give both sides fair play, the race took place along the furrows of a ploughed field. Davies, however, had two hedgehogs, one for each end of the furrow. Backwards and forwards the devil raced, only to find that the hedgehog always got there before him. At last, completely worn out, he gave up in disgust.

Davies goes to market

On one occasion Davies thought that he would amuse himself on market day by playing a few tricks on the people. While in a tavern, he caused a tankard to stick to the lips of the man who was drinking from it. After torturing his victim for a few minutes, he released him.

Outside on the street was a man selling china. All of a sudden the ware began to dance and caper about. While a man was looking out of the window of a nearby inn, and laughing at the china merchant's discomfiture, Davies clapped horns on his head. The man roared with fright when he found that he could not withdraw his head. At length Davies was satisfied with his prank, and caused the horns to disappear.

102

The dove and the raven fight for Davies's heart

When Davies was dying, he ordered that his heart should be placed on the mixen (dunghill), where a dove and a raven would fight for it. His friends would be able to tell, by the winner, where he would go after death. His orders were carried out, and the two birds appeared and fought, as Davies had foretold. The dove won after a fierce struggle, and by this token people knew that Davies had not gone to join the master whom he had served so well.

The burial of Davies

Davies had made one last compact with the devil. If his body was carried through a door, or along a road, or if it was buried either inside or outside a church, then the devil was to have his soul. Accordingly, when he was dead Davies was let down through a window, and carried over hedges and ditches. He was buried under the church wall, and was thus neither inside nor outside of the building. For the last time, therefore, Davies was one too many for the devil.

Watkins adds that according to tradition Davies was buried at Llanfair Waterdine church, near Knucklas. He remarks that a stone near the porch there to the memory of Andrew Davies (died 1780) bore a carving of two birds with 'some resemblance' to a dove and a raven. Several Davies

The Davies tombs at Llanfair Waterdine

tombstones stand close to the porch but some have weathered beyond legibility, including presumably that of Andrew.

In fact the Davies exploits in tantalising the devil are often attributed to a Jack of Kent who appears as early as 1595 as a character in a play by Anthony Munday. Until well into the twentieth century his deeds were widely known in Herefordshire, Monmouthshire and parts of Gloucestershire. David Price of Broad Meadow, Clyro, certainly knew of him, for he told Kilvert that Jack a Kent was a clergyman born in Cardiganshire, who held the living of Kentchurch in Herefordshire. He was related to the Scudamore family of that place. 'He denounced monkery and the monks in return spread abroad all the stories about Jack a Kent and the devil which gained such a hold on the minds of the people and are repeated now'.

Part of Jack of Kent's appeal lies in the joking aspect of his doings. The molecatcher who guided Kilvert to Craig-pwll-du (chapter 1) told him about Burroughs, 'the most pestilential practical joker that Radnorshire ever knew':

> He was a farmer - a fierce, wild man - and much dreaded by all the countryside. Once he drugged a farmer's beer so heavily with tobacco that the man was well nigh poisoned; another time he put quicksilver [mercury] into some apple dumplings boiling for the farmers' dinner at the Hundred House, and the dumplings leaped about till all the folk thought they were bewitched. Then, again at the Hundred House, Burroughs took the pudding out of the boiler and put in a live cat; when the servant came to dish up the dinner, she found only the cat's bones. Burroughs, after that, had to fly for his life, and the farmers rode after him terribly enraged, but could not catch him. Another day Burroughs enticed a man to come home with him, and made him very drunk: while he was in this state Burroughs forged a piece of iron round his neck with a long bar standing out horizontally. The man was obliged to walk home sideways, for the iron bar caught the hedges on either side and would not let him walk straight.

Such actions might well have been put down to sorcery in earlier times, and Watkins points out that his tales of Davies Sirevan came from 'the native district of the famous Doctor Dee'. By this he means Beguildy but Dee was born in London, though he had close links with Radnorshire.

John Dee

The remarkable Dr John Dee (1527-1608), mathematician and magician, astronomer and astrologer, antiquarian, geographer and philosopher, is said to have been the model both for Jonson's alchemist and Shakespeare's Prospero. He advised Edward VI, was accused and exonerated of practising sorcery against Queen Mary, and became Elizabeth's consultant. Isaac Casaubon, prebendary of Canterbury Cathedral, satirised him in a doggerel poem entitled 'A Dialogue between John Du and the Devil'. Almost four centuries later Robert Minhinnick in his poem, 'On a Portrait of John Dee', described him as 'This squalid agent of a vicious state' (1979).

John Dee (Ashmolean Museum, Oxford)

Dee claimed descent from Llewelyn Crugeryr, a thirteenth-century chieftain whose Castell Crugeryr mound can still be seen by the A44 just west of the Fforest Inn. The family surname came from Dee's grandfather, Bedo Ddu, so called because of his dark hair or complexion, who joined Rhys ap Thomas's army at Llanfihangel Nant Melan in 1485 and bore Henry Tudor's standard at the battle of Bosworth. Bedo subsequently

Castell Crugeryr

105

prospered in the service of Henry VII and bought the estate of Nantygroes between Pilleth and Whitton, where his son, Rowland, was born. Rowland, who changed his name to Dee, became head carver to Henry VIII, and his children played with those of the king.

Rowland's son, John, though he lived at Mortlake in Surrey, retained Nantygroes and visited it from time to time. He had cattle sent from there for his table, and welcomed visitors from Radnorshire. He claimed kinship with Blanche Parry of Bacton (Queen Elizabeth's maid of honour) and friendship with Thomas Jones of Tregaron (landowner, antiquary, genealogist and poet, as well as the model for Twm Sion Cati, 'the Welsh Robin Hood').

After going at the age of only 15 to St John's College, Cambridge, four years later Dee became a Fellow of the newly-founded Trinity College. As well as a Cambridge M.A. he had an LL.D. from Louvain University which gave him the title of doctor. He was also a clergyman, and at one time chaplain to Edward Bonner, the bishop of London. He was a genuinely learned man who helped to translate Euclid into English and wrote a preface which encouraged the study of mathematics. He advised on the exploration of the New World, and published *Memorials pertayning to the Perfect Arte of Navigation* (1577).

He also seems to have delighted in fostering the notion that he possessed supernatural powers. He conducted experiments in alchemy at Nantygroes, took an interest in astrology and horoscopy, claimed an ability to communicate with spirits, and left manuscripts, partly drawing on the

Nantygroes

apocryphal Book of Enoch, dealing with magic. John Aubrey, who knew several people who had previously known Dee, reported:

> John Dee etc conjuring at a poole in Brecknockshire, and that they found a wedge of Gold: and that they were troubled, and indicted as Conjurors at the Assizes.
>
> That a mighty storme and tempest was raysed in harvest time, the country people had not knowen the like ...
>
> That he layd the Storme [for] Sir Everard Digby.
>
> That the Children dreaded him because he was accounted a Conjurer.
>
> He recovered the basket of Cloathes stollen, when she [old Goodwife Faldo] and his daughter (both Girles) were negligent ...
>
> He told a woman (his neighbour) that she laboured under the evill tongue of an ill neighbour (another woman) which came to her howse, who he sayd was a Witch.

J.A. Bradney has described John Dee as 'perhaps the most celebrated man that came out of Radnorshire', yet to many he was primarily a sorcerer. His ghost is said still to haunt Nantygroes, together with that of his black cat.

Witchcraft

When Shelley was at Nantgwillt (see also chapter 1) in April 1812 he wrote: 'A ghost haunts this house, which has frequently been seen by the servants. We have several witches in our neighbourhood, & are quite stocked with fairies, & hobgoblins of every description'. His approach may be lighthearted but the five men

Nantgwillt, as drawn by R. Eustace Tickell in 1893

107

who wrote in 1825 to the chairman of magistrates at Talgarth were absolutely serious when they asked him to take action against Thomas Ralph because 'he hath a dominion over the evil spirit bewitching ... a pig of the property of John Hughes'. In addition, they claimed, Ralph had caused the deaths of numerous animals whose owners had offended him; and they concluded that 'indeed he is a terror and likewise dangerous to all the inhabitants of the neighbourhood in general'.

A similar state of mind is revealed in a story which dates to mediaeval times, though he found it still current in the early twentieth century:

> Many years ago the cattle and sheep of a well-known farmer, living on the Carneddau hills, kept dying of some mysterious malady, until at last his whole stock had practically disappeared. He consulted his neighbours and the wizards and charmers of the district, but to no purpose. At last he went to the parish priest who advised him to keep the carcass of the next beast that perished until the following Communion Sunday and to burn it in a bonfire in the middle of a spacious wood nearby, about the time of High Celebration. As luck would have it a beast died a few days before the Communion Sunday, and the farmer, all alone, carried piles of brushwood and timber into an open space in the wood, and thither, with the aid of his horse, he brought the carcass, and at the time appointed lit the fire which burnt away every trace of the beast except the heart.
>
> This the flames would not burn for it leaped out of the heat with marvellous force. The farmer, with the aid of a hayfork, struggled hard to keep this unruly member in the fire. While this was going on in the wood, a bent-up old woman with a wizened face disturbed the solemn service in the Parish Church just at the time of the consecration of the elements, by rushing out with indecent haste. She made her way straight to the wood and was horrified to find what was going on. 'In the name of heaven', she shrieked, 'what beest thou doing?' The farmer replied, 'and thou beest the cause of all my loss and trouble'. With a scared look she ran away and was never seen afterwards. The spell was broken and the strange cattle plague ceased from that day.

D.E. Owen comments that the heart of the victim gave the murderer a hard time in the old stories of Radnorshire, and that 'the belief is still [1911] strong that the human heart is almost indestructible'. He goes on to relate how an 'unworthy priest' abused the power he possessed over evil spirits:

The champion and hero of that parish [Llanbadarn Fynydd] was challenged to meet in battle the famous champion of Newtown who had never been vanquished. Deeming himself unequal to the occasion and yet unwilling to lose the confidence of his neighbours, the former went to the old Vicar of Beguildy and begged him to summon the evil spirits to maintain his reputation. The wicked old priest complied. On the day fixed a party started from Newtown in a spacious vehicle drawn by two powerful horses. They had not gone far before they found the roads literally covered with hares, over which the horses constantly stumbled and fell. Later on, while fording a brook, the vehicle was seriously damaged and the lives of the occupants imperilled. In fact, a series of most extraordinary accidents befell the Newtown champion and his supporters on their way to Llanbadarn Fynydd. Late in the day the conflict between the two heroes began; but from the start it was an uneven fight. The Newtown man was helpless. He was easily out-classed in strength, pluck, and prowess, to the great astonishment of all present. At last, the cause of all the trouble was detected. Hidden away in a yew tree was the old Vicar of Beguildy, with a huge book opened in front of him, directing the evil spirits to assist the Llanbadarn hero. As soon as he was discovered, he speedily escaped, and the Newtown party returned in great fear and disgrace.

Perhaps the sense of disgrace stemmed from having been worsted by underhand means. Deep resentment lies behind the victim of similar practice in another story repeated by Owen. A brother and sister farm successfully in the hills for many years, then stop working and going to church, even though the man is people's warden. Rumours begin to spread of the evil eye or a curse. Eventually the farmer acknowledges that he has been cursed by a conjurer and believes he can no longer succeed with anything he undertakes. He sells the farm and stock to become a labourer in a neighbouring parish. Only then does he feel the spell is lifted.

W.C. Maddox, a police inspector at Llandrindod, described in 1965 the case of

a man who reported the theft of certain property to the police. In so doing he suggested that the thief might be a well known character, much feared in the district for his so called evil powers. Secretly he was regarded as a conjuror. He was interviewed by the police with negative results, but as sometimes happens in cases of this nature fell out with the complainant over this matter. Shortly afterwards the complainant became ill and never worked again. For some years he suffered from lengthy periods of ill-health which eventually culminated in his death. There is no doubt that this man died from natural and not supernatural causes, but it was his deep rooted belief that his illness in the first place was due to a spell which had been cast upon him by an outraged conjuror, and he often told the writer that he wished he had never reported the theft to the police.

Maddox observed: 'It is no exaggeration to say that not so long ago the conjuror and the evil eye were potent forces in the lower strata of the farming community in Radnorshire'.

Owen believed that, unlike the vicar of Beguildy, the good priest could compel 'vicious spirits ... with the aid of certain very special incantations' to undertake various tasks—rather like those which Davies set the devil—such as gathering the feathers of a mattress after they had been scattered on a windy night, making a rope out of sand, carrying water in a sieve, or rolling a huge round stone to the top of a hill. Where even the best magic failed a priest had to ask a pious woman pregnant with her first child, emblematic of the Virgin Mary, to come to his aid. Then he could not fail. Owen says 'I have come across some very interesting stories illustrating this last statement'; but unfortunately (and tantalisingly) he gives no further details.

Protection against witchcraft might be provided by certain charms, one of which, dating from about 1700, is preserved in the church at Cascob, where it came to light in the nineteenth century. In faded but still legible sepia ink it runs:

> In the name of the Father, Son and of the Holy Ghost. Amen XXX and in the name of the Lord Jesus Christ who will deliver Elizabeth Loyd from all witchcraft and from all evil sprites by the same power as he did cause the blind to see the lame to walke the dum to talke. Pater pater pater noster noster noster ave ave ave Maria in secula seoulorum X on X Adonay X Tetragrammaton X Amen and in the name of the Holy Trinity and of Hubert ... Grant that this holy charm Abracadabra may cure thy survent Elizabeth Loyd from all evil sprites and all ther desises [?devices]. Amen X X X by Jah Jah Jah.

The curious mixture of Christian prayer and occult formula is followed by:

```
ABRACADABRA
 ABRACADAB
  ABRACAD
   ABRAC
    ABR
     AB
     A
```

Cascob Church

The idea behind this is that the threat of witchcraft or incidence of disease would gradually disappear in the same way that the inscription dwindled to nothing. Its first line was recorded elsewhere as early as the second century AD.

Another defence against witchcraft, dating from the same period as the Cascob charm, consisted of embedding three chicken wishbones in the plaster of a well. An example came to light at St David's House, Presteigne, only in 1950. In the same year, the skeleton of a small animal (presumably intended for the same purpose) was discovered in the plasterwork of a ceiling at Harford House in Presteigne. Over a century earlier, in 1830, workmen pulling down part of Dolfor Hall on the Montgomery-Radnorshire border found a vault with a horse's skull at each corner pointing northwards. These, too, were assumed to have been intended to ward off witchcraft. Others have been found in the footings of farms, houses, and even churches.

In the 1870s:

> Witches ... were plentiful, and used to dance a great deal on the top of Old Radnor Hill. One witch lived at Llwyn Cwmgwanon, near Clyro; she was so powerful and dangerous that people were afraid to go to her house lest she put the evil eye upon them. Another witch used to repair to Knill church [in Herefordshire] each Sunday and occupy herself with cursing the people as they came in to pray.

> Other witches lived at Bryngwyn and Llandeviron, and at Glasbury
> and Nantmel; and one haunted Clyro Hill for many a year in the
> guise of a huge hare, grey with age, which could neither be shot, nor
> caught with harriers and greyhounds.

So wrote Essex Hope, Kilvert's niece, in 1921, drawing on his diaries long
before they were published, and including some details from sections that
never were published.

Kilvert himself observed how branches of wittan (mountain ash) or
birch were placed over the doors of barns and houses on May Eve to keep
out 'the old witch', though he characteristically added, speaking for
himself: 'The young witches are welcome'. The practice survived well into
the twentieth century, and in some places an elder tree in the garden was
also considered a useful protector.

Thoughts of witchcraft may lie behind the Radnorshire story recounted
by Marie Trevelyan in the 1930s of the young man cruel to cats who threw
a stone at an unfortunate animal he saw crossing his path on his wedding
day. From that time on his health began to fail and he had to go away peri-
odically to recuperate. Some said that on these occasions he ran wild in the
woods, transformed into a cat. After he died they insisted that he continued
to prowl in cat's form. Naughty children were threatened with meeting him
so perhaps the story was simply invented by parents in the attempt to
restrain bad behaviour.

W.E.T. Morgan commented in 1925 that 'When Radnorshire women
bake bread ... they make a circle on it with their forefinger and the sign of
the cross ... to keep away the witches'. The practice is certainly recorded
at Cascob. Morgan also told the curious story of two sisters from
Painscastle who were invited to a grand wedding a hundred miles away.
Together with a man courting one of them, they went into a field and got
on the backs of calves which carried them in a flash to their destinations:

> At the wedding, no one saw them, but they thoroughly enjoyed
> themselves, partaking of all the good things. They had strictly
> warned the man not to speak until he had reached home again. At
> one spot of the journey there was a wide, deep trench, and the calves
> jumped it with the greatest ease. 'Well done, that isn't so bad for a
> cawv' [calf] cried the man, when the calf slipped away from under
> him and left him behind, many miles from home.

'Taffy' Prothero (born in 1901) was still telling in the 1980s the story of the evil eye (see page 108). The scene of the action is removed from the Carneddau to Hundred House. A wise man (or conjurer) gives advice on the burning of the heart, which takes place in Nant Wood. The witch compelled to reveal herself leaves a service in the chapel rather than the church. Yet the essence of the mediaeval narrative is intact.

Ghosts

According to Prothero ghosts in Edwardian Radnorshire were 'nearly as numerous and almost as well known as the fleshly inhabitants', and her childhood friend felt constrained to warn her that if she met one she should

make the sign of the cross. She tells of a waggoner whose horses one night suddenly attempted to gallop up Disserth pitch; when he glanced back from wrestling with the reins he glimpsed two silent figures, cloaked and cowled, in his gambo (cart). She knew one young man who after a night out with friends in Builth dared not walk homewards alone across the 'notoriously haunted' Wye Bridge. He hung about till dawn, caught a chill, and died of pneumonia. Prothero's parents, walking home near Hundred House after midnight, once saw a tall woman coming down the lane towards them as they approached their farm. 'Father moved his tongue to say "Good night. Are you in trouble? Can we help?" when - she vanished'.

Disserth Pitch, with the church below

A bridge near Hundred House was thought to be haunted. The grandfather of George Lewis's wife was making his way home that way on foot one night when he saw a pair of eyes glowing from the bridge. Many would have turned tail but he summoned up his courage and went forward—to find his neighbour's dog had come to meet him. A rather more spectral animal appears in another of Lewis's anecdotes. A mile north of Crossgates on the A483 there is a left turn to Abbey Cwm Hir. At the point where this road dips to a narrow bridge across a brook a black dog used to emerge from the right-hand hedge, dragging a piece of broken chain, as if it had just escaped. There was no gap in the hedge, and no local farmer at the time had an all-black dog.

Not far away, at Llidiart-y-dwr (Watergate) a sprung gate was avoided after dark by some, because when a person had passed through, the gate banged a second time after a short interval as though someone were following. Just as mysterious was the phantom female figure seen at Bryndraenog Farm, Beguildy, and no doubt others could be listed. Those who hid iron in life might return to look for it after death; at Llanelwedd it was considered unlucky merely to leave loose iron behind when a tenant moved out of a farm, since it might spell disaster to the next occupant.

After the funeral of a person—no details are given—who lived at Llanships Farm, Clyro, his or her spirit returned to search the premises. Plates repeatedly flew off the shelves in the kitchen, to be found unbroken on the floor. The phenomena ceased when the presumed object of the spirit's quest, a penknife, was discovered. The source of this story, an old woman, practised divination by bible and key. She opened the bible at the

Esylt Newbery (left) in 1889, aged 8, with her brother, Jocelyn, aged 6

verse, 'Where thou goest I will go', then closed it on her door key and named the person suspected of a theft, saying at the same time, 'Said Peter to St Paul, turn you or turn you not'. She firmly believed that the key would indeed turn when the right name was spoken.

Esylt Newbery (for whom see the previous chapter) relates that the house in which she lived as a child with her family in the 1880s—then the dwelling of the headmaster of the grammar school at Presteigne, though formerly the officer's quarters of a barracks, between the church and the river—was haunted by the ghost of a man from the regiment who had died of ill-treatment, possibly (though she does not say this) at the hands of one of the officers.

The classic ghost had either suffered injustice in life—or perhaps caused it. The unfortunate lady of Stapleton Castle (see chapter 8) falls into the former category, as does the ghost encountered by a leadminer at Cwm Elan in the 1870s. The story was told to W.B. Hamer by Old Clifton (for whom, see page 99):

> The Cwmelan mine was situated in a wild, lonely spot on the hill-side, nearly a mile to the rear of the mansion. With the exception of a small unoccupied and partly ruined cottage, adjoining the workings, and known as 'Cwmgwaithmoyn', not another dwelling was near. The men employed in the mine—and these were few—lodged at the farmsteads in the neighbourhood. The superintendent, or 'captain' of the mine was a Cornishman, named. J--- G --- , who, in spite of the mysterious warnings of his workmen, resolved to occupy the old cottage above referred to. Certain repairs having been effected, the 'captain' removed his effects into his new abode, and soon after went to live there. His first night in the cottage he never forgot. He slept well for some hours, and then awoke with a strange feeling that he was not alone. He felt certain that he had bolted the doors and windows, but the rustling of garments was unmistakable. Somebody, or something, was moving about. Presently there was a sound as of the moving of a table, and he distinctly heard the plates being taken from the dresser shelves and placed upon it. For a while these movements continued, and then a deathlike silence ensued. The same thing happened night after night for nearly a week. Although naturally a strong-minded man, J--- G---'s nerves soon began to feel the strain of these nocturnal disturbances. He, however, kept his own counsel, but began to dread the approach of nightfall. Matters at length came to a crisis.

'Captain' G--- had been spending the evening with friends, and, it was late when he got home. While eating his supper in the kitchen, which was his living-room, he had a return of the uneasy sensations that he had previously experienced. The same rustling sound that he knew so well was heard. It seemed to proceed from a small disused room which had formerly been a bedchamber. Presently the door of this room opened, and the 'captain' was dumbfounded on seeing a little old lady glide into the room holding out towards him a long bony hand. Thinking her attitude mendicant, he rose and placed a copper on her outstretched palm. To his horror the coin, securing no lodgement, dropped to the floor, and almost immediately the apparition vanished.

J--- G--- was so profoundly affected by the night's events, coupled with what he had previously gone through, that early next day he quitted the house, and shortly afterwards threw up his appointment and left the district. Many people wondered at this sudden departure. But soon the tale leaked out.

Not for many years had the Cwmelan ghost been seen. Old folk remembered their grandparents saying that a hundred years before an old couple with an only child - a daughter - lived in the old cottage. The daughter's affections had been won by a well-to-do farmer living close by. Arrangements for the wedding were made, but the evening before it was to have taken place the bride vanished, and although every enquiry was made no trace of her was ever afterwards discovered. Folks said she had fallen a victim to the jealousy of a former lover, who after went abroad. After the death of the old couple the cottage was left unoccupied. People said it was haunted. Tradition, however, kept green the memory of the unfaithful young woman; but whether the ghost which J--- G--- saw had any connection with her story will for ever remain a mystery.

The ghost of a man who perpetrated injustices has links with Llanbister. Jonathan Williams describes a fifteenth-century killing which took place there in a mansion called Llynwent:

> During the unguarded moments of a festive carousal, two cousins-german [first cousins], namely, John Hir, or John the Tall, son of Philip Fychan, and David Fychan, quarrelled about the extent of their Matrimonial inheritance, as parcelled out of the law of gavelkind [the custom of dividing a dead man's property equally among his sons], and fought with swords, in which combat, the

116

latter was run through the body, and died on the spot. His death, however, did not pass unrevenged, for the sister of the slain, named Ellen Cethin, who resided at Hergest Croft, in the county of Hereford, a woman of masculine strength, and intrepid spirit, hearing of the disastrous issue of this family dispute, and of the murder of her brother, repaired to the adjoining parish of Llanddewi [Ystradenni] on the day in which it had previously been fixed to hold a trial of archery. Disguising herself in men's clothes, she challenged the best archer in the field. This challenge was no sooner known than accepted by John Hir, who, entitled to the first shot, fixed his arrow in the centre of the target. Exulting at his success, and confident of the victory, he was followed by Ellen Cethin, who, instead of pointing the head of the arrow in a line with the target, directed its flight against the body of her cousin-german, John Hir, which it pierced, and went through his heart.

According to some sources, these events took place in 1430. Joseph Bradney claims that Elen Gethin (Ellen the terrible) was not the daughter but the sister of David Fychan ap David ap Cadwgan ap Philip Dorddu of Llynwent. She lived with her husband, Thomas Vaughan ap Rosser, not at Hergest Croft but at Hergest Court. (Both are just over the Herefordshire border near Kington). A frequent visitor at the Court was Lewys Glyn Cothi, one of the greatest Welsh poets of the time. When Thomas died fighting in the Yorkist cause in 1469—he was either killed in the battle of Banbury or captured and put to death afterwards—Lewys wrote a funeral elegy or *marwnad* which evoked his patron's fighting white-cuirassed like King Arthur at Camlan.

Thomas's body was brought back for burial at St Mary's Church on the hill above Kington. Elen—still alive in 1474 and residing at Nash, near Presteigne—eventually joined him there. Alabaster effigies of the pair can still be seen. Some time afterwards rumours began to circulate that Thomas Vaughan's unquiet spirit was abroad. Four hundred years on, Kilvert's molecatcher (see also page 104) explained:

It was believed that the crimes he had committed would not let his spirit rest, for his ghost haunted the wood, and terrified innumerable people; it used to take special delight in waylaying women riding home from market at dusk, leaping up on their horses and sitting behind them. At last strong measures were taken to defeat the ghost. Twelve or thirteen ancient parsons assembled in the court of

Hergest, and drew a circle, inside which they all stood with books and lighted candles, praying. The ghost was very resolute, and came among the parsons roaring like a bull. 'Why so fierce, Mr Vaughan?' asked one of the parsons mildly. 'Fierce I was a man, fiercer still as a devil', roared Vaughan, and all the candles were blown out except one, held by a very small, weak parson (also, says legend, named Vaughan). He hid the candle in his boot, and so kept it alight, all the time praying hard until at length the violent spirit was quelled, 'and brought down so small and humble that they shut him up in a snuff box'. The ghost made one humble petition—'Do not bury me beneath water'. But the parson immediately had him enclosed in a stone box, and buried him under the bed of the brook, and Hergest thenceforth was at peace.

On the contrary, people round Kington said that Black Vaughan continued to make appearances. In the 1930s his ghost was regularly seen by the pool at Hergest Court, and horses were known to refuse to pass the spot. Half a century later a visitor to the district, coincidentally called Jenny Vaughan, who knew nothing of her namesake, was terrified to see in Kington Church the ghostly figure of a bull outlined against the blue curtain covering the north door. The daughter of the present owner of Hergest Court told me that her father, who supplies organic milk to supermarkets, decided some years ago to have the pool filled in but abruptly changed his mind and dismissed the contractors when, as JCBs prepared to begin work, the water started to bubble ominously.

In 1860 shortly after a man had died in Green End at Presteigne various strange rappings, scratchings and the sound of footsteps were heard at nights in his empty house. Several Primitive Methodists decided to confront the phenomena but, gripped by sudden fear, they locked themselves into one of the rooms and spent the night there while the eerie noises raged round the rest of the house. The following night, with numbers swelled to between 30 and 40, they tried again. This time a large box seemed to move towards them of its own accord but when it fell over the creature which emerged turned out to be very much of this world, and under the influence of spirits of the alcoholic kind. The prankster in due course received the rather harsh punishment of 14 days' imprisonment with hard labour.

The incident illustrates a willingness to believe in ghosts and exorcism which may have been influenced by a celebrated case from Disserth which

Disserth Church interior with its box pews

became widely known throughout the county and is still remembered. It took place during the time of Rev. John Jones, who was the vicar of Disserth from 1781 until 1815. (He died in 1844 aged 89). The story has many similarities with that of Black Vaughan:

> Charles Lewis was a tanner, living at Henllys, in the hamlet of Trecoed. He was a dishonest scoundrel. It was well known that he was 'deceitful upon the weights' for he had two scales, the one giving double weight which he used for buying, and the other giving short weight which he used for selling. He amassed a big fortune. But in the midst of life he met with a fatal accident and was buried in Disserth Churchyard. The record of his burial is preserved in the parish register. This tragic event, however, was only the beginning of the trouble, for his nimble and particularly malignant spirit accosted every man who passed the Henllys after dark. He took fiendish delight in molesting men on horseback. Taking his place behind the rider, and terrifying the horse into a mad gallop, in low sepulchral monotonous voice he addressed the same remark to everyone: 'I am Charles Lewis of the light and heavy weights. Once I was a man, now I am a devil'.

After many months of fear and discomfort the farmers of the neighbourhood met at Llanelwedd and decided to ask old Parson Jones, of Llwynbongam [a house, now gone, near Bailey Einon], the saintly vicar of Cefnllys and Disserth, to lay this troublesome spirit. He consented and asked three neighbouring clergymen to come to his aid. A day was fixed, and late in the evening the four priests, followed by a large crowd of timid and anxious farmers, went to the Henllys. The clergymen entered the house and, after reading some special passages from the Old Testament, summoned the evil spirit to appear. He came rushing through a narrow passage like a mighty tempest and at once defied the priests. Parson Jones did not attempt to lay him there, for the place was much too cramped for conflict with such a vicious and nimble spirit. So, after uttering some incantations, he summoned the ghost to meet them in the parish church of Disserth.

An hour later the pale-faced crowd was anxiously watching the four priests, armed with books and candles, proceeding to the church. As soon as they entered, the spirit charged them with a mighty rush. The lights of the three assistant priests—all unworthy men—went out. Paralysed with fear, they crept out of church and joined the crowd. Parson Jones saved his light by sheltering it in the spacious upper part of his topboot. He was now left alone in the church face to face with this terrible spirit.

The conflict was long and doubtful but at last Jones prevailed. The evil spirit began to shrink and shrivel, until eventually he assumed the form of a bluebottle. In that form he was captured. Then he was further humiliated by being forced into the hollow of a large goose-quill. This was doubled up and placed in a silver snuff-box which was firmly fastened.

Parson Jones now emerged triumphantly and told the story of the conflict and conquest to the delighted crowd. He added that it was necessary to bury the spirit in a deep bog or well, for if they buried him in a dry place he would, after a limited period, regain his liberty and be seven times more vicious than ever. So the jubilant procession wended its way to Llyncoedeiddig and there the silver snuff-box, with the evil spirit of the dishonest tanner inside it, was tied to the top of an iron bar and forced down into the depths of the quaking mire.

Soon after this happy event the farmers collected enough money to place a tombstone over the grave of Charles Lewis in the church-yard. His name, age, and date of death was all that was written on it. The rest of the stone on both sides was literally covered with figures of dragons, snakes, lizards, toads, and everything loathsome and suggestive of the nether regions.

Such are the details first published in 1911 by Rev. D.E. Owen. They seem to have influenced the story told to 'Taffy' Prothero before the First World War of a sultry day in high summer when the church door at Disserth was left open during a service to let more air in:

> There was a very old clergyman there at the time, a truly venerable figure with white hair and a long white beard. He had been there since his youth, and was genuinely loved and revered by all. The service proceeded as usual, and he made his way to the pulpit to preach the sermon. He was just beginning to give out the text when there was a vivid flash of lightning and at the same time a very loud clap of thunder directly overhead, and also a heavy crunching sound on the gravel drive outside; and in through the open door there came a raving mad bull with bloodshot eyes and clouds of breath coming out of his nostrils which made his way up the aisle.
>
> The clergyman knelt down and said, 'Brethren, let us pray', and he proceeded to do so, aloud. The congregation of course followed suit and took to their knees, peering through the lattice work of their fingers at the bull, which seemed gradually to get less furious. Also in time it got smaller, and this went on until in time it was only a nice little bull calf. From then on it went through several metamorphoses, more than I can remember, but getting smaller all the time; sheep, hare, rabbit, mouse, etc., and in the end, a moth. Then it gave up and cried out with a loud voice and said 'O holy man, thou hast overcome me. Name thy punishment and let me be gone'.
>
> 'O evil spirit, a heavy punishment must surely be thine for desecrating this sacred place. But it is not for me to mete out punishment. I shall continue to pray that we be protected against thy presence here'.
>
> 'Your prayer is answered. I, of my own volition will take a vow not to come here for a period of nine hundred and ninety-nine years. But you must bury me deep down; not under earth and stone because for me they are but a flimsy covering. It must be in deep water'.
>
> A man in the congregation got up out of his pew and came up the aisle, took out his snuff-box, emptied it, dusted it out thoroughly with his handkerchief and held it open. The moth hopped in. The man snapped the lid to. Then they went to the blacksmith to get the

rim of the box soldered and a little ring and chain fixed, the other end fastened to a weight.

Somebody meanwhile had gone and got a pony and brought it to the church porch. They lifted the old clergyman into the saddle; a man took hold of the bridle and led the horse along the winding path up the hillside and everyone followed. The hill, and all the hills around, wearing a chastened look after the storm and still steaming a little from the heavy downpour and hot earth.

After a while they reached the top and made their way to the mawn pool. The strongest man in the parish went to the water's edge. They handed him the snuff-box and weight and he, with all his might, flung it into the centre of the pool. It sank, and the air bubbles came up, and kept on coming up. People looked at each other and said 'How very deep that pool must be'.

Prothero, writing in 1985, recalled that any child hearing the tale would want to know when the 999 years—the standard period of confinement for a restless spirit—would be up. The answer given would be: 'Well, certainly not in my time. But in yours? Well, I couldn't be sure about that'.

To this day George Lewis tells of the exorcism of a spirit which was haunting the church at Disserth. One version of the story is that the spirit was enclosed in a stone and thrown into a deep rocky pool in the River Ithon at Craig fain, some way downstream from the church; another that in the form of a fly it was captured in a matchbox and drowned in consecrated water in the font. Lewis personally remembers the vicar, called Evans, a tall, austere man wearing a wide-brimmed, low-crowned hat, who was brought in from a neighbouring parish for the exorcism. He seemed to be profoundly affected by the experience, which he would never discuss afterwards.

CHAPTER 6

Saints and Sinners

Of the 55 mediaeval churches in Radnorshire one, Ednol (near Kinnerton), is now a ruin and 31 have been more or less completely rebuilt. In some cases their sites were sacred for at least a thousand years before the coming of Christianity. They stand at the centre of networks of belief, custom and story. Carvings in wood and stone, and pictures on plaster and glass, all have their own tales to tell. Bells send messages, as do other forms of the church's music. Another important feature of parish life were customs such as bound-beating and fund-raising merrymakings. These last, however, are

Bleddfa Church, from the north-west

described in chapter 7; and the rites of baptisms, marriage and death in chapter 8. Funereal inscriptions and epitaphs bear words ranging from wry humour through resignation to profound pathos.

Sites and Saints

In the year 601 Pope Gregory ordered that sites such as springs, groves, mounds and circles which were revered by pagans should be sanctified where possible for Christian use. This may explain why Pilleth Church stands by a spring and why the churchyard at Discoed is surrounded by yew trees some 2,000 years old. Radnorshire has a particularly high proportion of circular churchyards, a pagan feature welcomed by Christians because it left no corner in which the devil might hide. Some were undoubtedly pagan sites adopted by Christians; others may have been laid out by Christians on the earlier pattern. The full list is: Beguildy, Bleddfa, Bryngwyn, Cascob, Cregrina, Discoed, Disserth, Glascwm, Kinnerton, Rhulen, Llanbister, Llanddewi Ystradenni, Llandegley, Llandeilo Graban, Llanelwedd (site of the old church), Llanfaredd, Llanifihangel Helygen, Llanfihangel Nant Melan, Llanfihangel Rhydithon, Llansanffraid-yn-Elfael, Llan-stephan, Llanyre, Nantmel, Old Radnor, Pentre, St Harmon, and Whitton. Of these, several have pre-Christian burial mounds in their churchyards and two, Bleddfa and Llansanffraid-yn-Elfael, have towers built on Bronze Age tumuli. The church at Llanfihangel Nant Melan appears to stand within a former stone circle (for which, see also chapter 1). Just over the Wye in Breconshire, a massive single

Llanfihangel Nant Melan churchyard yew atop one of the stones of an old stone circle

stone at Llanwrthwl is said to have determined St Gwrthwl to found the church by the south porch of which it now stands.

Christian burial sites could of course also lead to the establishment of churches. In defiance of Irish claims, St Bride was held to be interred in the Tomen Sant Ffraid and so a church was built nearby in her honour: Llansanffraid Cmteuddwr, close to Rhayader. This, though, was a twelfth-century foundation—and that of Llansanffraid-yn-Elfael, near Hundred house, fourteenth—whereas the golden age for Celtic saints was the fifth and sixth centuries.

The earliest dedication in Radnorshire is St Harmon, where the original church was reputedly set up in 429 by St Garmon or Germanus on land

The massive single stone at Llanwrthwl Church

granted by Vortigern on Waun Marteg. There is a tradition that the saint and his followers spent 40 days on the site in prayer for Vortigern's sins. Bedd Garmon to the east of the church purports to be the place of the saint's burial. In fact Garmon died (in 448) at Ravenna and his body was taken to be solemnly interred at his cathedral church of Auxerre in Roman Gaul. An alternative tradition suggests that he may have been a cousin of Vortigern's, and that he visited Gwrtheyrnion in 429, when he priested St Patrick, and again in 446-7. However, scholars now believe that a different Garmon was involved, a Breton of three centuries later, who spent time in Ireland and Wales before ending his career as bishop of the Isle of Man.

The Big Three of Welsh saints are David, Padarn and

Teilo, who travelled to Jerusalem together to be made bishops by the patriarch. Padarn, distantly related to Garmon, may have originated in south-east Wales. He is mainly famous as the founder of Llanbadarn Fawr in Cardiganshire but has three dedications in Radnorshire: another Llanbadarn Fawr, near Llandrindod; Llanbadarn Fynydd; and Llanbadarn y Garreg.

Teilo, another monk and bishop, born in Pembrokeshire, was so much revered that when he died at Llandeilo Fawr in Carmarthenshire a dispute arose as to whether his body should lie there, at Llandaf, or at his birthplace, Penally. The cadaver was miraculously multiplied by three—triply cloned, in modern parlance—so that each place could have one. His only Radnorshire dedication is Llandeilo Graban.

St David as shown on a cartoon for the decoration of the Central Hall of the Houses of Parliament

David is the sole Welsh saint to have been officially canonised and that was over 500 years after his death, in 1120. His day (1 March) is very widely celebrated in Wales, and a pressure group is attempting to persuade the Welsh Assembly to declare it a public holiday. David founded many churches in person, and others were established in his name. Glascwm Church claims to be a 'greater Dewi', a church personally founded by David, and those at Cregrina and Rhulen may fall into the same category. Five others—Colva, Heyope, Llanddewi Fach, Llanddewi Ystradenni and Whitton—may be 'lesser Dewi', or nonpersonal foundations. A poem by Lewis Glyn Cothi attributes the founding of Colva Church to David himself, but its origin probably dates to the eighth century.

*Cefn-llys Church, as depicted on a postcard in the early 1900s,
is dedicated to St Michael*

David's score in Radnorshire equals that of St Mary, who has Bettws
Disserth, Bleddfa (where she displaced St Brendan). Gladestry, Kinnerton,
Llanfaredd (replacing Mariaith), Newchurch, New Radnor, and Pilleth.
The total of eight does not include some later foundations such as the
parish church at Abbey Cwm Hir. Mary is by far the most popular saint in
Wales as a whole, with almost 150 dedications. Michael (Mihangel) comes
second, with almost 100, of which the following are in Radnorshire:
Beguildy, Bryngwyn, Cascob, Cefn-llys, Clyro, Discoed, Llanfihangel
Dyffryn Arwy (Michaelchurch-on-Arrow), Llanfihangel Helygen,
Llanfihangel Nant Melan, and Llanfihangel Rhydithon.

Brychan, who lived at Talgarth in the county to which he gave his name,
had, it seems, up to 63 children, many of whom became saints like their
father. Eiliwedd, one of his 24 daughters, founded Llanelwedd, though the
Normans changed the patron to Matthew. Another of Brychan's daughters,
Ceingair, gave birth at Glasbury to a son, Cynidr, who later started there the
monastic community or *clas* which gave the place the first part of its name;
the second came from the Old English, *burh*, fort or enclosure. Cynidr, who
enjoyed a special reputation for wisdom, probably baptised the faithful at
Ffynnon Gynidr, a spring on the common above Maesllwch. He may well
have been buried in or near the church, though in due course the Normans
built another of their own and dedicated it to St Peter.

At Llanbister the patron is Cynllo, who had a cell there in the sixth century. Like many early Welsh saints, Cynllo Frenin (Cynllo the King) had royal blood: his great-grandfather was brother to Helen, the mother of Constantine the Great. His father was St Gildas, the Jeremiah of Wales. Taliesin dedicated his first poem, 'Elphin's Consolation', to Cynllo. Popular belief held that no prayer of Cynllo's was in vain, and that his knees and the shoes of his horse left imprints on stone (*olion gliniau Gynllo* and *olion traul march Cynllo*) where they might be seen by those with the necessary discernment (or gullibility).

The rare eastern tower at Llanbister Church, a church dedicated to St Cynllo

Cynllo had three dedications in Radnorshire: Llanbister, Llangynllo and Nantmel. Rhayader was his, too, until the Normans changed it to St Clement. St Cynllo's Day is 17 July, and a poem of about 1460 by Lewis Glyn Cothi announced his intention of visiting Rhayader for that celebration, so it is clear that local people kept up the cult of their saint long after the Norman intervention in their church's affairs.

At Llanbister the church is unusual in having its tower at the east end, tucked into a steep hillside. According to local lore construction began in the normal way at the west end but at night the devil kept removing the masonry to the bottom of the churchyard. The builders decided to transfer operations to the east end where Christian influence was at its strongest, and so could combat the devil's power. It may, of course, simply be that the change arose from unsatisfactory geology at the west end. The move at Llanelwedd from Cae Henllan (Old Church Field) to the present site of the church, half a mile south, is unexplained.

Two more sixth-century saints, Cewydd and Maelog (or Meilig), together with the historian-monk, Gildas, were the sons of Caw, prince of Strathclyde, who travelled south after being driven from his lands by the Picts and Scots. Cewydd is considered to be a patron of the weather, a sort of Welsh St Swithin, and is known as Cewydd y Glas (Cewydd of the Rain). His day is, like Cynllo's, in July. He has strong associations with the cave at Aberedw later occupied by Llywelyn (see chapter 8), to which he walked past Maengewydd (Cewydd's Rock) on Aberedw Hill. The churches at both Aberedw and Disserth are dedicated to him, as is that of Cusop in Herefordshire.

Moll Walbee's Stone at Llowes

From his following a military career for a time, Maelog, who merits a brief mention in the *Mabinogion*, was known as Maelog the Knight. After changing to the religious life he studied with St Cybi on the Irish Aran Islands or with St Cadwg at Llancarfan in Glamorgan. He founded a monastic community on the common near Llowes where, according to Gildas, he died. The cross in the church, locally called Moll Walbee's Stone (see chapter 8), is mentioned in another poem by Lewis Glyn Cothi. It stood where the parishes of Llowes, Clyro and Llanddewi Fach meet, at a place called Croesfeilig, a name shared with a neighbouring farm. In the twelfth century the cross was moved down into the churchyard, and from there into the church itself in 1956.

Maelog was also the patron of Capel Maelog of which the foundations, which were discovered almost 200 years ago on Gors Farm in Cefn-llys parish, have been laid out near the lake at Llandrindod Wells. Another farm, Lower Caerfaelog at Llanbister, has the

The ruins of Capel Maelog relocated to Llandrindod Wells

remains of a monastic building which was the scene of an ecclesiastical conference in 722. In the same parish Croes Cynon Farm bears the name of another saint, Cynon, who, according to tradition, had a hermitage at Craig Cynon and drank the water of Nant Cynon.

Other saints are even more obscure. We do not even know whether Ano of Llananno was male or female, and he/she occurs nowhere else. The church at Llanyre has been variously allocated to a mysterious sea god, despite its distance from the sea, or to an otherwise-unknown virgin martyr. Alternatively the founder is said to have been been Llyr Merini, the father by Gwendoline (herself the martyred founder of Talgarth Church) of Caradoc Freichtig (for whom, see chapter 8). Tegla may be the same person as Thecla of Iconium, of whom one manuscript 'Life' preserved in the library at Lambeth Palace includes accounts of miracles connected with the church at Llandegley. Thecla, a possibly fictional figure whose cult was suppressed by the catholic church in 1969, is said to have been converted by St Paul himself. When an attempt was made to burn her alive a providential downpour of rain quenched the fire; when she was thrown to wild beasts in an arena the animals refused to touch her; when after 72 years as a (well-preserved) hermit in a cave she was approached by men intending to ravish her she prayed for deliverance and was swallowed by the rocks. Just how she came to be associated with a remote Radnorshire village remains a mystery.

Rood Screens, Rude Women, and Other Objects

In mediaeval churches the rood screen separating the chancel from the nave took its name from the cross (or rood) which surmounted it. Some screens, elaborately carved and showing traces of original paintwork, remain

a striking feature of churches such as Aberedw, Beguildy, Llananno and Old Radnor. Others were removed in whole or part at the Reformation; and at least nine fell victim to the excessive zeal (or vandalism) of Victorian restorers.

Llananno's tiny church stands by the murmuring waters of the River Ithon. Its spectacular screen of the late fifteenth or early sixteenth century is considered by some to be the best in all Wales. A mass of intricate carving includes biblical figures, fruit

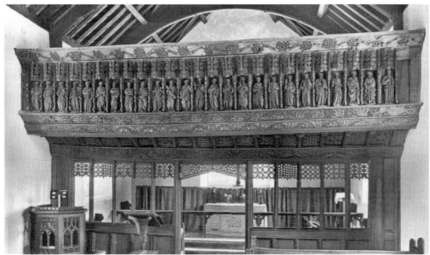

Llananno Church (top) with its rood screen (below)

Serpent at the south end of Llananno's rood screen

and flowers, leaves and tendrils. A winged and scaly serpent or dragon with a vine stem issuing from its mouth may be a reminder, amidst the fertile profusion of nature, of the presence and power of evil. On the simpler, reverse side of the screen are some curious, grotesque heads which exude the feeling of world-weary, chastened humanity.

In a similar position on one of the bosses of another fine screen at Beguildy there is a carving of a head with vegetation emerging from the mouth, a classic Green Man. These figures are not common in Radnorshire, though they can be found in wood and stone across Britain, and also in Europe, dating from Roman times to the Middle Ages. Fanciful claims have been made that the Green Man is a pagan fertility spirit but it seems more likely that it represents wicked or lost souls.

Similar controversy has surrounded carvings of a genitalia-displaying female figure known as a sheila-na-gig, from the Irish

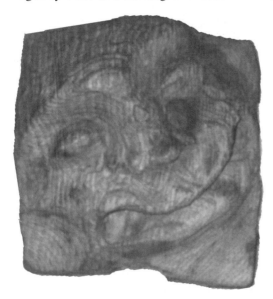

One of the grotesque heads on the reverse side of Llananno's screen

Sheila-na-gig, Llandrindod Old Church

expression, *sile na gig*, meaning immodest woman. This, too, has been taken to be a pagan fertility symbol but the more cautious view considers its depiction of the human body as ugly and deformed to be a desire to give warning of the perils of the flesh. The sole example in Radnorshire is in the old parish church of Llandrindod Wells where the carving on a flat stone now kept in a windowsill may have been part of the fabric before the restoration of 1895. It is possible that the immodest and ugly woman turned in local eyes into a tutelary goddess. The evidence comes from a story still remembered in Llandrindod. Early in the twentieth century the sheila was due to be taken to Cardiff and studied there. She was carefully carried out of the church and secured with ropes to a waiting cart. As soon as the conveyance started to move off the ropes parted and she fell to the ground. The plan to move her was abandoned.

Churches, for many centuries the only public building in a parish, attracted a variety of other objects, both sacred and secular. At Cregrina the paws of the last wolf to be killed in Radnorshire—at Penarth wood, in early Tudor times—were nailed to the church door. A healing charm of the eighteenth century (see chapter 5) hangs on the north wall of the nave at Cascob. Curative powers were attributed to a staff of St Curig's once kept in the gallery at St Harmon Church. Gerald of Wales wrote about it at some length:

It is completely encased in gold and silver, and the top part has the rough shape of a cross. Its miraculous power has been proved in all manner of cases, but it is particularly efficacious in smoothing away and pressing the pus from glandular swellings and gross tumours which grow so often on the human body. All those who suffer from such vexatious afflictions will be restored to health if they go to the staff in faith and offer an oblation of one penny. It happened in our time that a person with a tumour handed a halfpenny to the crosier: the result was that only one half of his swelling went down. Soon afterwards he completed his oblation by offering the staff a second halfpenny, whereupon he was completely cured. Another man came to the staff and promised faithfully that he would give a penny at some later date. He was cured, but on the appointed date he failed to pay. To his consternation his tumour swelled up again. His sin was pardoned, for he trebled the oblation and in great fear and trembling had the faith to pay threepence, with the happy result that he was completely restored to health.

Unfortunately, the staff's ultimate fate does not seem to have been documented.

The font at Old Radnor is said to have been hewn from what was originally a fifth monolith at the site of the Four Stones in Walton (see chapter 1). A Roman centurial stone from Castell Collen, inscribed *Valflavini*, has been built into the porch of the church at Llanbadarn Fawr, where, incidentally, Gerald of Wales spent a night in 1176 and was met the next morning by Cadwallon ap Madoc, his wife, Eva, and his son, Maelgwyn.

The font at Old Radnor Church

When rebuilding took place in 1879 a Norman arch was preserved, on the right-hand capital of which is carved a dragon with open mouth. Dragons feature a good deal in churches, where they represent evil; a knotted tail signifies their defeat, since the tail was thought to be the source of their power. The archangel Michael is particularly associated with the conquest of evils and hence the slaying of dragons.

Rev. Daniel Parry-Jones, who lived in the county from 1926 until 1935, wrote of Radnor Forest:

> Deep in its fastnesses dwelt the dragon. I often spoke to an old man who lived high up on the slopes of the Forest and who maintained that though he had never seen it he had heard it breathing. Was it because of the dragon that our Christian ancestors ringed it round with St Michael churches one of which was my own church of Llanfihangel Rhydithon?

Well within living memory terrifying roarings have been heard coming from the Forest on certain winter nights, but these have been explained as being caused by the wind. This slightly deflating insight came in conversation with George Lewis, who then added the poetic suggestion that Radnor Forest was first ringed with castles but the dragon (devil) took no notice until churches were built, whose power proved stronger.

Rev. D.E. Owen passed on the story of a different dragon, the last in Radnorshire:

> Ages ago, one of these vicious and powerful brutes slept every night on the tower of Llandeilo Graban Church, after making dreadful devastation during the day. Many brave men tried to destroy the monster but their attempts were always futile, and sometimes even fatal to themselves. At last, the parishioners offered a rich reward to anyone who would capture and slay this destructive brute which measured three yards and one inch long. After many vain attempts on its life it became 'curster' than ever. An ingenious plough boy, attracted by the handsome reward, devised a plan that proved successful. He made a dummy man out of a large log of oak, and, aided by the local blacksmith, armed it with numerous iron hooks, powerful, keen, and barbed. Then he dressed the dummy in red and fixed it firmly on top of the tower. At dawn the following day the dragon first saw his daring bed fellow and dealt him a violent blow with his tail, which was badly torn by the hooks. Infuriated by the pain, he attacked the dummy with tooth, claws wings and tail, and finally wound itself round its wooden foe and bled to death.

No dragon is depicted at Llandeilo Graban but at Llanbadarn y Garreg a stone in the church shows a two-humped beast with flipper-like

Llanbadarn y Garreg which contains a stone with a carving resembling the Loch Ness Monster

appendages, long neck and small head, which seem reminiscent of the Loch Ness monster. Some have suggested that notions of dragons derive from folk-memories of dinosaurs, so this is perhaps unsurprising.

Another mysterious stone, formerly outside, now stands in the church at Bryngwyn. It dates from between 600 and 800, and bears an inscription as yet undeciphered, in Ogham characters. It also carries a sort of diagram which may be a phallic symbol and a heart, or possibly a mandala—a diagram with various possible meanings including that of the wholeness of self. The motif of a dot within a circle, which occurs five times, is said to be a symbol of totality.

On a more mundane level, two churches, Llanfihangel Helygen and Disserth, retain the box pews which were once commonplace. They were allotted to householders and farmers who paid a yearly rental for the privilege of using them, but quarrels arose from time to time. In 1700 at Disserth, a woman claiming rights to a pew first sat on the lap of another one occupying it, then dragged her out. Six years earlier Nellie Jones was presented, perhaps in connection with a similar dispute, for 'shoving a straw up her neighbour's nose' during a service.

For more serious offences people ran the risk of being required to do penance, which involved standing draped in a white sheet in the church porch during a service. There are particulars in the church register at Knighton—and no doubt elsewhere—of people made to do such penance. Barnaby Lloyd, Richard Young, Catherine Rogers and Elizabeth Felton are listed. No date is given, nor indeed any other details, though the mixed names might suggest sexual misdemeanour. The penance and excommunication of James Cartwright 15 years later similarly lack detail.

Bells and Bass Viols

As if to reinforce the message given when they ring, church bells often have traditional inscriptions such as 'Come away without delay' (at Colva), 'I to the church the living call/And to the grave I summon all' (Llanfihangel Rhydithon and Old Radnor), 'Peace and Good Neighbourhood' (Knighton, Presteigne and Old Radnor), and 'Prosperity to this Parish' (Boughrood, Gladestry, Knighton, and again, Old Radnor).

According to a belief mentioned by Kilvert enchanted oxen conveyed three bells to Glascwm from Llanddewi Brefi in Cardiganshire, where David himself preached in 519. Another bell at Glascwm, wrote Gerald of Wales, had miraculous powers:

It is supposed to have belonged to Saint David and is called a 'bangu'. In an attempt to liberate him, a certain woman took this handbell to her husband, who was chained up in the castle of Rhaiadr Gwy, in Gwrtheyrnion, which castle Rhys ap Gruffyd had built in our time. The keepers of the castle not only refused to set the man free, but they even seized the bell. That same night God took vengeance on them, for the whole town was burnt down, except the wall on which the handbell hung.

The mandala stone in Bryngwyn Church

It seems likely, though, that such a bell was by no means unique to Glascwm. Writing on Llanfaredd, Roger Williams comments that 'a small handbell called Bangu was kept in Welsh churches, which the clerk or the sexton took to the house of the deceased on the day of the funeral'. It was then carried in the funeral procession and rung at intervals on the way to the

137

church. Aberedw's version of the same bell, dating from 1654, is now in the National Museum of Wales.

To return to Llanfaredd, the village had two bell ringers whose calling is remembered in the placenames of Letty'r Clochydd Isaf and Uchaf—Lodging of the Lower and Upper Bellman. Parish records often list payments to ringers on special occasions, and at Presteigne there is still a daily curfew bell. In 1565 a local woollen manufacturer, John Beddoes, gave land—later known as Bell Meadow—to provide the necessary funds from its rent. A bell was rung morning and evening, initially in the winter months but within a few decades, all the year round. Just before the First World War the day bell was discontinued and the 8.15 pm curfew limited to five minutes. Bell ringing of every kind was suspended during the Second World War because with one or two pre-publicised exceptions it would have signalled a German invasion. The curfew came back in 1945. 'Presteigne is one of the few places in the country', writes the local historian, Keith Parker, 'where the curfew is still rung on a regular nightly basis'. Income from the Bell Meadow no longer suffices to pay the ringers but the shortfall is generously made up by the musician, Mike Oldfield.

Esylt Newbery described the chime of bells at Presteigne Church which played 'The Sun is sinking past' at 9 a.m., and then 'at three-hourly intervals throughout the day, till it got it right at 6 p.m.'. On Sundays a peal of eight bells summoned the congregation 'but at five minutes to the hour [of service] came the substitution of two tinny little bells which were universally known as "the ting-tang"'. After the service 'loaves of hot bread were given away in the church porch to "the deserving poor"'.

One former bell custom was shared with Montgomeryshire. Rev. Parry-Jones relates that when he was inducted as vicar of Llanfihangel Rhydithon in 1926 he was asked to ring one of the church bells to announce that he had taken up his appointment. 'Much attention is paid by parishioners to the number of tolls the new incumbent gives to the bell', he writes, 'for it is an indication to them of the number of years he means to stay among them'. He rang seven times but stayed for nine years.

Music within churches was provided by organs in the few places fortunate to possess them such as Old Radnor, where the fine instrument of the early 16th century may have come from Worcester Cathedral. In their history of the church Sinclair and Fenn suggest that the existence of such an organ 'cannot be unconnected with the fact that John Bull, the charismatic composer and organist', was born in the parish (in 1563). After a

The gallery at Llanbister Church

distinguished career, patronised both by Elizabeth I and James I, Bull left London for the Continent in 1613 under a cloud, either as a catholic recusant or to escape charges of 'incontinence, fornication, adultery and other grievous crimes'.

In general, Radnorshire church musicians led less colourful lives than John Bull. Like Thomas Hardy's 'Mellstock Quire', singers and instrumentalists performed on secular occasions during the week and on Sundays sang and played from the wooden gallery or loft constructed in the west end of churches. These structures have now gone for the most part. The singing loft at the west end of St Mary's, Newchurch, was taken down in 1857. The fine gallery of 1716 still exists at Llanbister, where parts of some of the instruments heard there—two bassoons and a double bass with bow—are kept in a glass case fixed to the north wall of the nave. A flute and a clarinet have been preserved at Presteigne. A flute, clarinet and pitch-pipe are displayed at Aberedw, where Rev. A.G. Adamson (incumbent 1887-1903) noted:

> Will Meredith (Gwernalltcwm) played the Bass Viol; Jas. Jones (Llanbadarn y Garreg), the Tenor Viol; Charley Hawkins, the Fiddle; and Williams, (Hendre), father and son, the Pipe or Flute. [William Williams died in 1897 at the age of 75]. Only the players and singers had books, and the people would only listen. The players could not always agree. There would be a struggle to get possession of the church, and those who struck up first would be left in possession.

Disputes and rivalries among church musicians undoubtedly hastened their own demise. It became the fashion to replace them with the more manageable, if less flexible, barrel organ—so called because for a given tune a wooden cyclinder with projecting pins was inserted, and a handle then turned. At Knighton an ensemble consisting of violin, flageolet and bass viol was superseded in the 1830s by a seraphine (which the *OED* defines as 'a musical instrument of reed kind, invented by John Green in 1833'). The violin, clarinet and cornet players managed to hang on at Llanbadarn Fawr for another 20 years. When Kilvert made his first visit to St Harmon in May 1876 he was depressed to find 'a bare cold squalid interior and high ugly square boxes for seats, a three-decker pulpit and desk, no stove, a flimsy altar rail, a ragged faded altar cloth, a singing gallery with a broken organ, a dark little box for a vestry and a roof in bad repair, admitting the rain'. However, he found the people friendly and hospitable. He kissed a pretty girl 'on her blooming cheek and sweet lips', and accepted the living. Incidentally, she was still alive in 1947 at the age of 84, at the Walsh Arms, Llanddewi. At Llanfihangel Rhydithon a barrel organ took over in the west gallery (which covered a third of the chancel) but both organ and gallery were swept away in 1891.

Until about the same time the *plygain*—the word derives from *pulli cantus*, Latin for cock-crow, and refers to early morning service—lingered in parts of Radnorshire. Congregations, both in church and chapel, assembled at five or six o'clock on Christmas morning and sang carols, often in Welsh, until daybreak. The custom, which some date back to pre-Reformation or even Celtic times, prevailed at Rhayader until early in the 19th century, when 'abuse ... caused its abolition'. So wrote Jonathan Williams. According to Maddox the problems at Rhayader were caused by men who sat up drinking all night and then disrupted the service with 'riotous conduct'. He gives no details, save for an example from Garthbeithio in Montgomeryshire, where during a *plygain* service a man in the west gallery threw a rotten turnip at the vicar. At the end, as was customary, the parson went down the aisle to greet parishioners by the door as they left. Then, he quickly locked the door, ran up the steps to the gallery, and 'broke his walking stick across the back of the offender'. This was in the days of muscular christianity.

When churches gave up the *plygain* it continued in chapels and even, where there was no chapel, in remote farmhouses. If it were a pre-Reformation custom, deriving from the aurora (dawn) mass, it is ironic that nonconformists kept it going. The Primitive Methodists of Presteigne persisted with the *plygain* until about 1890, and went home singing carols through the streets after the service.

Other early religious habits which survived until the 1960s, this time among church-goers, included men occupying one side of the church seating, women the other. Until early in the 19th century men would bow to the altar as they entered the church, and women would curtsey. Some old people still used the saints' days as landmarks in the year, such as St Barnabas (11 June) or Becket's Feast (27 May). Until the 1830s congregations at Llanfihangel Nant Melan would not merely kneel at communion but would prostrate themselves before the consecrated bread and wine.

In a revival of religious fervour which took place during the second half of the 19th century, and coincided with the refurbishment or restoration of many churches, sprigs of yew and box were brought as decoration for the Palm Sunday and Easter services, and sometimes also at Whitsun. Holly, ivy and various evergreens were preferred at Christmas.

Rogation Day, the first Sunday after Easter, was one of the occasions favoured for beating the parish bounds, with parishioners led by their parson who stopped from time to time for readings from the gospels. The Gospel Oak at Clyro which Kilvert mentions would have shaded parson and flock for many a generation. In Gospel Field on Fullbrook Farm at St Harmon similar proceedings were held beneath another tree, now long gone.

A practical result of such exercises was that a parish's boundaries were firmly imprinted in the minds of participants. Those of Knighton, for example, in 1742 and again in 1803 were:

> from an elder tree or bush growing on the back side of Francis Mason's house, who is now deceased; thence to an ash, late of one Meredith Edwards, barber, deceased; and thence to the further side of Black Meadow, beyond the river Tame [Teme], and so over Tame to Cappero Meadow, late in the possession of Jeremiah Bayliss; thence to a stone bridge in the highway leading from the town of Knighton to Presteigne; thence to an oak in a parcel of land of Mr Barbley; thence to the top of Frith Wood; thence to a crab tree near St Edward's Well; so over a common called the Garth, unto a gutter near Whitterley, with the compass of the Lord's Meadow, late in the possession of Richard Evans, deceased; and so to the farther side of a meadow called Clasby; thence over the river Tame; and so to a house wherein Thomas Hodges, now deceased, formerly dwelled; and so to the elder bush aforesaid.

*Door at Rhulen Church with
its sanctuary ring
to the left of the handle*

Another outcome was the provision of free refreshments. The churchwardens' accounts at Llangynllo record the expenditure of three shillings a year for 'ale for the parish round' during much of the 18th century. At Disserth, perhaps under the influence of temperance campaigning, in 1863 'cakes for perambulating the boundaries of the parish on Ascension Day' cost the churchwardens the large sum of £1 2s 0¹/₂d.

A tangible reminder of times long past is the sanctuary ring in the door of Rhulen Church. From the Anglo-Saxon era people wanted for crime or debt could avoid arrest by taking shelter in churches for up to 40 days. This right was drastically limited in the sixteenth century and abolished in the seventeenth. Gerald of Wales mentions that sanctuary applied 'not only in churchyards but outside, too, within the fences and ditches marked out and set by the bishops to fix the ... limits'. There seems to be no record of when sanctuary—*braint* in Welsh—was sought at Rhulen, but in 1558 four men and a woman took refuge at Llanfihangel Nant Melan after escaping from the gaol at New Radnor. (The Llanfihangel churches seem to have been particularly favoured by sanctuary-seekers). In the end, though, of the members of the party, Hugh ap Harry of Gwaithell was hanged, Meredith David Goch of Nantmel and Rhys ap John of Llanbister died in captivity, David ap Thomas of New Radnor and Joanna *ferch* [daughter] Morgan of Knighton were pardoned—by which time the latter was already dead. Their alleged crimes are not known, except for Meredith David Goch, who stood accused of horse-stealing.

The Dead and the Dancers

Large numbers of Radnorshire churchyards have empty expanses on the north or back side, unpopular because of negative associations, and indeed considered to be heavily under the devil's influence. (At Kerry, as the clergyman entered the church the north door was opened so that the devil could leave by it). Paupers and wayfarers who expired in the parish might well be interred on the north side. At Llanfihangel Helygen, a tiny, isolated church between Llandrindod and Nantmel, an infant called Michael Seymour was consigned as recently as 1944 to the outermost limit of the empty north side of the churchyard, presumably because he died unbaptised. The tiny, lonely grave evokes both pity and anger. In the half-century that has since elapsed only two more burials have taken place in that side of the churchyard. By contrast, William Howard Woods, who died in 1997 at the age of 81, has chosen to rest at the farthest western limit of the two-acre churchyard at Glascwm, beneath a line from Dylan Thomas: 'And death shall have no dominion'.

At least the dead, wherever they are, now rest in peace. Formerly the ground favoured for burials to the south and east of churchyards was used and re-used over the generations. The bones which inevitably came to light were collected and placed in charnel houses or, in the case of Presteigne, in a 'skullery' beneath the high altar. Another expedient was to re-bury bones, fairly haphazardly. The church accounts at Llangynllo have entries such as these:

> 1720 For burying the bones 2s. 6d.
> 1782 Paid raising and mending the pavement 3/-, and putting
>   yp of the pulpit and burying ye bones 15/-

Of Pilleth an observer remarked in 1847:

> In digging out graves great quantities of human bones are always discovered, and it is conceived that there can be but little doubt of this having been the resting place of many of those who fell in the battle [of 1402; see chapter 8].

In 1664 Sir Henry Williams of Gwernyfed donated land for a new church at Glasbury, the former building, with its graves, having been washed away by the Wye. In conformity with ancient custom he had to demonstrate that he relinquished the land by cutting a turf which he placed in a fold of the bishop's gown and said: 'I resigne upp all my interest in this circuit of ground, to be a buringe-place for ever for the dead of this parishe'. Such a use of a turf may hark back to Saxon times, when a turf from land being granted to a monastery was sent along with the deeds to the archbishop for placing on the altar, as confirmation of the grant.

The bishop, William Lucy of St David's, then consecrated the plot 'to be a restynge place for the bodyes of those who shall be buried here, untill the last day of doome'. (Unfortunately the church lasted only until 1836 when it was replaced by another). The bishop went on to warn parishioners that no 'heathen people' should be given burial, and that 'from henceforth here must be none of yo'r parishe feastes, nor lawe courtes, nor musterings of soldiers, nor prophane and common uses be exercised'.

This gives a very good idea of the alternative uses to which the empty north side spaces were put. The parish feasts which took place there are described in chapter 7. Dancing also went on there, at various times. Two figures carved in stone set into the external walls of Bryngwyn Church at the south-east corner may show dancers, one male and one female (see illustration on page 166). One wonders whether they engaged in the kind of activity Gerald of Wales described from neighbouring Breconshire:

> You can see young men and maidens, some in the church itself, some in the churchyard and others in the dance which threads its way round the graves. They sing traditional songs, all of a sudden they collapse on the ground, and then those who, until now, have followed their leader peacefully as if in a trance, leap in the air as if seized by frenzy. In full view of the crowds they mime with their hands and feet whatever work they have done contrary to the commandment on sabbath days. When all is over, they enter the church. They are led up to the altar and there, as they make their oblation you will be surprised to see them awaken from their trance and recover their normal composure.

A much later traveller, Benjamin Heath Malkin, touring in 1804, wrote:

> The custom of dancing in the churchyard, at their feasts and revels, is universal in Radnorshire. ... Indeed, this solemn abode [the churchyard] is rendered a kind of circus for every sport and exercise. The young men play at fives and tennis against the wall of the church. It is not however to be understood that they literally dance

over the graves of their progenitors. This amusement takes place on the north side of the churchyard, where it is the custom not to bury. It is rather singular, however, that the associations of the place, surrounded by memorials of mortality, should not deaden the impulses of joy in minds, in other respects not insensible to the suggestions of vulgar superstition.

The great churchyard yews signified not so much mortality as immortality. The oldest and biggest in Radnorshire, at Llanfaredd, reached 36 feet in girth. Other churchyards boasted their own venerable specimens, 14 of them at Llansanffraid-yn-Elfael, 11 at Cefn-llys and eight (formerly ten) at Llanfihangel Nant Melan. Beneath one yew at Heyope 600 people gathered for a service in 1865, and it is appropriate that this is one of the many villages which planted a tiny sapling in March 2000 to mark the millennium and in the hope that it will last through to the next and beyond.

Malkin mentions two big specimens at Aberedw, 'evidently of very great age, but in unimpaired luxuriance and preservation under the shade of which, an intelligent clergyman of the neighbourhood informed me, that he had frequently seen sixty couple [*sic*] dancing, at Aberedw feast, on the 14th of June. The boughs of the two trees intertwine, and afford sufficient space for the evolution of so numerous a company within their ample covering'.

The use of churchyards for both sacred and secular purposes seems to show a healthy, matter-of-fact attitude towards death which is often paralleled in inscriptions and epitaphs.

Under the Green Stone
Several tombstones now fixed to the outside north wall of the chancel at Aberedw have inscriptions beginning with the evocative formula: 'In hopes of joyful resurrection under the green stone'. Despite such words the messages chosen by (or for) the dead in their epitaphs can be gloomy.

Plaques inside the north wall of the nave at Rhulen to four members of the Probert family from Cwmpiban are uniformly lugubrious:

> Our Life begins with trouble here
> Our days are but a span
> And Death you See is allwayes near
> So Vain a thing is man
> [Mary, died 1760, aged 38].

145

Rhulen Church

> Ready repent thy Minutes
> Swiftely fly
> Prepare thyself for Death
> And Learn to Die
> [Thomas, died 1757, aged 26].

> Who can withstand God's dreadful hand
> he Spares not young nor old
> All liveing must return to dust
> thou reader art but mould
> [James, died 1756, aged 66; Mary, his wife, died 1769, aged 74].

Moralising is common. The gravestone of another Probert, Thomas, a tailor who died in 1773 at the age of 44, is now in the porch of Cefn-llys Church:

> Young men quickly behold and see
> How quickly Death hath conquered me
> Redeem your Time make no Delay
> On Earth uncertain is your day.

146

John Price of Penybont (died 1798, aged 73) tells us from a tablet in the chancel at Llanbadarn Fawr:

> Thus, thus it is, we all must tread
> The gloomy regions of the dead,
> Nor bloom of youth nor wealth can wave
> Our mortal bodies from the grave.

A slightly more bitter reference to wealth comes in the traditional verse chosen by John Boore (died 1856), who is buried at Cregrina:

> This world is full of crooked streets,
> Death is a place where all men must meet.
> If Paradise was a thing that men could buy
> The rich should all live and the poor should die.

In the same churchyard lies David Pritchard who before he died at the age of 80 in 1878 planted a yew tree to mark where he wished to be buried. His epitaph runs:

> This yew by me set here so nice,
> Before my spirit died,
> Now decks the grave where I must lie,
> Till God shall raise the dead.
> Let none cut down with ruthless hand,
> Or hurt this blessed tree,
> On sacred ground it humbly stands,
> A monument to me.

All too many inscriptions record lives cut short. A tablet on the south external wall of the chancel at Llanbister commemorates the two Davies children, Richard (died 1807, aged 9) and Eleanor (died 1813, aged 6):

> Tho' Infant years no pompous honors claim,
> No loud parade, or Monumental fame:
> To better praise the last great Day shall rear:
> The spotless Innocence, that slumbers here.

A wooden plaque in Heyope Church commemorates John Handson, who died in 1796 at the age of 11. The inscription breaks up words and

147

lines to suit the width of the board and its decoration: 'Affections tender, and his Tem/Per mild, A loving and obedient child,/A tomb and verse/is all I now can give And here my/Child thy name shall ever live'.

Deaths in childbirth were by no means uncommon, but it is unusual to find a mother and daughter, side by side, as at Disserth, who both died in the same way, perhaps because of some congenital problem. Sarah Hughlings died in 1771, aged 37:

> By various, various ways and means
> We leave this brittle frame behind,
> The child bed's agonising pain
> My soul to God I have resigned.
> Ransomed by His Son's Blood most dear,
> Who for my sins vouchsafed to die.
> Therefore dear Friends your sighs forbear,
> I dwell with Him in endless Joy.

(In the pronunciation of the eighteenth century the last word would indeed have rhymed with 'die'). The unfortunate woman's daughter, also Sarah, the wife of Thomas Jones, herself died in childbirth in 1802.

Accidental death inspired numerous epitaphs. William Johnson (died 1823, aged 17) lies in the churchyard at Presteigne:

> My death so suddenly and quick,
> Occasioned by a horse's kick.
> My parents dear, do not repent [?regret],
> My soul so quick to Heaven was sent.

Headstones to the left of the church entrance at Knighton record the deaths of cousins, Thomas and Edward Hope, aged 21 and 18 respectively. 'Injudiciously taking shelter under an Oak' in 1778, they were struck by lightning. Each has his epitaph. Edward's reads:

> At thy powerful voice, O Lord,
> Tremendous thunders roll,
> And pointed lightnings at thy word
> Dart swift from pole to pole.
> Reader think not thy judgement seized
> Two youths so honest could expire,
> Victims so pure Heaven saw well pleased
> And snatched them in celestial fire.

The hard winters of earlier times also claimed victims such as Tom Rogers who served as a fifer with the Radnorshire Militia for 50 years and then became a Chelsea Pensioner. On the way home to Presteigne in the winter of 1798 he became lost in the snow less than half a mile from the town, and perished. Some 30 years earlier (in 1767) John Chandlour, a shepherd from Llanfihangel Rhydithon, went up in a blizzard to the hills above Dolau to bring down his sheep. When he failed to return his brother Thomas went in search of him. When Thomas in turn did not come back it must have taken great courage for Edward Chandlour, the brothers' cousin, to set off

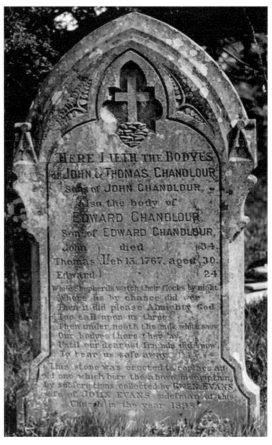

The Chandlour stone

into the teeth of the storm. All died. They were 34, 30 and 24 respectively. A stone raised to them by public subscription (and renewed in 1898) stands by the east end of the church. It bears these words:

> While shepherds watched their flocks by night
> Whereas by chance did wee
> Then it did please Almighty God
> To call upon us three.
> Then under neath the milk white snow
> Our bodyes there they lay
> Until our dearest friends did know
> To bear us safe away.

149

Such calm and dignity are not always observed in epitaphs. A stone unearthed in an unnamed churchyard in the Elan Valley during the construction of the reservoirs is said to have read:

> I plant these shrubs on your grave, dear wife,
> That something on this spot may boast of Life.
> Shrubs may wither and all earth must rot,
> Shrubs may revive but you thank God, can not.

Perhaps surprisingly, an even more scurrilous verse came from a clergyman, Rev. Samuel Phillips (1754-1807), who was himself both born and buried at Bleddfa. He intended it—though only on paper—for a cantankerous old maid:

> Scorning and Scorn'd, she passed her life away,
> An useless lump of animated Clay;
> Now Spite and Envy rule her frame no more,
> But here it lies - more useless than before.

In all Radnorshire only seven funerary inscriptions in Welsh have been recorded. One of them was noticed only in 1955 on a fragment of gravestone built into a wall at Howey. It commemorates Catharine Price and concludes with: '*[Yma yr hu]naf yn llwch y llawr [hyd ddyd yr] Adgyfodiad mawr rhoir im newydd*'—Here I rest in the earth's dust until the day of the great Resurrection new [?life] is given me. A gravestone in the south-east corner of the churchyard at Llanyre, after identifying Mary Neale, who died in 1802, aged 78, adds: 'N.B. Been in the Armada'. The rather enigmatic words may mean that she had voyaged in a ship of that name. Then follow these lines:

> *Mae amser i ryfel*
> *Ac amser y heddwch*
> *Tae amser i drafel*
> *At dy y bedd, ac amser i orphwys.*

The translation is:

> There is a time for war
> There is a time for peace
> Were there time for travel
> To the house of the grave, and time for rest.

Opposite the priest's door in the churchyard at Llowes a gravestone bears these words:

> *WILLIAM BEVAN OR*
> *VIDOWLOYD DAN Y*
> *GARREG SYDD IM*
> *MA YN GORPHWYS*
> *AY OYDRAN OYDD*
> *84 MHYLNEDD AC Y*
> *MADDVIS AR BYD HUN*
> *Y 17 DYDD O EBRILL YN*
> *Y FLWYDDYN, 1684.*
> *MISERERE MEI DEUS*

[William Bevan of Fedwlwyd is resting here under this stone His age was 84 years and he departed this life on the 17 day of April in the year 1684 God have pity on me].

Perhaps the most famous epitaphs in the county are those to Mary Morgan, who in September 1804 killed her newly-born baby daughter in her room at Maesllwch Castle, where she worked as undercook for Walter Wilkins, the MP for Radnorshire. Some seven months later, shortly after her 17th birthday, she was sentenced to death by Mr Justice Hardinge, and hanged at Presteigne in Gallows Lane.

The case had some disquieting features. The MP's son and namesake was on the grand jury which found a case to answer against Morgan; and also possibly on the petty jury which found her guilty of murder. (A document gives the names of 13 jurors but is unclear as to whether the 14th was either Wilkins junior or Charles H. Price). There is evidence that Wilkins helped Morgan to conceal her pregnancy; and it is possible that she expected some help from him at the trial, in the shape of a letter to the judges, and this may explain why she seemed curiously unconcerned.

Her apparent lack of contrition may have determined the judge to persist with a sentence of death where in such circumstances he might normally have commuted it to a term of imprisonment. Hardinge appears (as Hardsman) in these lines from Byron's poem, *Don Juan* (canto iii, 1819):

There was the waggish Welsh Judge, Jefferies Hardsman,
In his grave office so completely skill'd,
That when a culprit came for condemnation,
He had his judge's joke for consolation.

Hardinge does not appear to have joked about Mary Morgan, indeed he seems to have felt remorse after her death, which, he said in a letter to the bishop of St Asaph, she met 'in a most affecting manner, with calm intrepidity and with devout resignation'. According to local tradition the judge visited Morgan's grave every time his duties subsequently took him to Presteigne. (He died in the town in 1816). He wrote both a Latin epitaph for her and a poem, 'On seeing the tomb of Mary Morgan'.

He had ordered that after the hanging her body should be 'dissected and anatomised'—that is, handed over to the surgeons at a medical school—but, and this is perhaps a measure of local sympathy for her, she was buried in a corner of the rectory gardens adjacent to the churchyard. By one of the ironies of

The epitaph to Mary Morgan erected at the expense of the earl of Ailesbury

history this unconsecrated plot later became part of holy ground when the churchyard was subsequently extended. A lengthy, pompous and sanctimonious epitaph, erected at the expense of the earl of Ailesbury, a friend of Hardinge's, justified the sentence on 'the victim of sin and shame for the Murder of her bastard child'. It still stands, as does a second stone to Mary Morgan which merely (mis)quotes a biblical text: 'He that is without sin among you/Let him first cast a stone at her'. Presteigne's historian, Keith Parker, suggests that this memorial was erected between 1816 and 1818 as a counter to the Ailesbury epitaph, but one wonders whether the latter could have been a response to the former. According to Esylt Newbery the old sexton who at the end of the nineteenth century usually showed visitors round, 'would make sure they had read Mary Morgan's epitaph, then casually remark: "You see, the judge was the father of her child"'. A striking comment, but pure fiction.

While acknowledging that 'documentary sources afford no evidence of overt local sympathy' for Morgan, Parker refers to oral indications:

> W.H. Howse, in his conversations with elderly residents uncovered many local traditions connected with Mary Morgan which had been handed down over the generations: that the householders in Scottleton Street drew the blinds out of respect for her on the morning of the execution and that if money could have saved her, she would have had 'a wagon load', that Mary, wrapped in a winding sheet, was unconscious when lifted from the cart at Gallows Lane. In one of his notebooks W.H. Howse records the tradition 'that initially the authorities were unable to find a farmer willing to provide a cart to carry Mary Morgan to Gallows Lane, nor a waggoner to drive it. The strong local tradition of an attempt to obtain a reprieve also suggests that the Mary Morgan case had excited local sympathy. Mrs Parris [who wrote a paper on the subject in 1983] has demonstrated that there is no evidence that a pardon or reprieve was granted or even sought, nevertheless the tradition persists that Sir Samuel Romilly [campaigner for law reform], or her young defence counsel Richard Beavan, or an unknown gentleman rode to London, obtained a reprieve or pardon, but arrived back in Presteigne too late to halt the execution as his horse went lame.

The time-honoured theme of a fatally-delayed reprieve is also mentioned by Stephen Coleridge, writing in the *Westminster Gazette* for 4

June 1898 under the title of 'Pitiful Welsh Tragedy Re-told'. Coleridge states that the unknown person who sought a reprieve for Morgan paid for her tombstone, which may be another indication of its having been erected prior to Ailesbury's epitaph.

According to Jennifer Green, writing in 1987, flowers were placed on Morgan's grave by an unknown hand every year on the anniversary of her death, 13 April. Interest in the unhappy Mary has certainly continued. In 1957 a radio feature, 'Mary Morgan's Story', by Gwyn Jones was broadcast. Over 40 years later a film on her was being made.

Perhaps, though, one should give the last words to other epitaphs. That of Thomas Burchlate, who died at Presteigne in 1850, aged 68, and had served as a soldier in Egypt, the Iberian Peninsula, and at Waterloo, runs:

> Praise on tombs are titles vainly spent
> A man's good name is his best monument.

Essentially the same couplet is to be found on the plaque at the east end of the chancel at Colva to William Stocking (died 1779, aged 39). Stephen Haywood (died 1820, aged 58) takes his leave at Clyro with a warning:

> Farewll wife and children dear
> From all affliction I lie here
> This grave is all my bed you see
> Where you must shortly be with me.

Even more laconic are the words reported from an unidentified grave at Llandrindod Wells by W.H. Howse:

> Him as was has gone from we
> Us as is must go to he.

CHAPTER 7

Fairs and Feasts

The recent emergence of car boot sales and farmers' markets is in some ways a reversion to older styles of trading. Fairs and markets were once established by royal charter, though some, perhaps of very ancient origin, were merely confirmed. The fairs, particularly, were eagerly awaited as social highlights of the year: when buying and selling were over, people looked to enjoy themselves. The fairs may have developed, at least in some cases, from the feasts or wakes which, instead of being austere prayer meetings to commemorate a church's foundation, became increasingly devoted to pleasure. Indeed, rowdiness and drunkenness caused many of them to be abandoned, though churches of late have revived feasts in a more sedate form.

This chapter also considers horse racing and fox hunting, each of which had a passionate following in rural Radnorshire. The latter pursuit, which dates at most from 250 years ago, is now controversial, a position underlined by two letters juxtaposed in the correspondence columns of the *Brecon and Radnor Express*'s first issue for January 2000: one was headed a 'A millennium call to end cruelty', the other 'The cost of a fox hunting ban'.

Ballads which once chronicled epic fox hunts are among the few examples of street literature in Radnorshire. The oral tradition of song, too, is sparsely recorded, which is tantalising because references to singing abound. Instrumental music seems to have been plentiful, and there was a great vogue for dancing. Venues for this included churchyards, private houses, and also the many inns, taverns and public houses of Radnorshire. These have certainly dwindled over the years but they remain an important feature of social life in the county.

Fun of the Fair

Royal charters for annual fairs date from as early as 1225-6 at Presteigne and 1305-6 at New Radnor. Over the centuries other places acquired their own fairs, and an almanac published at Hereford in 1831 listed five at Rhayader alone (on 6 and 27 August, 26 September, 14 October and 3 December), four each at Howey and Knighton, three at Painscastle, Penybont and Radnor, and two at Presteigne. Two more began at Gladestry in 1840 but lasted barely a decade.

Fair-goers had a reputation for rowdy behaviour such as the 'stand-up street fighting' and the 'disgraceful practice of breaking the public lamps' of which the *Hereford Journal* complained at Knighton in 1849. Even so, new fairs continued to be established. Evan Watkin of Nantmel regretted the creation of a May Fair at Rhayader on the day before Penybont's, thus threatening the existence of the latter's 'glorious old fair'. His description of the occasion at Rhayader in a letter to the *Hereford Times* (published because of a mix-up only in August 1857) provides useful insight into such events:

> The fair morning dawned - it was fine - stock sold exceedingly well, and wages were high: all the complements of a fair came together. The standings were set up, but not without considerable scuffles between Mr Tape and Mr Shoelace, which Mrs Gingerbread put an end to by driving them both out of the field.
>
> The young people, and some old ones, spent the evening in walking back and face through the streets, or visiting one public-house after another. John and Jenny wandered into a room with a glass of gin, where they were followed by Tom and Kate, with a host of others whose names I could not find, or do not remember. Now and then you could meet Billy taking five or six young lasses to have a share of his pint of beer. The girls thought it better to be treated in sixes and sevens than not to be treated at all. Most of the people went from the town drunk or sober before morning, but some remained several days, to drink the remainder of the casks and flasks; and *mine hosts* were very glad to see them, however drunk, if they had any money. One consequence of this fair was that a man went home, beat his wife, and then jumped on his head into the river to rise no more.
>
> I believe upon the whole this new fair had as little fighting and squabbling as any I remember, thanks to the new police I suppose; but, as for that, fighting had descended in our last fairs to clogs and pattens in the hands of women.

FAIRS AND FEASTS

Despite a stated aversion to fairs, Watkin took the trouble to go to Penybont the following day so as to compare with Rhayader:

> Some thought that it was not so numerously attended but still I could not help wondering at the number who came together in that barren spot. A person seeing it on any other day could never believe that so many would come together. Well, they did come, full the wide road for half a mile. Never did I see so many thousands mingled in such higgeldy piggeldy way, roving to and fro through each other like madmen. To the great danger of flounced dresses and fragile forms they walked away every one right before him, as if in a great hurry to reach a particular spot, and then turned back again before they had been anywhere. The head inn was extended to twice its size by a curtain tent extended outside, and filled to excess with drinkers among whom I observed the vicar of ----- and his intended.
>
> To get anything to eat there at such a time as this was quite out of the question, the drinkables bringing so much more profit to mine host than the adibles [*sic*]. It is true there were little cakes in various tents, but all so dry as if they had been baked the first summer after the deluge.

Watkin then abruptly moved to consider the hiring of workers which took place at the same time (see also chapter 2), and then concluded with the fervent hope that such fairs would soon come to an end:

> I think it a great pity that hiring should *not* be accomplished by some method besides in fairs, for both masters and servants here have no chance of knowing whether they suit each other or no. This, likewise, gives an excuse for hundreds to go that have no business. I was very much surprised to see those two young women with sky-blue trimmed bonnets, black falls [veils], light drab mantles, with brown trimming, and stripe dresses in the fair. They appeared superior to most of the young lasses in the place, but still they stood in the worst places looking at those filthy and demoralising sights called shows. These are the parts of fairs next to spirits (alcoholic); could both these be expelled 300 degrees beyond the bounds of this globe, our fairs may then be places of harmless amusement. As far as I could judge, not more than five per cent had any business in that fair. The other 95 were mere idle spectators and pleasure hunters. I regard this fair as a cesspool of vices or centre of immorality, from

which the country all around is demoralised. Not until the judgement of the great day will it be known how much evil and immorality has originated in such fairs as this. It was here that many a lad drank his first half-pint and commenced a life of drunkenness. Here many a fine young woman commenced the path which led her to disgrace and ruin. Here did many a father teach his son a trick that made his gray hairs sink in sorrow to the grave; and many a mother has had to weep all her days because her daughter went to the pleasure fair. The old feasts on saints' days are now done away with, and I hope the pleasure fairs will soon follow their wake. Markets are useful, but pleasure fairs benefit none but those whose work it is to pander to the vices and profit by the crimes of their fellow-creatures.

The thought may be inconsistent moving as it does from 'glorious fair' to 'cesspool of vice', but the words are powerful. Yet they contrast with accounts published the following year in the same newspaper of May Fairs at Presteigne and Knighton. The former, though 'one of the best for live stock we ever remember' was disappointing with regard both to hiring and the pleasure fair, which 'like most other of our old-fashioned "sports and pastimes", seems year by year growing "small by degrees and beautifully less"'. The anonymous contributor much regrets the decline, but in doing so describes former attractions:

Those giants, eight feet high, that were able to put 'the house they live in' upon their shoulders; the giantesses - specimens, at least, upon the canvas (by the bye, often the best part of the exhibition), of gorgeously-dressed mammoth beauties with flowing flaxen hair and blue satin slippers; those male and female figures—the little woman with a tiny arm thrust out of the upper storey window of her house half her own height ringing a bell, to astonish the open-mouthed gaping rusties: the little gentleman (and, of course, to heighten the interest, they were always husband and wife) would exhibit a tight little pair of legs clad in black silk breeches, silk stockings and pumps, through a window of his own cub [hutch] house, and then carry it round the stage, to the cries of the showman to walk up and see the living 'feenomenon', accompanied with the din of gongs, horns, drums, not omitting the never-to-be-forgotten speaking-trumpet, with which half a dozen 'proprietors' would be in rivalry, seeing which could turn out the greatest wonders encouraged by the shouts and laughter of the crowd, and the more substantial gathering of their pence. The Miss Biffens, the Hottentot Venuses, the living Cannibals (who, to keep alive in a civilised country at all, were obliged to feed on raw flesh), the conjurors, jugglers, fire eaters (to whom 'Professor' Anderson was but an apprentice), learned pigs, performing horses, fortune-telling ponies—all are gone, not a shadow left—and May fair, which served the boys and girls with a never-failing source from which to draw supplies and stories for the year of wonders seen and admired, has been by the ruthless march of Time—and, shall we say, improvement—swept, with other rustic gatherings, from the scene; and, in its place, we have—what? blue-coated and belted policemen, solemnly promenading up and down and right and left, advocates for the march of enlightenment and improvement. Our Broad-street on Monday last, hitherto the scene of crowds of 'shows' and show-seekers, presented a deserted appearance: in fact, quite that of an ordinary day. ... One solitary representative of the show class, one 'merry-go-round', one 'up and down', a rifle tube, a few nut and cake stalls, pedlars' tables, and basket depositories, and Presteigne fair is described. The weather was delightful, and all passed off quietly.

A week later at Knighton 'an incessant fall of rain, throughout the whole of Monday' did not prevent an 'influx of pleasure-seekers and others'. Stock prices proved 'much superior to those of any neighbouring fair', but another writer lamented past times:

> In the pleasure fair, although the attendance was large, small provision had been made for the amusement of our country friends: the wonderful exhibitions which usually grace our May fair were absent. No giants 20 feet high - in portrait; no live lions or tigers; no circus company in long procession, were here. Some small exhibitions, with horn and drum and glittering representation of something which you did not see inside - if you were so foolish as to invest your twopence in the speculation; and no end of 'cheap John' carts, wonderful riding horses, &c., the only novelty being a sort of water-wheel with boxes appended, in which some score of rustics were alternately elevated and brought low again, amid immense applause, were the only public amusements provided.

Despite such gloomy reflections fairs continued. Penybont Fair was described by W.J. Bufton of Llandrindod in 1897 as 'one of the most celebrated in Wales'. Hirings seem to have persisted until after the Second World War (see chapter 2). Stock fairs of various kinds went on until the early years of the twentieth century at least. W. Watkins of Nantywellan remembered the big gatherings at New Radnor on 28 and 29 October each year. The event became known as Radnor Goose Fair, not because geese were sold but because they were on the bill of fare at all the inns and eating places. It was also 'proverbial for rough weather'. Sheep were sold on the first day, cattle and horses on the second, the latter including 'all classes from the best cart horses, hackneys, cobs, mountain ponies, and foals'.

Watkins also attended stock fairs at Knighton:

> The large fair for live stock was in March when some of the best cart horses and cobs were shown. The cattle were mostly stores - barren cows, young bullocks, and a very few fat cattle, but there were few sheep at this time of year. Michaelmas fair, on the first of October, was the great store ewe fair, when sheep taken from this parish [Llanfihangel Rhydithon] left home as early as two or three in the morning. This was necessary as the buyers from a long distance came the night before; the market commencing soon after daylight. The same applied to the cattle fair on the second of October. This was the time when the big bullocks were shown.

Newbridge Horsefair, c.1905, as shown on a postcard

Some of the best were from The Farm, Bleddfa, The Moat, Beguildy, and the Great House, Llangunllo.

At Presteigne the Candlemas (2 February) Fair started for stock in 1812 was later restricted to horses. From 1895 it combined with a horse show, and in 1914 merged with the annual show of the agricultural society. Minna Barron remembered its being held in the big field below the Warden, accompanied by sheepdog trials and tugs-of-war: 'We used to see the magnificent great shire horses being led through the streets, their coats gleaming and tails and manes done up in intricate plaits ... with coloured ribbons'. The horse fairs at Newbridge-on-Wye on 17 October and 12 November were described by Bufton as being among the biggest in the principality. The November event featured in the national press—the *Sunday Pictorial*—in 1934. These fairs survived the Second World War but died out in the 1950s.

Wintry weather seems to have been no deterrent to those attending such gatherings. The fair at Rhayader on 3 December, famous equally for dressed pig carcasses and glue-like mud, was known as Dom Fair, after the Welsh, *Ffair Domlyd* (miry fair). Its attractions included auctions, cattle sales, waxworks and Wild West shows. People also stocked up there with winter provisions.

Ironically, perhaps, the pleasure element in fairs—once entirely subsidiary to the main business—lasted longest. Elizabeth Clarke remembered how colliers travelled by train to the May Fairs at Rhayader, proclaiming their intention of enjoying themselves by sporting pound notes tucked into their hatbands. John Hereford's very readable novel, *The May Fair* (1948), is set during a day at Rhayader, flimsily concealed as Aberelan. Mona Morgan's family favoured Hay, with 17 May marked as a red-letter day in her childhood calendar:

> Booths and stalls spread down from the clock tower and the street was thronged with people. ... The novelty of being in a crowd excited us. We hurried from stall to stall, trying to see everything at once. The crack of rifles guided us to the shooting galleries where we found men levelling guns at moving targets or aiming at white balls rising and falling on jets of water.

She goes on to mention a coconut shy, try-your-strength machine, chair-o-plane, switchback and roundabout.

May Fairs are still held at Hay as well as at Knighton, Rhayader and Presteigne but it is doubtful whether they inspire the wonder and delight of days gone by.

Feasts and Wakes

Despite Evan Watkin's claim (see above) that 'the old feasts on saints' days are now [1857] gone by', these parish events survived a great deal longer, and are still not entirely gone. In origin they were vigils or wakes held for prayer on the saint's day appropriate to each church, except when this fell in winter, in which case an alternative date would be adopted. After prayer followed pleasure, in the shape of feasting and celebration. These events were centred on the church and churchyard, though as the secular side became increasingly prominent they were often moved elsewhere.

Richard Suggett has contested the view of the *gwylmabsant* (patron saint's festival) as a survival from pre-Reformation times. He argues instead that 'the annual parochial revel was in essential respects a new phenomenon' which reached its heyday only in the eighteenth century. Early in the twentieth, D.E. Owen's parishioners at Llanelwedd remembered such events with affection:

> Within living memory no feast was considered in any way complete without a special service and sermon. The feast service was quite as popular and well attended as the harvest thanksgiving service is today, and a vast majority of the hill-folk would welcome its revival now. Two years ago one vicar resuscitated this service in his parish with the result that, though it was not widely advertised, the spacious old church was crowded with people, many of whom had come on horseback from distant places, to attend a service similar to those which their parents and forbears had attended for many centuries. Unfortunately much drinking and fighting always attended the feast, with the result that the clergy joined the revivalist preachers to put a stop to the whole thing. An attempt was made in some parishes (Llangunllo in particular) to retain the religious side of the festival and to abandon the social, commercial, and riotous accretion, but the young people could not be taught to sift and separate what had been so very closely wedded for many centuries.

There are plenty of examples of such accretion. In Radnorshire, according to Howse, 'fights at the fairs and wakes were an essential part of the day's pleasure, and there are still [1949] people who remember the

Presteigne with the Warden, as shown on a postcard

scenes of combatants, stripped to the waist, hammering at one another with their bare fists, while their friends and admirers looked on and shouted their encouragement'. The Warden's Wake at Presteigne on 20 June drew big crowds to wrestling, drinking booths and various competitions including skittling for a pig, but the event, wrote Barron, 'became rather disreputable and caused so many fights and so much drunkenness that it was stopped soon after 1900'. ''Tis no festival unless there be some fighting', according to a popular saying. 'On the Welsh border', writes Suggett, 'it was the custom at the Wake to settle by fighting all the quarrels of the past year'.

Llanigon—just across the Wye in Breconshire from Llowes and Glasbury—held its feast on the first Sunday after 20 September. Old inhabitants gave this account in 1925 to Rev. W.E.T. Morgan:

> A great deal of dancing went on to the strains of the fiddlers, the two gipsy brothers Leigh, or old blind Ukin, the harpist, landlord of The Harp, in Glasbury, or John Price, fiddler, the butcher, from Glasbury. Old blind Ukin, the father of Molly Ukin, played the harp at these feasts for the people to dance, and his daughter often carried it and played it herself at the Swan. The blind harper carried his harp by a string on his back.
>
> The women sometimes acted as seconds for their husbands in their fights, or at any rate cheered them on to deeds of valour. When young Jack Thee (John Jones) had a memorable and most

Dancing on the Green (Sikes)

sanguinary encounter with old John Walker, Nancy, his wife, carried out jugs of beer for the combatants, and urged her husband on with the inspiring words 'Lay to him, Jack, and if thee gets bested I'll carry thy bones home in my apron'.

Before the change of calendar in 1752 Disserth Wake was held on the first Sunday in July, but afterwards moved on a week. The old wake in the churchyard came to an end in the late nineteenth century, though a modern and rather more sedate revival still takes place on the time-honoured day. In 1744 an anonymous visitor from Shropshire described seeing people 'genteelly dressed' doing the dance called 'Burthers Squire Jones' in a barn by the riverside. However, the main action took place elsewhere:

> The churchyard, though large, was filled with people of almost all ages and qualities. ... The church is a strong building and pretty large, against the tiles of which were a dozen lusty young fellows playing at tennis, and as many against the steeple at fives. They played very well, but spoke (as almost every one else did) in the Welsh tongue. On one side of the church were about six couples

dancing to one violin, and just below three or four couples to three violins, whose seat was on a tombstone. In short, the whole was something whimsically odd. We here saw common games of ball played against the sacred pile, and there also music playing over the bones of the deceased. We were in the middle of a merry, noisy throng, without knowing the language or indeed almost anything they said.

The same man went on the following day to the wake at Aberedw, where he again saw dancing, by the well-to-do in a booth made of twigs and branches (presumably to keep the sun off), and by the ordinary people in the open churchyard. As late as 1917 in their guide to Aberedw Tudor and Lloyd note that dancing having started after service on the Sunday would go on 'as long as it was light'. They add that the local J.P., Squire Pugh of Blaenmilo, was very fond of dancing, and that the 'Feast would go on in full swing on Monday and Tuesday - only to start again the following Sunday at Llanfaredd'. According to the present rector, Rev. Alan Charters, the big church porch accommodated a band which played for up to 60 couples of dancers. The game of fives was played against the west wall of the tower.

Attitudes to the wakes such as that of Squire Pugh became increasingly unusual as drinking and fighting increased. Rev. David Lloyd, vicar at

Disserth chuchyard, showing the space used for dancing

Carvings of dancers set into the south-east corner of the outside walls of Bryngwyn Church (see p.144)

Llanbister, became so exasperated at rowdy behaviour at the wake that he publicly prayed to God to send a thunderstorm on St Cynllo's Day (17 July). The Almighty obliged with a spectacular downpour, and thereafter, we are told, celebrations became more restrained.

Lloyd, a native of Llanbister, was vicar there for over 40 years. As well as being an inventor, he played the violin and the organ. His musical compositions included a march, 'The Loyal Cambrian Volunteers'. His published writings included not only sermons, but poems and essays. He died in 1832, agred 80.

Preferred fare for the wake at Llanbister was new potatoes followed by rice pudding. The rice was baked with plenty of raisins in big pans called steins (from the Welsh, *stên*) until it became thick, then cut into cake-like slices. The steins were set along the church wall from the gate to the Stores so that people could help themselves. Ale and cider washed down the food.

In the 1840s the Society for the Suppression of Sunday Wakes strongly campaigned against what it saw an unseemly behaviour. A somewhat uncharitable Rhayader resident in a letter to the *Hereford Times* in 1857 expressed satisfaction that 'the old dames' who had previously sold such delicacies as cakes, tarts, puddings, gooseberries and plums in the church-yard on feast day (9 August) were by then 'deposited in the same, and their

evil habits buried in oblivion'. The writer added that 'This year compara-
tively few of our youth ... visited the temple of Bacchus before attending
the evening service' on feast day.

On the other hand, a feeling of regret at the passing of old times
emerges from an account of the previous year, relating to Gladestry:

> Lord's Day, August 31st, being the anniversary of our ancient
> Sunday Feast, which some years ago received the patronage of the
> surrounding neighbourhood, all classes uniting to perpetuate its
> celebration with glass and pipe, and with dance and song, the
> prolongation of which sometimes extended through three or four
> days, was this year celebrated with a public baptism of a young man
> in the stream.

The immersion mentioned was not a ducking, attended with horseplay, but
a solemn ceremony of the kind described in chapter 4.

At New Well, a now-deserted hamlet in the parish of Llananno, the
wake lingered, attracting people from a wide area on the third Sunday in
July (or the Sunday nearest the 17th). The Green, a natural amphitheatre,
provided space for dancing, foot races, and football played with a pig's
bladder. Wrestling and boxing took place in a specially erected ring, the
contests stimulating brisk betting. Ale, beer and cider were consumed in
large quantities, together with plenty of food.

Drunkenness and disorder led to adverse publicity, and local Baptists
relentlessly campaigned against such events. John Jones, writing in 1895,
remarked: 'Formerly there were wakes held at Llanbister and New Well on
Sundays and on these occasions there was leaping, wrestling, fighting and
drinking. Happily these evils have ceased'. In the same book, *History of
the Baptists in Radnorshire*, Jones expressed pleasure at developments in
another Llananno hamlet with the intriguing name of Maes yr helm (Field
of the helmet):

> The neighbourhood of Maesyrhelm like other neighbourhoods in
> which the Gospel was not earnestly and faithfully preached was
> very dark and wicked when the little band of Baptists began to hold
> their meetings. Card playing, dancing parties, wakes and pitched
> battles were very prevalent. Since the commencement of the Baptist
> cause in the neighbourhood of Maesyrhelm the religious and moral
> state of the country is in some respects much improved.

The more tolerant Kilvert refers in neutral terms to the Clyro Feast of 1874 but the rough old celebrations were not in keeping with Victorian opinion in general. As Bryan Lawrence has observed, 'It was the drink in the end which killed this [New Well] Wake as well as many others in the area for they gradually deteriorated into orgies of drunkenness and disorder and few survived mid-Victorian times'.

Horse Racing and Fox Hunting

It is scarcely surprising, given Radnorshire's rural character, that horses had (as they still do) a passionate following in the county. The name of Race Course Field on Church House Farm at Gladestry commemorates one former sporting venue. Bailey Hwlin Farm at St Harmon also had a racecourse, though trouble there put an end to meetings in 1852. Punters could have transferred their allegiance to Penybont, New Radnor, or Glascwm; or for that matter to bigger courses.

From the time of Queen Anne meetings were held annually on Bailey Hill, some 1,500 feet above Knighton. In 1862 these moved to a site east of the town and flourished there for some 20 years. Presteigne's meetings took place at Broad Heath. At a meeting in 1849 the *Hereford Journal* listed the Presteigne and the Broadheath Stakes in the morning, the Farmers' and Scurry Stakes in the evening. Racing at Broad Heath was suspended for 12 years after disorder in 1851, and ended altogether in the 1880s. A revival at Discoed in 1945 reverted to the earlier site in the 1950s, but this, too, came to an end a few years later. Trotting races, though, are still held there, and at Monaughty Poeth.

Race meetings began at Llandrindod in the 1750s and lasted until 1914. A revival in 1949 proved short lived. Trotting races continued on the Ddole until the 1990s, when they moved to Penybont. Oddly enough, Bufton's *Illustrated Guide to Llandrindod Wells* (1897) does not mention horse racing, though its list of attractions does include otter hunting: 'The several rivers and tributaries in the district, in which the otter plentifully abounds, afford capital privileges for hunting. Mr Forster's hounds meet on various occasions during the season, in the vicinity'.

A pack of otter hounds, established at Presteigne in 1814, was disbanded in 1838. Some 30 years later the Hon. Geoffrey Hill established another, the Hawkestone (called after the family seat in Shropshire), which operated round Presteigne until at least 1956, and possibly until 1982, when otters became a protected species.

Colonel Price of Lyonshall, master of the Radnor and West, 1868-92

Records of fox hunting in Radnorshire go back to the late eighteenth century. If one may deal with the later period first, in the 1830s Walter Wilkins of Maesllwch Castle kept a pack of hounds which hunted in Breconshire and Herefordshire as well as Radnorshire. Close by, at Glasbury, an annual hunt during the following decade pitted the hounds of Thomas Pugh of Blaenmilo (Squire Pugh again) against a bag fox—an animal caught and then released to act as a quarry. Presteigne had a series of packs, starting in the 1840s. In the 1860s the picturesquely-named Captain Bevan of Old Gittoes and Jack the Rat were in charge; at the end of the decade the Radnorshire and West Herefordshire Hunt—which still exists—came into being. During the Second World War some 40 of its riders joined the Home Guard and formed a mounted detachment which patrolled the Radnorshire uplands. The hunt's annals are full of accounts such as this:

> On February 25th, 1889, the hounds met at Corton. Colonel Price [of Lyonshall, master 1868-92] found at once in Paradise Wood, close to Presteigne. The fox ran through the North Wood past Barland and Evenjobb on to Litton Hill, where the hounds pressed him hard. Running through the Forest Wood they got on to Radnor Forest, which at that time was not planted with trees. Keeping along the Radnor Forest and leaving Creigiau on their left, they ran down to Llandegle [*sic*] and over the rocks down to Cwmbrith. Carrying on down the valley they caught their fox in a little spinney close to Howey. This was an 18 mile point and the colonel vowed that they never changed foxes nor did he ever touch [whip] the hounds.

The earliest pack in Radnorshire was maintained at Llanfihangel Nant Melan by Thomas Butts, who died in 1793 at the age of 65. One of its epic hunts was chronicled in a 19-verse ballad:

Members of the Radnor and West on Home Guard patrol duty

FAIRS AND FEASTS

Squire Butts's Hounds

Ye Gentlemen of note and fame, and men of low degree
Who take delight in Fox-hunting, pray listen unto me;
A story true I tell to you concerning of a fox,
How we went over mountains high, through valleys, woods and rocks.

We started for the 'Bfedow [Aberedw] hill, one morning fair and gay,
Early before bright Phoebus rose; 'twas scarce the break of day;
We rode away straight for Alltgoch, bold Reynard for to find,
And there we hit upon the trail which he had left behind.

Old Snowball he ran down the hill, 'twas he that found him then;
To chase the fox was his delight, like Captain o'er his men;
And soon as he threw up his nose he knew it was a fox,
And ran him straight, boys, through the woods and o'er the mighty rocks.

Bold Reynard hearing how the dogs came rattling down the wood,
Awoke straightway out of his sleep and on his legs he stood;
Said he, 'They are the Rhiwey hounds by their echo loud and shrill,
Before they shall to me come nigh I'll cross Llandilo hill'.

O then the fox left cover straight and up the hill he goes,
Saying, 'I do not care for friends or either fear my foes'.
Said he, 'I'll go to Llanbedr woods and there I will take ground,
I value not the huntsmen all, nor do I Squire Butts' hounds'.

The huntsmen then came riding upon the hilly plain,
And then they halloo'd - 'Hark him! Hark! Come wind him boys, again'.
Little Ringwood he laid to him then and Windsor with his sound;
I know there are not better dogs in England to be found.

Singer, Primer, Trimbush, Teaser - these dogs began to hunt,
And little Tidings did engage to lead them in the front.
'I'm leader tho' I'm old and grey, this cause I will maintain,
If he'll stay on the face of ground this day I'll have him slain'.

Old Music would not stay behind but came bowling down the hill,
And hunted him through every bog and every little prill [brook];
The fox stood listening in the wood within hearing of the dogs
A-chasing him most merrily o'er the Higley bogs.

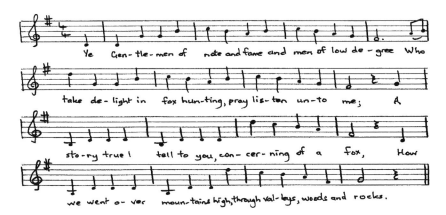

'I think I hear the beagles hunt, they do pursue me still;
To Llanbedr's woods I'll bid adieu and cross for Glascomb's hill,
But first I'll call at Painscastle where I may shelter find,
If I find none I will go on and leave my foes behind.

'For well I know the dogs are stout and they'll hunt me like the wind,
But I'll tread light upon the ground and leave no scent behind'.
Painter and Dido did agree to lay on him still,
And made the groves and valleys ring going over Glascomb hill.

Cleary and Farnons now came in, for the dogs were hunting cool,
And scarce could drive him down above Llanhilling Pool.
But Painter bold the chase did hold and bravely wagged his tail,
For he was stout and would ne'er give out and ne'er was known to fail.

Oh! when the fox took cover straight, 'twas in Ca[e]banal's wood,
And there he staid to rest awhile and thought it for his good,
But Primer soon came to his den and off in view he goes,
And faintingly crept up the hill in presence of his foes.

He then went for Llanivan straight as fast as he could go,
Saying, 'Is there any shelter here to hide me from my foe?
If you this day my life will save I'll promise and fulfil
Ne'er to come near your father's [feather'd] fowls, nor lambs upon the hill'.

And now the dogs laid on him quick and made him sadly shail [falter],
He thought to go to Radnor's rocks but his heart it did him fail,
Said he, 'I will not stop nor stay whatever me betide,
And ne'er will look back again till I cross the Forest wide'.

172

The dogs again laid on apace and sorely did him chace,
He did not know which way to go, nor where to hide his face,
But cross'd straight o'er the hill to part of Blethvaugh [Bleddfa]'s plain,
And there most sadly 'gainst his will this famous fox was slain.

'Farewell, now to friends at home, the young ones all adieu.
I fear I never shall again return to visit you,
I feel my body doth decay, my tail hang feebly down,
And I shall soon become a prey to every hungry hound.

'Farewell, likewise, to geese and ducks and lambs and fowls also'.
For Ranter caught him by his back and would not let him go;
And then came quickly thundering in the rest of Ranter's crew,
And this famous fox was forced at last to bid this world adieu.

Go, Gentlemen, here ends my song, likewise a jovial chace,
The fox did strive his life to save, but the dogs laid on apace;
They hunted him twelve hours or more, through parishes thirteen,
And brought him low unto their bow when chaced to Blethvaugh Green.

As for the master of the hounds, I wish him long to live
In healt and wealth and happiness, may all things with him thrive;
For he's a gentleman by birth and well he can abide
To ride his horse a-foxhunting with beagles by his side.

A more prosaic summary of the 16-mile itinerary would be from the south side of Aberedw Hill over Llandeilo Hill and Llanbedr Hill almost to Painscastle; left over Red Hill and Glascwm Hill to Gwaunceste Hill; past the Mawn Pool to LIynheilyn Pool; across the road to Caebanal; then, leaving Llanifan to the left, up over Radnor Forest; next, with Creigiau Rocks to the right, past Shepherd's Well, Llaethdy and Rock Dingle, to flat ground near Bleddfa. The ballad is said to have been written by the squire's wife, Lucy, but if she did so she had a remarkable knowledge of traditional texts, with their verbal formulae, internal rhymes, and devices such as the fox's giving his own commentary and valediction. It presumably circulated in both oral and written form. Richard Parry, the Kington historian, who dated the hunt to 1762, had a manuscript copy entitled 'The Best Hunting Song in South Wales, The Rhiwy Hounds'. Some of the place names are garbled. For example, Alltgoch in verse 2 has become Earl Oak. A printed version, 'A Favorite [sic] Fox Hunting Song, For Herefordshire and

A FAVORITE
FOX HUNTING SONG,
For Herefordshire and Radnorshire.

COME all you gentlemen of fame of high and low degree,
That takes delight in fox hunting come listen unto me,
A story true I'll tell to you, concerning of a fox
They hunted him over mountains high thro' valleys woods & rock

As we went over the Breddo hill, one morning fine and gay,
Bright Phœbus was not disclosed, 'twas scarce the break of day
As we came near unto a cover, bold Reynard for to find,
We cross'd him upon a trail, that he had left behind.

Bold Snowball hunted in these woods he had so fine a scent,
He takes delight in fox hunting, as a captain over his men,
As soon as he threw up his nose, they knew it was a fox,
Come let us run him out of these mighty woods and rocks.

There's Finder, Trimbo Trimmer & Dexter they began to hunt,
But little Tiding did engage to go in the fore front,
There's Leader bold & grey, their course they'll maintain,
If he goes over mountains high, this day he shall be slain.

Bold Reynard being in these woods, and hearing of the dogs
Awak'd him out of his sleep, and on his legs he stood,
I think I hear these ruly hounds, with their voices loud & shrill
Before they shall me come nigh, I'll cross Llandiloes hill.

Now I'll take for Lambed woods, and there I'll take ground
I value not your huntsmen all, nor 'Squire Butt's hounds,
Altho' I know the dogs are stout, they'll run me like the wind.
I'll tread so light on the ground, I'll leave no scent behind.

Bold Reynard being in Lambed woods & hearing of the dogs
awak'd him out of his sleep, and on his legs he stood.
think I hear these beagles, pursuing of me still,
I'll bid adieu to Lambed woods, and cross for Glascomb Mill.

Now I'll take for Pain's castle, some shelter to find.
If I find none, I'll go and leave my foes behind,
The huntsmen all they drove him up until the hills lay plain,
Hark in my dogs, hark in they cry'd, let's run him once again

Little Ringwood lay to, and Windsor bore the sound,
I'm sure there are no better dogs, in England to be found,
Dido and Famous did agree to hold on him still,
They made the woods & valleys ring going down Glascomb hill.

There's Leader bold the chase will hold by swaying of his tail
He runs so stout he ne'er gives out nor never knew to fail,
But little Famous did come in as the dogs was hunting cool,
They scarce could drive him down the brow from Llanellings pool.

Bold Reynard coming down the brow but sorely did him rail
Resolv'd to reach the Radnor's rock but his heart did him fail,
If you'll spare me this day, I'll promise and fulfil,
Never to touch your feather'd fowl, nor lambs upon the hill.

So farewell my young ones all, I bid this world adieu,
I'm afraid I shall come no more to visit you.
I feel my body do decay, my daring strength comes down,
I fear I am become a prey, to yonder hungry hounds.

So farewell to geese and ducks, and little lambs also,
Bold Ranter caught him by the back, and would not let him go
The dogs they all came thundering, the rest of Ranter's crew
They swore unto the fox that he must bid this world adieu.

They hunted five hours and more, through Parishes thirteen
They brought him low unto their bow, & he died on Blerver
green.　　　　　　　　　BY T. HARRIS ROSS.

A street ballad sheet

Radnorshire' (in 14 verses, like Parry's version, though not all the same)
appeared in about 1850, with authorship claimed by T. Harris of Ross (on-
Wye). No tune is specified in any of these, nor has one survived in oral
tradition. I have, however, supplied a possible melody.

Balladry and Balls
Radnorshire is by no means famed for ballads, but a second epic of fox
hunting has survived. 'Cerdd Newydd, am yr enwog Helwriaeth, wnaith

Cwn John Lewis, Esq., a Nantgwillt, Ar ol y Llwynog' (New Song on the famous Hunt the Hounds of John Lewis, Esq., of Nantgwillt, According to the Fox), a worn and battered sheet preserved in the National Library of Wales, bears the imprint of 'Norths, Printers, Brecknock'. The North brothers, William and George, were in partnership at Brecon from 1783 until 1821. The sheet must have been in existence though, by about 1810, when Edward Mills, a bandmaster from Llanidloes, wrote (or arranged) the tune (which, incidentally, later became popular with both ballad and *plygain*-carol singers under the title of 'Dydd Llun y Bore'—'Monday Morning'. This was only two years before Shelley's arrival at Nantgwillt, though one must resist the temptation to speculate that he might have heard the ballad. Its eight 16-line verses relate a hunt, as the subsidiary title indicates, from the point of view of the fox. One of them runs:

Trwy unplwy ar ddeg,
Yn landeg ar redeg mynegaf i chwi,
Aeth y cwn gwirglod, mewn llawnder yn llu;
Trwy ran a dair Sir,
Mai'n eglur gwn clodfawr rai hynod ei hoîn,
Gallwn feddwl 'n ddiammai bod ei pene pewn pown;
Llanwrthwl llanwrthie, a Nantmel ddiammai,

175

Llandewi maen ole mewn brintiau or bron,
Llananno, Llanbister, Saint Harmon drwy burder;
Y rdedfant ai hyder, mewn llawnder yn llon,
Llangirig lle gore duhintiau 'drw hon,
Llanidloes llwyn odiaeth, Tref Eglwys lle helaeth;
A Llanbrynmair glanwaeth iach doreth ar dir,
A Carno plwy cornfawr lle hwylwd ei elor;
Heb Dy nag Esgybor, na gwibor ond gwir,
Brechinog, Maesyfed, Trefaldwyn, tair Sir.

Through eleven parishes
Running handsomely, I will relate to you,
The hounds of true fame went, ina great number;
Through parts of three shires,
Conspicuous were the hounds of great praise, or remarkable vigour,
I would imagine without doubt that their heads ached;
Llanwrthwl, Llanwrthie [?], and Nantmel no doubt,
Llandewi [Ystradenni] altogther of bright honour,
Llananno, Llanbister, St Harmon through purity,
Thye run boldly, happily together,
Llangurig full of excellence, Trefeglwys a large area,
And comely Llanbryn-mair with healthy stock on its land,
And Carno, parish of the loud horn where he met his death,
Without house or barn, or [?]prize but truth,
Brecon, Radnor, Montgomery, three shires.

(translated by Tegwyn Jones)

It is interesting that such a ballad was printed outside the county but not surprising, since Radnorshire's population could scarcely sustain the publication of such material. Curiously enough, though, a sheet dealing with a ploughing match in Carmarthen—'Cân i Ymdrechfa Aredig Waunllanau', by Myrddin Glan Gwyli—was printed and published at Presteigne by one Moses Zachariah Job. It is preserved at the University of Wales, Lampeter.

A proposal to extend the railway line to Knighton aroused some local opposition but the decision to go ahead was celebrated both by poems and a ballad, 'The Mid Wales Railway'. It is not clear whether the latter was ever printed. I am indebted to Keith Parker for this copy, which derives from manuscript:

The Mid Wales Railway

We had a railway meeting
In the Year of Fifty Nine
Some came to oppose it
As you will quickly find
If Satan's Agents were not there
I'll tell you who were seen -
ROBINSON the Engineer
Along with Mr GREEN.

There was another in the room
The truth we can't deny
Who did his best 'long with the rest
To stop the railway by.
This is the talk that we do hear
Whenever he is seen
He ought to learn to do us no harm
In the hands of Mr Green.

In Rhayader there were many
The truth I do declare
Afraid the Act would not be passed
Sunk almost to despair.
But now they are as cheerful
As any King or Queen
They sing 'Hurrah we've won the day'
In spite of Mr Green.

On the second of September
In the Year of Fifty Nine
The first Sod of the Railway
Was cut by Mrs Pyne.
And though it rained in torrents
Each heart was filled with joy
To see her brother, GIBSON WATT
'Long with her youthful boy.

Success attend the railway men
The promoters of the line
When they are cutting through the hills
To find lead and copper mines

And treasures in abundance
I hope there will be seen
For to enrich the gentlemen
Who conquered Mr GREEN.

When we have the railway
They'll come from everywhere
Some will stay at the Borough Inn
And others at the Bear
And in the Lion Castle
Some scores there will be seen
With their heads out giving a shout
'We've conquered Mr Green'.

The people from St Harmons
Will come to Rhayader Town
Some will shop at the Lamb
And others at the Crown
The people from Vain Marteg
Will fill tile Oak and Harp
And they will side up in the train
And be home before 'tis dark.

The lads and lasses of this place
Now vow and do declare
When comes the rail they will not fail
To be at Llanidloes Fair
And there they will be singing
'God Save Our Gracious Queen'
Each tells his dear 'We did come here
In spite of Mr Green'.

The hides will come from Liverpool
To Rhayader for to tan
Passengers will come flocking in
To the Lion and the Swan.
And in Cwmdauddwr Arms brave boys
Some hundreds will be seen
And Cornhill will have its fill
In spite of Mr Green.

When we have the railway
We'll flourish by degrees
We shall have from Liverpool
Flour, Fish and Cheese.
Everything that we do want
Will come along the line
Farmers will be thronging here
To fetch their coal and lime.

Now I'm going to take a walk
And then conclude my song
And call up at the Eagle
To see the mighty throng
To be singing and rejoicing
They think it is no sin,
So 'Michael Price' cries 'order'
For 'Thomas Price' to sing.

The Mr Green mentioned was afterwards Sir Richard Green-Price, mentioned below. Incidentally, the railway reached Knighton in 1861, and opened to Llandrindod four years later.

Until at least 1965, when they were the subject of an article by R. Stedman Lewis, printed sheets bearing a song and a ballad were pasted to the inner doors of Coed-y-mynach (Monk's wood), a farmhouse two miles

*The railway viaduct over
Rhaidr Gorge,
from an old postcard*

south-west of Rhayader. One, dated 1886, celebrates a bard called Graienyn; the other, of 1877, commemorates the birth of Gwlithyn (Dewdrop), 'a daughter of the mountains'. Both were written by Amgeiniad Ellan, but nothing more is known of either author or subjects.

The pieces are somewhat fey— the second, for example, begins: 'On the banks of the Ellan,/Away from the sea,/Comes the fairy Gwlithyn,/To stay with me'—and they are far removed from the earthiness of street ballads such as 'A new Election Song on the Great Victory in Radnorshire'. This was 'Printed only for the Vendor, John Patteshall Cooper' and the first line of the chorus shows that the melody intended was that of a popular song of the day, 'Tommy, Make Room for Your Uncle'.

The sheet must have been produced after Sir Richard Green-Price of Norton won the Radnorshire County parliamentary seat for the Liberals in the general election of April 1880 (defeating the Tory candidate, Mr R. Baskerville Rickards Mynors of Evancoed) and before the bye-election of May in the same year, when S.C.E. Williams—incidentally, a relative of the historian, Jonathan Williams—won Radnorshire Boroughs for the Liberals.

A NEW
ELECTION SONG
ON THE
GREAT VICTORY
IN
RADNORSHIRE.

Ben Dizzy you have lost the race,
By getting into such a sweat,
You Liberals of Radnorshire
You are alive and kicking yet.
A dissolution have took place,
Which has put them to the rout,
For the Liberals they have walked in
And the Tories have walked out.

Chorus

So jingo make room for the Liberals,
Their majority is making you sweat,
You had made the country miserable
By getting us into a mess.
Hurrah for our Liberal member,
We give him three hearty cheers,
We've got in our choice, Sir Richard Green Price,
As Member for Radnorshire.

The Tories had six years rule of the land,
What they promised they forgot,
But now they've caught you understand
Like flies in a treacle pot.
You know they are a crafty, cunning crew,
Looking for what they can gain,
Trying their best to get over you,
Like the Jews of Petticoat lane.

Dizzy make room, &c.

What good did they do in Zululand
By loosing our soldier's lives,
Causing distress on every hand,
With orphans, widows, and wives.
And then in Afghanistan
Have not they placed the fool,
For it must be well known to you
The pickle we are in Cabul.

Dizzy make room, &c.

The Tories have done the best they can,
But of course I mean for themselves,
There has been a nice picking for every one,
But they are laid on the shelves.
Dizzy is were poor Moses was
When somebody blew out the light,
But now he has got the sack my boys,
Everybody says it serves him right.

Dizzy make room, &c.

John Bright has bothered the Tories so,
For their gammon he will not stand,
They'd all be just in their glory
If they'd take them by the hand,
Against all their brag and bluster,
He will struggle with all his might,
For we mean to be led by GLADSTONE,
Lord HARTINGTON and BRIGHT.

Chorus—

So cheer up now you Liberal boys,
With a hearty good hurrah,
For Sir Richard Green Price is our M.P.,
For the Liberal cause to-day.
To Mr S. C. E. Williams, our Liberal candidate,
We likewise give him a hearty cheer,
We try our best to put him in
For the Boroughs of Radnorshire.

Printed only for the Vendor, JOHN
PATTESHALL COOPER,

Ben Diz-zy you have lost the race, By get-ting in-to such a sweat, You

Li - be - rals of Rad-nor-shire You're a-live and kic-king yet. A

dis- so-lu-tion have took place, which has put them in a rout, For the

Li- be-rals they have walked in And the To-ries have walked out. So

jin-go make room for the Li-berals, Their ma- jo-ri-ty's ma-king you sweat, You had

made the coun-try mi-s'ra-ble By get-ting us in-to a mess Hur-

rah for our Li-beral mem— ber, We give him three hear-ty cheers, we've

got in our choice, Sir Ri-chard Green Price, As Mem-ber for Rad-nor-shire.

Less controversial were the words written on Llandrindod's health-giving properties by D. Arthur Davies, which were published on a post-card. No date is given, though the copy I found in a Cornish secondhand bookshop was franked in 1918. The tune specified, 'Mi gollais y trên' (I missed the train), was turned up for me by Dr Phyllis Kinney 'in the extensive ms. collection of Thomas David Llewelyn (1828-1879), a very well-known harpist and collector from the Aberdare area. ... His nom-de-plume was "Llewelyn Alaw" and he is invariably referred to in Wales under that name'. No other example of the melody has so far come to light.

A further ballad turned up only in 1991, though it dates from some 200 years earlier. When Phil Rogers set about renovating Cefn Faes Uchaf Farm near Rhayader he noticed a crevice in the oak lintel over an inglenook. With great care he extracted its contents: a broken sword point, a few tiny wooden pegs, and a crumpled scrap of paper. Perhaps these were a child's hoard of little treasures left behind because of sudden death, a hasty move of house, or merely forgetfulness.

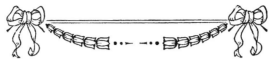

Doctor Llandrindod.

BY D. ARTHUR DAVIES.

He's not on the " Panel," by George! but he's free,
'Mid the fair hills of Radnor to heal without fee ;
So my pen's always ready, your attention to call
To Doctor Llandrindod, the doctor for all.

They come from the seaside, from city and town,
To consult him in thousands, all " fagged " and
"run down ":
But health, strength and beauty, return to them all,
By paying old Doctor Llandrindod a call.

At fishing or boating your time you may spend,
Of tennis, and bowling, and golf there's no end ;
Drink freely the waters whatever befall,
For Doctor Llandrindod provides these for all.

The baths and the waters will heal without doubt,
Rheumatic', sciatic', neuritis and gout:
Most stubborn diseases before him will fall,
So Doctor Llandrindod gives good hope for all.

Tune—" Mi gollais y trên."

Published by Hughes, Llandrindod Wells.

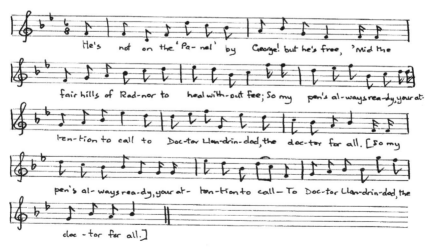

The postcard on Llandrindod's health-giving properties

When Rogers painstakingly unfolded the piece of paper he found the fragile and tattered, but still legible remains of a ballad sheet measuring $3\frac{1}{2}$ by $11\frac{1}{4}$ inches. This, with gaps shown in square brackets, is the text:

The Enchanted Piss-pot
A NEW SONG
Sold by Thos. Davies, High Town, Hereford

The Lincolnshire Farmer had a fair wife
The Clerk of the Parish loved her as his life
In pleasure of love they would frolic and play
Till her loving husband got jealous they say.

Then straight to the cunning man away they [he] did go,
To know whether he was cuckold or no.
Says the cunning man, if my counsel you'll take
Tomorrow right pleasant sport I will make.

There's an oak half a mile out of town,
To keep yourself warm take your cloak and your gown,
And in this same [tree] you shall lodge all the night
Tomorrow I'll show you a delicate sight.

The farmer resolved the project to try
With the conjuror then he did comply
He then told his wife he must ride out of town
With a sorrowful sigh she began to look down.

'The Enchanted Piss-Pot': the remains that were found

His back being turned for her gallant she sent
That they might revel all night with content
Before the next morning there came a sad rout
[W]hich the conjurors charms had brought out.

The conjurors scholar got in by skill
[W]here he lay as safe as a thief in a mill
He fixed such a charm to the piss-pot [at last]
That if they should touch it they should [surely stick fast]

THE FOLKLORE OF RADNORSHIRE

The next morning to make water [the Clerk did] arise,
The pot was found locked between bo[th his thighs]
The farmer's wife rose up in her shift,
[For to] keep her kind lover out of great strife.

[His] delicate ware in her right hand she took,
[But] her left hand was seized to the side of the pot,
[She] bawl'd and she pull'd till her arms did ache,
[And] they both stuck as fast as a bear to a stake.

[Then in] this sad case with her feet she did knock
[Her da]ughter immediately ran up in her smock
Come girl and help us and make some excuse
For the piss-pot's bewitched and we [cannot] get loose.

Pretty Nancy endeavoured to set them both free
[But as soon as she touch'd it, they stuck, to it all three
[T]he conjuror open'd the door, it being day,
And his conjuring pipe he began to play.

Stripp'd naked in their shifts through the town they did prance,
When they were met by a lusty bold tailor [by chance],
Who would needs break the pot, being lusty and. strong
But as soon as he touch'd it, went prancing along

Thus piping he led them along the highway
Till he came to the place where her husband did [stay]
And hearing a noise peeps out of the oak,
Like a man so affrighted these words then he spoke.

[It's] you my friend Richard, the good Parish C[lerk]
I[t's] you thats cuckl'd my wife to the heart
And for the offence I'll be now satisfied
Or immediately whip off your nutmegs he cried.

The Clerk he offer'd to give him ten pounds
[For the trespass] he said he had made on his grounds
[Th]e Farmer no less than a hundred would have
[And the] Clerk he gave it, his nutmegs to save.

184

They sent for apparel and when they were done
They went to an Ale house to [laugh at the fun]
The Farmer no less than a hundred would have
And the other he paid it his nutmegs to save.

Thomas Davies, whose name appears at the head of the sheet, was a Carmarthen man who moved to Hereford in 1788 to work as a journeyman printer, and set up in business on his own account seven years later. The ballad dates back to the 1690s, when it appeared in London as 'The Lancashire Cuckold: or, The Country Parish-Clark betray'd by a Conjurer's Inchanted Chamber-pot. To the tune of *Fond Boy*'. The Hereford text of a century later still fits the tune if the second couplet is repeated. As late as 1975 the ballad's longevity in oral tradition was demonstrated when Hugh Shields recorded a version from Eddie Butcher of Magilligan in Northern Ireland.

Printed ballads went into oral circulation in Radnorshire, too. In 1870 Kilvert was intrigued to learn that Mr Philips, parish clerk at Colva and landlord of the Sun Inn (now Colva Farm), knew three songs. It turned out that he had forgotten one of them, 'King James and the Tinker', but he promised to 'try to think of him'. He remembered 'Dives and Lazarus' and 'the ballad of our Saviour and the Three Children', and wrote out the words for Kilvert. 'Dives and Lazarus', a fierce and vengeful piece about reward after death for the poor and punishment for the rich, was widely printed on ballad sheets. The third item—probably a version of 'The Bitter Withy', which deals with Christ's chastisement by his mother for drowning some rich lords' sons who had snubbed him—did not appear in print until 1908. Kilvert noted that 'the two old songs [were] imperfect but very curious and of some merit', and on 3 March 1870 at Hay Castle 'I read aloud to them my Colva Ballads which interested them much'. It is most unfortunate that they did not survive in his papers.

Records like these of the oral tradition of singing in Radnorshire are extremely rare. One possibility is that sympathetic observers did not come along at the right time. Another is that evangelical campaigners came down heavily on all forms of music other than the sacred. Whatever the reason, we are left with the merest vestiges. Kilvert mentions 'We won't go home till morning'. Such references to song titles are unusual, quotations from songs even more so. Mona Morgan recalls part of a 'farm workers' ditty':

> Saturday night is my delight,
> And so is Sunday morning;
> Sunday night comes far too soon,
> And beggar to Monday morning

A family called Mills which originated in Laethdy, broke into song when they thought of slaughtering a pig:

> Oh how sad and grieved was we
> When we killed the Mochyn Du [little black pig].

The Croose brothers of Huntington preserve a curious fragment of song learned from their mother, who came from Hundred House, but thought that it derived from Pantydŵr or Llangynllo. The tune is 'Land of My Fathers':

> The pointer, the setter, the spaniel, the hound,
> Go loose into covert with nostrils unbound;
> But muzzle the sheepdog he has a bad name
> For rabies and killing of game.
> [Chorus]
> Dogs, dogs, they muzzle the low-bred sheepdogs.
> They shall not kill the snipe on the hill,
> Nor pheasant, nor partridge, nor hare.

One of the brothers, Mr Kinsey Croose, later wrote another verse:

> The fierce pit bull terrier, the doberman too,
> Rotweiler, Alsatian, to mention a few,
> Will have to be muzzled, but oh what a shame,
> To treat the poor sheepdog the same.
> [Chorus]
> Dogs, dogs, don't muzzle the friendly sheepdogs.
> They will not kill any game on the hill,
> The milkman and postman they'll spare.

If dancing was also targeted by hard-line religion it seems to have resisted better than singing. As early as the seventeenth century John Aubrey observed: 'In Herefordshire &c: parts of the Marches of Wales, the Tabor and pipe were exceeding common: many Beggars begd with it: and the Peasants danced to it in the Churchyard, on Holydayes and Holy-day-eves'.

From the 18th century to the early 20th, both public and private balls were held an a great variety of occasions, including race meetings, hunts, agricultural trade and friendly society gatherings. 'Quadrille parties', wrote W.H. Howse, 'began to be popular at the end of the 1840s, and dance bands from that period until the end of the 1880s were usually known as Quadrille Bands'. There is a record of the quadrille being danced to the Welsh harp at Llandrindod in 1859. The harpists and fiddlers who played for dancing at village feasts have been mentioned earlier.

The fiddle was very popular. Kilvert noted on 18 October 1870, with his usual knack of evoking atmosphere:

> A wild rainy night. They are holding Clyro Feast Ball at the Swan opposite. As I write I hear the scraping and squealing of the fiddle and the ceaseless heavy tramp of the dancers as they stamp the floor in a country dance. An occasional blast of wind or rush of rain shakes my window. Toby [his cat] sits before the fire on the hearthrug and now and then jumps up on my knee to be stroked. The mice scurry rattling round the wainscot and Toby darts off in great excitement to listen and watch for them.

The dances at the time would probably have included polka, waltz, quadrille, lancers, gallop, schottische, with Sir Roger de Coverley to close the ball.

Earlier in the same year Kilvert's imagination was exercised while he was out walking between Clyro and Newchurch. He came across 'the old long low brown cottage of Whitehall', by then derelict. The sight prompted these reflections:

> Here were held the Quarterly Dances. What fun. What merry makings, the young people coming in couples and parties from the country round to dance in the long room. What laughing, flirting, joking and kissing behind the door or in the dark garden amongst the young folks, while the elders sat round the room with pipe and mug of beer or cider from the Black Ox of Coldbrook hard by. Now how all is changed, song and dance still, mirth fled away. Only the weird sighing through the broken roof and crazy doors, the quick feet, busy hands, saucy eyes, strong limbs all mouldered into dusty the laughing voices silent.

The Baskerville Arms,
the Swan of Kilvert's time

Inns

Kilvert had occasion to regret his proximity to the Swan at Clyro, when people swarmed round the 'door and steps, laughing, talking loud, swearing and quarrelling in the quiet moonlight', or worse, lay 'by the roadside at night drunk, cursing, muttering, maundering, and vomiting'. In short, he saw outside the public house 'the World and the Flesh reeling about arm in arm'.

At least the Swan is still there (now called the Baskerville Arms), unlike the Black Ox (see also chapter 2) which had gone even before Kilvert's time, like others since. Even so, Radnorshire still had on average one pub for every 285 people. Llanbadarn Fawr, claimed to be the most central village in the county, once had four inns, of which one remains, the Llanbadarn Hotel. Since the mid-18th century over 40 such establishments have come and gone at Knighton. By the 1940s the town had a mere eight, not counting the Chandos which in 1880 during the heyday of the Blue Ribbon Army—the Band of Hope—became a temperance hotel.

Rhayader has had at one time or another 25 inns, Cwmdauddwr, six. On market days men from certain districts congregated in particular establishments. As one Rhayader rhymester put it:

> The people of Wern Marteg [Pantydŵr]
> To town they will come;
> Some of them are at the Lamb,
> And others at the Crown.
> The people of St Harmon
> Will fill the Oak and Harp,
> And ride upon the railway train
> And get home before it's dark.

The Radnorshire Arms, Presteigne, in the 1920s

Other inns acquired a wider reputation. Presteigne's Radnorshire Arms was originally a private house built in 1616, probably on the site of an earlier structure, for a John Bradshaw—whom rumour (erroneously) connected with his namesake, one of the signatories of Charles I's death warrant. Later the house became an inn, possibly called the Crown. Tradition provides it with secret rooms and underground passages leading to the Warden (site of Presteigne Castle) and—even more far-fetched—beneath the River Lugg to Stapleton Castle.

The inn's name at Aberedw gave rise to the jocular saying that the nearby church tower was the highest in Wales. A stranger who heard the remark and questioned it would be triumphantly informed: 'because it's higher than the Seven Stars'.

Several pubs, including the Swan (still open) at Knighton and the Oak (closed in 1912) at Presteigne, were once renowned—or notorious—for their cockpits. Birds, carefully bred, fed and trained fought there in matches organised by the local gentry, who wagered heavily on the results.

Roger Williams, in 1937, described similar proceedings elsewhere:

> There exists the cockpit which up to eighty years ago was the scene of great armageddons of birds. At that time Llanelwedd was a village, with cottages clustering round the church, and the building which is the vicarage today was then a commodious village inn, which for one

week each year was packed with sportsmen who indulged in cock fighting. Here the championship of the three counties, Herefordshire, Breconshire and Radnorshire was decided every year.

For the combat the natural spurs of the birds were removed and replaced with silver or steel spurs called gaffles. By the Welsh rules, 32 birds were cast into the pit and sixteen pairs began to fight. The defeated birds were successively removed until the two triumphant cocks alone remained. From tiers of seats around this spot people watched the final pair in deadly combat. In those days Welsh people were very superstitious, and many of them would not allow the birds to enter the ring until the pit had been sprinkled with salt, which they believed would break the spell of any exercise of witch-craft and make the fight a fair one.

Other efforts to this end included writing a particular verse from the bible—'Taking the shield of faith wherewith ye shall be able to quench all the fiery darts of the wicked'; in Welsh, 'Wedi cynryd tarian y ffyd â'r hwn y gellwch diffoddi holl bicellau tanllyd y fall' (*Ephesians* 6.16)—on a slip of paper to be wrapped round the bird's leg as a spur was fastened. Alternatively, earth from a churchyard could be sprinkled throughout the cockpit. At Clyro 'sometimes when a fight was arranged the owner of the cock would bury a prayer book under the turf in the cockpit ring, believing that the other cock would refuse to fight'.

Rev. Jonathan Williams, the early historian of Radnorshire, charac-terised cockfighting as a 'brutal and barbarous diversion'. Parliamentary acts of 1835 and 1849 outlawed the sport, though it continued clandes-tinely until the twentieth century and is still not extinct. The Llanelwedd pit, some 200 yards north-east of the church, is now filled and part of a car park. Robert Gibbings, visiting before that development, in 1942, found that people still bred gamecocks, which 'they cared for like greyhounds'; '"We don't fight them any longer", one owner said to me, "but we like to keep the sport alive", whatever he meant by that'.

According to Keith Parker, at Presteigne 'illegal cockfighting also continued into the early twentieth century, notably at a sawpit near the Burgage'. Cock Field on Boatside Farm at Aberedw recalls the cock-fighting which the grandfather of the owner in 1969 remembered there. Another field at Cregrina, the Plock, has similar associations.

However, to return to the pubs, one should point out that they also played host to more pacific sports such as skittles and quoits, the pastimes of singing and dancing—and, of course, eating and drinking.

CHAPTER 8

Signs of Strife

'We be very historical round here and they don't teach it in the schools neither', said a roadman encountered by H.J. Massingham somewhere between Kington and Old Radnor. He was presumably referring to anecdotes and tales of historical events passed down through the generations by means of oral transmission. Over two hundred years earlier Daniel Defoe remarked; 'The stories of Vortigern, and Roger of Mortimer, are in every old woman's mouth here'. Such traditions might be reinforced by the names of fields or other features of the landscape such as Soldier's Tump (Beguildy), Cwm y Rhaidd (Spear Valley, east of Llandrindod) and Tir y Beddau (Land of Graves, Llowes), though sometimes the background story faded from the collective memory.

Radnorshire is now a peaceful place but many echoes remain of its blood-boultered history of invading Romans, Saxons, Normans and English; of Owain Glyndŵr's powerful bid for independence; of struggles between king and Parliament during the Civil War. Other campaigns have also left a mark: for example, those of protesters against 19th century road tolls who invoked the name of Rebecca, and the salmon poachers who later adopted it.

Romans
Not until the 70s AD did the Romans finally subdue Wales, making Julius Frontinus governor. It was he who had the great fortress built, a mile north of Llandrindod, which became known as Castell Collen (Hazel Castle). Other Roman strongholds in Radnorshire included those at Clyro, Hundred House (Colwyn Castle), Llanddewi Ystradenni, Llanelwedd, Llanfihangel Helygen and Nantmel.

Caer Caradog, or Caratacus Camp, near Knighton, from an old postcard

Fleeting glimpses of the Romans' 400-year stay remain in local lore, and in some cases have been confirmed by archaeological finds. The Barn Meadow on Maestrayloe Farm at Discoed is said to be the site of a Roman fort; a field called the Camp on Wern Farm at Disserth is believed to have a Roman connection. Again at Disserth, Coed-mawr Farm is thought to be crossed by a Roman road, like Parciau Farm at Clyro, while Upper Noyadde Farm at Llowes has a field called Roman Road meadow.

A tradition still current says that in Roman times a battle took place at the Crag and Van Rocks on Bryn Farm at Disserth. Two farms at Llanbister each have a Soldiers' Well, thought to have been used for drinking by Roman soldiers at Lower Caerfaelog and for washing their wounds at Drainllwynbir by others. Caer Caradog, a hill three miles north of Knighton just over the Shropshire border, is one of several claimants to be the scene of the last stand against the Romans in 51 AD of Caradog, otherwise styled Caradwg or Caratacus. The Romans could have forded the River Teme a mile below Knighton, gone up a valley to a place now called Five Turnings, then stormed the hill from the west where the slopes are least steep. Another story places the battle at Coxall Knoll, to the east of Knighton, with Caradog marching there from Wapley Hill. A further variant puts his starting point at Crug-y-byddar, some eight miles up the Teme from Knighton. This last place-name means Deaf Man's Mound, and may have its own interesting story. The Roman general, Magnus Maximus, who claimed the empire in 383, appears in Welsh mediaeval legend as

Macsen Wledig. Some Welsh rulers who established themselves on Roman sites claimed descent from him. They included Maelgwyn (died 547) of Gwynedd and in due course Rhodri Mawr (died 878), who ruled not only Gwynedd but much of central Wales, including Powys. King Arthur himself, who used cavalry against the Saxons, may have been Roman-trained.

Saxons

According to Geoffrey of Monmouth, Vortigern and Aurelius Ambrosius were brothers to Uther Pendragon, and hence uncles to Arthur. Vortigern is known to the Welsh as Gwrtheyrn, which means high king and may originally have been a title. In the fifth century he ruled Gwrthrynion, part of Rhwng Gwy a Hafren (Land between Wye and Severn) later known as the Hundred of Rhayader. Vortigern became king of large parts of Britain and gave land in c.430 to the Saxon invaders, Hengist and Horsa, in return for their military support against the Picts and Scots. (The Venerable Bede says that Horsa was killed in battle by Vortigern, but others have questioned whether Hengist {meaning stallion} and Horsa {meaning horse} existed at all). Vortigern then handed Kent over to Hengist in exchange for his daughter, Rowena, whose first meeting with the British king is described by Geoffrey of Monmouth:

> While he was being entertained at a royal banquet, the girl Renwein came out of an inner room, carrying a golden goblet full of wine. She walked up to the king, curtsied low and said: 'Laverd King, was hail'. When he saw the girl's face, Vortigern was greatly struck by her beauty and was filled with desire for her. He asked his interpreter what it was that the girl has said and what he ought to reply to her. 'She called you Lord King', answered the interpreter, 'and did you honour by drinking your health. What you should reply is 'drinc hail'. Vortigern immediately said the words 'drine hail' and ordered Renwein to drink. Then he took the goblet from her hand, kissed her and drank in his turn. From that day to this the tradition has endured in Britain that the one who drinks first at a banquet says 'was hail' to his partner and he who takes the drink next replies 'drinc hail'.

Although Vortigern married Rowena—or by another account, Sevira, daughter of Magnus Maximus—people objected to his taking a pagan wife. The Welsh marked him down both as a drunkard and—for ceding land—as a traitor. He also stood accused of committing incest. In due course he was deposed. According to one account he then fled in *c*.450 to Caer Wtheyrn in Ceredigion, where he was consumed by fire from heaven. Radnorshire tradition takes the view that he took refuge first at Craig-pwll-du, then either at Bwlch Llys in Ysfa, near Nantmel, or at Castell Gwrtherin in the parish of Llanbister. 'This solitary spot', wrote Jonathan Williams of the last place, 'constituted the last resort of this traitorous and wretched king'. Unfortunately, the exact location is not entirely clear.

Williams suggests a spot near Arthur's Marsh marked by a row of stones called Caermenin or Croes y Noddfa (Cross of Refuge).

Romano-Celtic jewellery discovered at Cerrigwynion, near Nantmel, is claimed to have belonged to one of Vortigern's wives. The 'superbus tyrannus' (haughty tyrant), as Gildas called Vortigern, was execrated for centuries after his death. The monks of Abbey Cwm Hir and Capel Maelog are said to have prayed that Vortigern should be punished for his sins.

After Vortigern the leadership of resistance to the Saxons passed to Ambrosius, and later to Arthur. By one account Arthur was born to

Vortigern burned alive in his tower, from a fourteenth-century MS. in the British Library

194

Ygraine (otherwise known as Fior) at Crug-y-byddar, where Uther Pendragon had a castle. Guinevere or Gwenhwyfar, whom Arthur married, came from a few miles away at Cnwclas Castle. Cnwclas means green mound, but the castle was otherwise known as Caer Gogyrfan after Guinevere's father, the giant Gogyrfan, Cogran Gawr or Ogrfan Gawr. Gogyrfran, whose name derives from *ocur fran* (evil raven, the bird of ill omen and death), was one of the gods of the underworld. He owned the cauldron out of which the three muses had been born and, despite his name, acted as a patron of bards. Tradition holds that Arthur fought giants near Cnwclas—perhaps he fell out with his in-laws—and also, in his eleventh and penultimate battle, at Nant y cawr, near the source of the Claerwen on top of Mount Egant (see chapter 1).

Not far away from Cnwclas on Monaughty Poeth Farm is Bloody Field, but this is thought to take its name from the battle of 1146 in which Hugh Mortimer defeated and killed the lord of Painscastle, Meredydd, son of Madoc.

One of Arthur's chief advisers was Caradoc Freichtig (strong arm), son of Llyr Merine, founder of Llanyre Church, and Gwen, the martyred foundress of the church at Talgarth (see chapter 6). Caradoc, a close friend of Padarn, had a son called Hyfaidd, whose name features in the folk etymology of Maesyfed (see chapter 3). Hyfaidd's daughter, Rhiannon, one of the ladies of Arthur's court, lived at Cil Manawg in Llanfihangel Rhydithon. Trystan, Arthur's gloomy knight, is associated with the parish of St Harmon, where the Moel Hywel is claimed to be called after another of the round tablers.

A son of Arthur's, Gwair, has given his name to Esgair Gwair, a ridge on the Brecon side of the River Elan. Nearby, on Carngafallt is a great heap of tumbled stones called Carn Cabal. Arthur's dog was called Cabal, and its footprint, made when hunting the swine, Troynt, can be seen on one of the stones. Arthur, says the story, built the cairn himself and put the marked stone on top. If ever it were removed it would find its own way back.

Over a period of several centuries, Saxon encroachment left its marks on field and place-names. In 1056 an Anglo-Saxon army, led by Ralph, earl of Hereford, and including Leofgar, the fighting bishop of Hereford, crossed the Wye near Glasbury. The Welsh, under Gruffudd ap Llywelyn, met the invaders near Painscastle and overwhelmed them. Fleeing men were harried over a wide area back towards Glasbury and also further west, so that one name given to the battle was Gwaith Machawy

(Machawy Work, the reference being to the river now called Bachawy). Among the dead was Leofgar, who had been in office only 11 months. He is said to be commemorated in a field at Glasbury called Bishop's Stocking, though the second element of this does not mean stockade, as one writer claims, but land cleared of trees. Another tradition says that a bishop was caught and killed by his enemies at Tarren yr Escob (Bishop's Knoll) in a remote corner of Glasbury parish near Capel y Ffin. Some say this was Leofgar.

Normans and English

At Painscastle the earliest stronghold was probably Roman, and a tessellated pavement came to light there in the nineteenth century (see chapter 5). Caer yn Elfael, as it was then called, stayed in Welsh possession until the Norman Conquest, and after that often changed hands. Its present name derives from the Norman, Payn Fitz John, who ordered the construction of a stone castle early in the twelfth century, through he did not live to see it completed.

During the course of a successful campaign in 1196, the Welsh prince, Rhys ap Gruffydd, took the castles of Colwyn (at Hundred House, north of the Edw: the castle of the same name south of the river came later), New Radnor (after a battle fought, according to local tradition, on what is now Water Street Farm), and also Painscastle. He was soon ejected from the last stronghold by Roger Mortimer, who handed it back to William de Braose.

The railway viaduct at Knucklas with the hill behind on which the Mortimers built one of their many border fortresses

The Norman motte at Hundred House

Both Painscastle and the second Colwyn Castle were known for a time as Maud's Castle, after William's wife, the formidable Maud de St Valery.

Both William and Maud were hated by the Welsh. After 1176 William bore the label of 'Ogre of Abergavenny' when 70 men and women, his guests at a banquet, were massacred on his orders. His abduction of a young woman of royal Welsh blood (see chapter 1) could hardly have helped his reputation. Having conceived a grudge against Traiarn Bychan (the Younger), he lured him to Brecon and there had him tied to a horse's tail, dragged round the streets, then beheaded and his body suspended from the gallows. Traiarn's cousin, the mellifluously-named Gwenwynwyn, swore to take revenge, and laid siege to Painscastle. After three weeks a Norman relieving force fell on the attackers and killed some 3,000 of them. Sir Walter Scott covered these events of 1198 in his novel, *The Betrothed* (1825), which gives the name of 'la Garde Douloureuse' to Painscastle. Writing in 1923, Mrs M.L. Dawson observed: 'The memory of this great battle, though fought over seven hundred years earlier, lingers in the traditions of the countryside to this day, and the inhabitants of the district still tell in awe-struck tones of the great slaughter when the river Bachawy "ran with blood", and told the terrible tale to the inhabitants of the lower valleys'.

The disaster for Welsh arms was partly attributed to the malign influence of Maud, described by Camden as 'that very shrewd, stout and malapert, stomackful woman'. Stories circulated about her for centuries, under her local name of Moll Walbee — aided by occult powers, she built Hay Castle in a single night; she was of giant stature and carried stones in her apron; when one of these, seven feet long, fell into her shoe she plucked it out and flung it three miles off into Llowes churchyard (where it remained for many centuries though it is now preserved inside the church). Long before the days of William Tell she compelled a Welsh chieftain called Madog to place an apple on his young son's head and shoot it off with an arrow.

Other stories record the unpleasant end of both William and Maud. In 1206 William received a signal mark of favour from King John, the lordship of the three Monmouthshire castles of Skenfrith, Grosmont and White Castle. A few years later the king began to doubt his loyalty, and in 1210 demanded his children as hostages. Maud peremptorily refused, saying that John 'basely slew his nephew, Arthur, whom it was his duty to protect'. William fled, first to Ireland, then to

Moll Walbee's Stone at Llowes

France, where he died in abject poverty in 1211. Maud and her oldest son fell into John's hands, and were imprisoned at Windsor. (Some accounts, incorrectly, say Corfe Castle). There, they were callously starved to death. They were shut in a dungeon (specially built by hundreds of masons, says one story) with a sheaf of wheat and a piece of raw bacon. When the door was opened again, 11 days later, both were found dead. The boy's cheeks were half-eaten.

Some of the liveliest existing traditions are concerned with the thirteenth century Llywelyn ap Gruffudd, the last native Prince of Wales (officially-appointed, that is), who was possibly born at Llyswen on the Breconshire side of the Wye. Late in the reign of Henry III Llywelyn's relations with the Crown were cordial but under Edward I the English invaded Wales in 1276 and again six years later. On the latter occasion Welsh resistance was strong until Llywelyn was killed, on 11 December 1282, near Builth. A clutch of sometimes-conflicting stories have come down from that time: Llywelyn takes refuge in the cave at Aberedw which now bears his name, though it was previously associated with St Cewydd (see chapter 1); or he is tricked into a meeting with the Mortimers in the village, presumably at the castle, where he is struck down from behind and then dragged, mortally wounded, to the cave. Alternatively, he finds himself surrounded at the cave and realises that he has been betrayed by the Aberedw blacksmith who re-shod his horse with the shoes reversed to leave false tracks in the snow. (The motif of reversed horse-shoes runs from classical antiquity through tales of Hereward the Wake to Wild West films, but I am told by knowledgeable riders that a horse shod in this fashion would very quickly go lame). The blacksmith, Madog Goch, is tortured or bribed to reveal Llywelyn's where-abouts, and ever afterwards becomes known by the contemptuous sobriquet of Min Mawr (Big Mouth).

Another story says that when Llywelyn is surprised at the cave he bursts through the enemy ranks on his horse, crosses the Wye, and seeks refuge in Builth Castle, only to be turned away by his erstwhile friend, John Giffard. He then looks to rejoin a band of his men posted on the River Irfon but is forced to dismount when his horse becomes exhausted. A lone enemy happens upon him, brings him down with a spear-thrust, and passes on. Shortly afterwards the soldier, a Lincolnshire man called Adam de

Llywelyn's Cave, Aberedw

Francton or Frampton, returns to search his incapacitated victim, finds on him a letter in cypher and a privy seal, and recognises Llywelyn. A different source says he finds Llywelyn's Croes Nawdd (Cross of Protection), a relic purporting to be a fragment of wood from Christ's cross.

Francton cuts off Llywelyn's head, though before doing so allows a passing white friar to administer the last rites. The head is sent to Edward I who has it crowned with silver or ivy to mock Merlin's prophecy that one day Llywelyn would wield the sceptre of Brutus, and has it displayed on London's Temple Bar. Meanwhile, soldiers drag the body a short distance and bury it in unconsecrated ground at what came to be called Cefn y Bedd (Ridge of the Grave). The place, just to the west of the village of Cilmeri, is now marked by an imposing monument. However, Llywelyn's body does not lie there, but at Abbey Cwm Hir, where it was later taken.

For over seven hundred years the accusation of *bradwyr* (traitors) was levelled against the people of Builth and even more those of Aberedw for their perceived part in Llywelyn's death. As recently as 1992 when Rev. Alan Charters was preparing to move all of 12 miles from Talgarth to Aberedw his parishioners remarked on his 'going to join the traitors'. Later still, a man playing rugby for a Builth XV in South Wales found himself attacked after a match when he unwisely mentioned that he came from Aberedw.

In a passionately-felt but closely-argued book, *Appointment in Aberedwy* (1992), Anthony Edwards has attempted to reach the truth behind both official accounts and traditional notions. His conclusion is clear: Llywelyn was 'induced to walk into an ambush and was captured and beheaded near Aberedwy'. One of those who persuaded Llywelyn to go to Builth was Madog ap Cynwrig, otherwise known as Madog Mîn, archdeacon of Anglesey, who read him a letter purporting to come from various southern magnates with offers of support. (His pseudonym seems to have transferred to the Aberedw blacksmith). Roger Mortimer, feigning a quarrel with John Giffard, asked for Llywelyn's help in attacking the castle at Builth.

The plot, hatched by Edward I and planned by John Peckham, arch-bishop of Canterbury, and Roger Lestrange, army commander in Wales, had the aim of luring Llywelyn and his army towards Builth, then detaching Llywelyn to Aberedw. When Llywelyn's army was encamped at Rhosferig Hill, a mile or so north-east of Llanganten, a messenger arrived from Roger and Edmund Mortimer, whose forces were at Llanelwedd,

The remains of Abbey Cwm Hir

inviting Llywelyn to a meeting at Aberedw to discuss a combined assault on Builth Castle the following day.

The plan worked. Accompanied by a Cistercian monk and an escort of only 18 men, Llywelyn went to the rendezvous where, as he conferred with the Mortimers one of Lestrange's men struck him down from behind. The rest of the party was immediately killed, save for the priest, who was kept with the wounded Llywelyn in Gruffudd ap Owain's dungeon (which is possibly the place now known as Llywelyn's Cave). A messenger sent to Lestrange at Builth to ask for instructions returned with an order for summary decapitation. Llywelyn was allowed to make his confession to the priest before both were killed. (Richard Body struck the blow which ended Llywelyn's life; his fellow Shropshireman, Stephen de Frankton, took part in the ambush).

Llywelyn's head was taken first to Builth, then to Edward I at Rhuddlan. Afterwards it was paraded through the streets of London on a pole, then displayed for many years at the Tower. His body may have lain for some time in the dungeon (or cave) at Aberedw before being taken, possibly with the knowledge of Edmund Mortimer, for burial at Abbey Cwm Hir.

On the day after Llywelyn's death his army, on receiving a forged order, moved to attack Builth Castle but was trapped at a ford over the River

Irfon. Some 3,000 foot soldiers and 160 horsemen were killed. On the English side there was not a single casualty, and it is probable that the Welsh were massacred after laying down their arms on a promise of being allowed to disperse. Some managed to escape, and a speculative scenario postulates their arriving at Abbey Cwm Hir and being given shelter on condition they take Llywelyn's body back to Gwynedd. Some six miles north-west of the abbey they abandoned the corpse at Prysgduon (on what is now the long-distance footpath called Glyndŵr's Way). A tradition first recorded in 1590 says that as they washed in a waterfall (pistyll y geiniog) the soldiers were reproved by the spirit of Gronw ab Ednyfed for failing to save Llywelyn.

Llywelyn, known to this day as 'ein llyw olaf' (our last leader) or simply as 'yr olaf' (the last), was one of the ancestors of Owain Glyndŵr, whose supporters in 1400 proclaimed him as Prince of Wales, in opposition to the rule of Henry IV. The ensuing rising spread to the whole of Wales. In Radnorshire Glyndŵr set about destroying the power base of the Mortimers, who though they, too, were hostile to Henry IV, had for centuries been among the most ruthless oppressors of the Welsh. He captured and destroyed a whole series of castles, including Cefn-llys (where in a variation on the theme of the Trojan horse his men gained entry by purporting to deliver a waggon-load of wood), Colwyn, Cymaron (at

Cefn-llys Castle site on the ridge, seen from the churchyard by the Ithon

202

Llanddewi Ystradenni), Knucklas, New Radnor, Painscastle, and, just over the Herefordshire border from Presteigne, Stapleton.

Destroyed in this context means burnt, since there would not have been time to demolish stone structures. Whole towns were fired, too, such as Presteigne and Knighton. Churches were not spared either: with their strongly-built towers they could house useful garrisons. Along with others in neighbouring parts of Herefordshire and Shropshire Glyndŵr's forces damaged churches at Bleddfa, Cascob, New and Old Radnor, and Pilleth. Abbey Cwm Hir was wrecked; its patrons were the Mortimers and its monks were rumoured to have passed word of rebel movements to the English.

The 'worthy gentleman', Glyndŵr, in Shakespeare's phrase, well educated and a

The well-known putative portrait of Owain Glyndŵr at Kentchurch Court. Many people think the portrait depicts St Jerome, because of what appears to be a cardinal's hat hanging from the back of the figure's neck, and lions (an animal associated with St Jerome) which some can espy in the background

patron of poets, had a ruthless side which he shared with other soldiers of his day. When New Radnor Castle fell in 1401 after a siege the governor, Sir John Grendor, was spared, but possibly not the garrison. Leland, visiting Wales in the late 1530s, wrote:

> Radenor partely destroied by Owen Glindour, and the voice is that, as he wonne the Castel, he took a iii score men that had the Garde of the Castel, and causid them to be heddid on the brinke of the

New Radnor's castle mound looming through the mist

Castel Yarde, and that there sins a certen Bloodworth growith there
wher the Bloode was shedde.

Bloodwort is a name used for several plants, but the Bloody-veined dock
(*Rumex sanguineus*) was probably intended here. There is no evidence that
Glyndŵr personally ordered any slaughter at New Radnor, nor even that he
was there. Nevertheless a testimony to the accuracy of the oral tradition,
already over a century old when Leland passed that way, was provided in
the 1840s when, during the rebuilding of the church, a group of 60 skele-
tons came to light, together with the same number of separate skulls.

On 22 June 1402 Glyndŵr and his lieutenant, Rhys Gethin (Fierce
Rhys) were on Bryn Glas (Green Hill) above Pilleth with an army which
awaited the assault from the Lugg plain below of Edmund Mortimer's
much larger force of Shropshire and Herefordshire men, supported by a
contingent of Welsh archers. Soon after battle was joined, these archers,
possibly in a preconcerted move, went over en masse to Glyndŵr, who
won a decisive victory. Mortimer was captured (he later joined Glyndŵr
and married one of his daughters), and between 800 and 1,000 men—half
his army—were killed.

Glyndŵr won the battle but lost the war; and history is written by the victors. The Benedictine monk and chronicler, Thomas Walsingham, who died in *c*.1422, suggested that Welsh women mutilated the English dead on the battlefield. His account was then taken up by later historians, including one who in turn influenced Shakespeare, Holinshed, writing in the 1580s:

> yet did the women of Wales cut off their privities and put one part thereof into the mouthes of everie dead man, in such sort that the cullions hoong down to their chins; and not so contented, they did cut off their noses and thrust them into their tailes as they laie on the ground mangled and defaced.

He added that 'The dead bodies might not be buried, without great summes of money given for libertie to conveie them awaie'.

The story seems unlikely. The bodies of the fallen were routinely stripped of their clothes and weapons but the mutilation described would have brought no gains and would have taken tremendous time and effort in view of the numbers involved. One wonders, too, who would have paid the bribe for burial, with the dead men's comrades dispersed in hostile territory or captured. The Welsh have never accepted the allegations; one man, interviewed as recently as the 1990s by Elissa Henken, summed up their views '*Felly mae o'n myth wedi'i creu gan y Saeson i arbed 'u balchder*' (So it's a myth created by the English to save their pride).

Pilleth Court, Church and Wellimgtonias marking the burial site

Whatever the truth of the story, the corpses were buried in the grave-yard of Pilleth Church and in a place on the hillside marked since the mid-nineteenth century by a stand of Wellingtonia trees. Traditions concerning Owain Glyndŵr have proved, perhaps not surprisingly, more tenacious in Welsh-speaking areas than in eastern Wales, though support for him in Radnorshire was strong. He and Rhys Gethin are said to have spent the night before Pilleth either encamped above Water-break-its-neck or lodged at Monaughty. There is still a belief that one of Glyndŵr's daughters lived in an old house at St Harmon which is now part of the outbuildings at Bryn-cenarth Farm. Penarth Mill in the same parish is believed to have stood since Glyndŵr's day.

Something of the supernatural persisted in his reputation: he was never captured; never betrayed, despite the huge reward offered; never surrendered, even when amnesty was eventually granted. The place of his death and burial continues to be the subject of speculation. In his poem, 'On Radnor Forest', A.G. Prys-Jones wrote in 1934:

> And here men say he vanished in the dawn
> Leaving no sign save a half-opened door,
> His baldric and his naked sword forlorn
> In some lone shepherd's hut below the moor.
> And so he passed, but Radnor Forest still
> Hides in her wind swept acres, secret lore
> Of him whose heart beat one with moor and ghyll,
> The hero-heart of Wales that beats no more.

One of Glyndŵr's daughters, Alice, married a Scudamore of Kentchurch Court in Herefordshire, just across the River Monnow from Wales; another, Margaret, married a Monnington of Monnington Court. In 1999 John Scudamore of Kentchurch revealed a secret handed down in his family for all those years by pointing out a mound behind the outbuildings of the farm at Monnington Court (Vowchurch) as the site of Glyndŵr's grave. Bones subsequently removed by members of the Owain Glyndŵr Society await carbon dating at Bournemouth University. One irony is that the land where Glyndŵr has possibly rested for so many centuries now belongs to the current Prince of Wales since it has just been acquired by the Duchy of Lancaster. Another is that walkers pacifically tramp Glyndŵr's Way, a long distance footpath tracing a route trodden by the hardy soldiers who for a brief time achieved virtual independence for Wales.

Mat's Children

Resistance to English rule did not end with Glyndŵr's defeat but in the next century Henry VIII's Act of Union formally joined Wales with England and, incidentally, created Radnorshire. Four years later, in 1540. as a judge rode to Rhayader to preside at the assizes he was waylaid and murdered by a gang of outlaws known as Plant Mat. Jonathan Williams take up the narrative:

> A Cardiganshire banditti, composed of disbanded soldiers, had long concealed themselves in an inaccessible cavern near where the Devil's Bridge now stands. From hence they sallied out, imposed contributions on the adjoining country and, to their depredations sometimes joined the occasional effusion of human blood. They were distinguished by the name of Plant Mat, or the children of Mat. Leaving their lurking-place in the obscurity of the night, and having arrived an the right bank of the Wye, they waited their opportunity safely concealed in a thick grove of oaks which grew on an estate named Dderw, in the parish of Cwmddaudwr Llansantffraid; where, being informed by their spy that the judge would repair at a certain hour on the ensuing morning to the church at Rhayader, previous to his entering on the business of the sessions, they sallied forth, crossed the river at Waun-y-capel, met him at Maesbach, fired their pieces, and shot the venerable man through the heart. During the moments of amazement, with which the suddenness of the transaction overwhelmed the attendants, the villains were able to effect their escape, and returned over the hills to the cavern. The whole country rose against them; the murderers were besieged in their rocky den, and, after a desperate resistance, taken, and executed.

As a result of the incident the assizes were removed from Rhayader to Presteigne (though this place was thought to be 'among the thickest of the thieves'). The name of the outlaw band remained in local memory, to be revived at Cefn-llys. There, at Cwmbrith in 1805 a farmer who had sold cattle at Builth Fair during the day was confronted at night and shot dead. The assailants then demanded money from his daughter who, when the commotion began, had dropped it into a wash tub. When the thieves failed to find the cash they wrenched the woman's wedding ring from her finger and decamped. The leader was later caught, and hanged at Presteigne. So ended the second wave of Plant Mat.

Civil War

Some two centuries after Owain Glyndŵr Radnorshire suffered again during the struggles between king and Parliament. One of the earliest skirmishes in the conflict took place at Presteigne in 1642 when a raiding party of Parliamentary troops from Hereford, acting on information from William Jones of Nantmel, a supporter of theirs in Presteigne, killed three royalist soldiers and arrested six leaders, including Charles Price, MP, of Pilleth Court. In the following year a further raid freed Jones, who had been imprisoned by royalists and robbed of his possessions.

In 1644 Royalists who had fortified the ruins of Abbey Cwm Hir were besieged there. They surrendered, as did the garrison at New Radnor, battered into submission by cannon. Seeking to protect local communities from the depredations of both sides, many Radnorshire men joined the clubmen, a vigilante force. In 1645 a body of them, 15,000 strong, marched to the walls of Hereford to demand that the governor (then Royalist) curb the excesses of his troops in the surrounding area. Some people sought to protect their property at least from Royalist plundering by planting Scotch pines as a badge of their allegiance to Charles I, and these became known as 'Charlie trees'. It seems unlikely that such trees could have survived for over 350 years, and existing examples may be connected with droving routes (see chapter 2).

After his crippling defeat at Naseby in 1645 Charles I twice passed through Radnorshire, some of his movements being attested by tradition rather than historical record. When Charles was Prince of Wales, James I granted him North Wood, between Presteigne and Beggar's Bush, and he hunted in the area, staying in a lodge at Barland. He therefore knew the locality well. In August 1645, on a journey to Oxford from South Wales via Brecon and Ludlow he travelled with 3,000 men through Painscastle and Newchurch. William Pritchard of Cefn y Blaen, near Rhosgoch, gave to Kilvert this remarkable account, drawn from oral tradition, in 1870:

> I have a jug that the king once drank out of at Blaen Cerdi. He had breakfast that day at Brecon, dined at Gwernyfed and slept at Harpton, passing through Newchurch. His army was with him and riding two and two in the narrow lanes that reached from Pen Vaen in Newchurch, through the village up to Blaen Cerdi. At Blaen Cerdi all the farm people, boys and girls ran out to see the king pass. The king was afoot. He stopped opposite the house and asked my ancestress Mary Bayliss to give him something to drink. She went

into the house and fetched him milk and water in this jug which has been handed down with the tradition in my family.

The chair on which Charles sat to drink was preserved at least until the 1950s at Walton Court, Old Radnor.

A different source, Sir Henry Slingsby, puts Charles' overnight stay not at Harpton but in a yeoman's house at Old Radnor:

> the king lay in a poor chamber, and my lord of Lindsey and others by the kitchen fire on hay. No better were we accommodated for victuals ... When the king was at his supper, eating a pullet and a piece of cheese, the room without was full, but the men's stomachs were empty for want of meat; the good wife troubled with continual calling for victuals, and having it seems but one cheese, comes into the room where the king was, and very soberly asks if the king has done with the cheese, for the gentlemen without desired it.

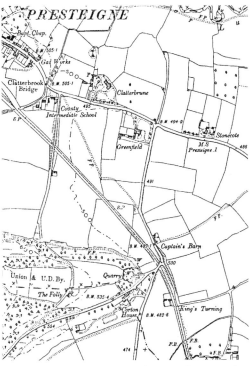

One variant of the story says that Charles 'stopped' at Stones, the seat of Maurice Lewis; another, that he put up at an inn, the Bush, which because of its frugal fare he dubbed the Beggar's Bush, a name retained by the hamlet one mile north of Evenjobb. Yet again, he is said merely to have sheltered from a shower at the Bush, as he did a short distance earlier at what became called Royal Gate, now Railsgate. In a pool near the latter place a sword found in the mid-nineteenth century is supposed to have been cast away by Charles in an effort to conceal his status, which would have been bizarre indeed if he were being escorted by 3,000 soldiers.

A map of the area to the south-east of Presteigne showing the 'King's Turning'

Charles apparently went on to Knighton, by-passing Presteigne, but he did stay there in September. A room at Lower Heath Farm, two miles east of the town, was long shown as the place he spent a night (or possibly two), but in the context of his further movements the 'house of Master Andrewes' at Presteigne makes the better claim to have provided hospitality. It seems that Charles sent off his main force towards Knighton over the Lugg Bridge, then went with a small escort towards the south-east as a feint. Next he turned sharply to north-west (at a point just beyond the present traffic island where the B4355 and 4362 roads diverge), crossed the Leominster road, forded the Lugg and joined up with his men, possibly at Stapleton, before crossing Stonewall Hill on the way to Knighton and Newtown. The place where he changed course is still known as King's Turning.

Some incidents at Willey, just north of Stapleton, may also date from September 1645, but only if the narrative which Jonathan Williams gives, presumably from oral tradition, intends harvest instead of hay making:

> On a certain day, whilst Mr Legge, of Willey Court, and all his male domestics, were occupied in the hay field, these reforming marauders took the opportunity of pillaging his house, and brutally treating the females that were preparing dinner for the labourers. Mr Legge, wondering that the dinner was so long protracted beyond the usual hour, returned to his house to know the cause, and found it

View from Bryn-y-Castell towards Knighton, from an old postcard

Hopton Castle

completely plundered and his domestics bitterly lamenting the base usage they had received. His indignation stimulated him to immediate revenge. He assembled his workmen, who armed themselves with pitch-forks, and, commencing at their head in pursuit, he overtook the villains, attacked them without hesitation, killed one on the spot, and wounded and dispersed the rest. The pitch-fork with which the soldier was run through the body, and nailed to the ground, remained for many years with the family a favourite relic.

According to tradition, the encounter between the furious Colonel William Legge and the band of soldiers took place on the outskirts of Knighton at Bryn-y-Castell, the site of the old castle (now a recreation field). The affair was very minor compared with the massacre at Hopton Castle, some six miles north-east of Knighton, in 1644. The Roundhead garrison surrendered to besieging Royalists, but only after protracted resistance. Save only the governor and his second-in-command, all the defenders were slaughtered in a particularly ruthless application of the unwritten rule against over-zealous resistance. Two maidservants were forced to watch, and one of them went mad. The bitterly ironic phrase, 'Hopton justice' or 'Hopton quarter', continued in use in Radnorshire for several generations.

After the Civil War many of Cromwell's soldiers settled in Radnorshire, where they formed several strong communities of Dissenters, though not the first in the county. It has been suggested that John Bradshaw who owned the Radnorshire Arms at Presteigne was one of the signatories to Charles I's death-warrant. However, the regicide John Bradshaw was a Cheshire man with no connection with Radnorshire.

According to Jonathan Williams, the future Charles II, whom he characterises as 'a thoughtless and voluptuous monarch', followed 'the same circuitous route as his father had used before, through Presteign, Knighton, etc., into Staffordshire' after the battle of Worcester in 1651. Kilvert's informant, William Pritchard of Rhosgoch, passed on this story:

> * Charles II was in hiding for some time in this country and went about in the disguise as a lady's servant. Once when he was in the pantry with the butler of the house where they were staying he asked the butler if he would give him a glass of wine. The butler said in a meaning way 'You are able to command what wine you like'.

Another narrative which mentions Charles II was published in the 1940s after coming to light in a notebook discovered in a farmhouse near Presteigne. It seems to me like a nineteenth century confection, especially as Stapleton Castle was slighted in 1645, but it may be worth summarising:

> Hankin Stapleton of Stapleton Castle drowns in the river while he is stag-hunting. His young wife, left with an infant son, Everard, appoints a steward, Morgan Reece, to manage the estate. Unbeknown to her, Reece institutes an oppressive and self-serving regime affecting tenants and servants.
>
> Some years on, realising that Everard is becoming aware of his exactions, Reece persuades Lady Stapleton to send him to boarding school. Six months later comes news that Everard has disappeared, and three months after that his mother is found dead with her throat cut, apparently by her own hand. (We suspect Reece, and learn at this stage that shortly before her death she not only rejected Reece's proposal of marriage but accused him of abducting her son).
>
> Reece leaves to join Cromwell's side in the Civil War, and is rewarded by the grant of the Stapleton estate. Shrieks are heard in the castle at night, and the ghostly figure of the late Lady Stapleton is seen there.
>
> Ten years pass. Charles II is restored to the throne. A traveller (in fact, Everard) arrives at Wigmore, asking for news of the Stapletons. He learns of his mother's death, and of her spirit appear-

ances. (We learn that at boarding school he received a message that he mother wished to leave the country to escape the troubles of the Civil War and that he was to meet her at Cardiff. When he arrived there he was bundled aboard a ship which then sailed, only to sink in a storm. He was picked up by a vessel bound for Virginia, and there befriended by a Puritan widower and his little daughter, Mercy. In due course he left for Holland, accompanied by Mercy disguised as his page, and offered his services to Charles II, who knighted him.

Everard decides to spend the night in Stapleton Castle, which has been empty for six years, to see whether his mother's ghost appears, taking with him Mercy, still in page's dress. They wander through the rooms until they reach his mother's bedchamber with its still-bloodstained floor. Everard hears a shriek, sees a prostrates bleeding figure on the floor—and faints. Mercy tends him. Reece arrives the next morning. Everard confronts him but is overpowered and on the point of being killed when a faithful family retainer, Pritchard, shoots Reece.

Lady Stapleton, exonerated of suicide, is solemnly re-interred in a vault at Presteigne Church. Charles II confirms Everard's right to

Stapleton Castle in 1850

Stapleton but he cannot bear to live there; he leaves it, untenanted, in the charge of Pritchard, and departs with Mercy.

An alternative, and altogether shorter version of the dark deed at Stapleton, is that a husband murders his wife there because of her alleged infidelity. Before she dies she swears that in proof of her innocence white violets will bloom round the castle at Christmas time. They have done so ever since.

Until well into the twentieth century few local people cared to pass the castle at night, and the children of Presteigne chanted this rhyme about its ghost:

> Lady Bluefoot, all in black,
> Silver buttons down her back.
> Harigoshee! harigoshee!
> Lock the cupboard and take the key.

Rebecca and her Daughters

'And they blessed Rebekah and said unto her, Let thy seed possess the gates of those that hate thee'. This verse from *Genesis* provided a *nom de guerre* for those who objected to the turnpike road system with its costly tolls. A different explanation is that the Rebecca nickname was given to an early leader of the movement, Thomas Rees, whose great bulk obliged him to borrow as a disguise during the first action on the Cardigan-Tenby road at Esfailwen the clothes of a woman of similar size, Great Rebecca of Llangolman, Pembrokeshire. Like the Luddites of 30 years earlier the Rebeccaites blacked their faces and donned women's clothes as a form both of ritual and disguise. Their campaign of smashing tollgates began in western Wales in 1839 and spread to Radnorshire four years later. Gates were destroyed at St Harmon, Newbridge, Howey and Glasbury. At Rhayader, where seven roads met and nine gates controlled access, the property of unpopular magistrates and clergymen also suffered, and in a novel sanction illegitimate infants put out to nurse by wealthy men were returned to their fathers.

Both military and metropolitan police were called in to patrol the town. An unusual contemporary view of events is provided in letters written by John Davies of Gwardolau, a mile north of Rhayader, to Thomas Lewis Lloyd of Nantgwillt, who was away with his family in Boulogne:

An artist's impression of an attack on a tollgate,
from the Illustrated London News *of 11 February 1843*

A party of Rebeccaites sawed off the posts of the Cwmtoyddwr Toll
Gates, broke the Gates to atoms and then threw the wood into the
river. The attack was made about 1 o'clock in the morning by
(according to some accounts) about 40 to 50 persons in female
attire; others state the number at 100 or 150, but those who wish to
make the number larger were I fear themselves of the party. It is
generally supposed that they were all Llanwrthwl and Cwmtoyddwr
men ... It is currently reported about Rhayader that most of Mrs
Evans' tenants [from the Noyadd] were engaged in its and some
people go so far as to say that they know those who impersonated
Rebecca, but they will not tell.

John Davies, adding that 'I fear that Llanwrthwl Folks are nearly all
Rebeccaites, and am pretty sure that Edward Rees of Dolfallen is the chief
Rebecca of this District', supplied the further names of Griffo, Jack
Tyngraig, Davies Vrondorthy, Thomas Talwrnmeanog and his son—the
last two substantial landowners in Llanwrthwl, just south of Rhayader.

The great fear generated by Rebecca activities is illustrated by the stir
occasioned when a woman dressed in riding costume was seen sketching
the workhouse at Knighton and taken to be a Beca planning an assault. It

turned out that she was a perfectly respectable person with an artistic bent, but not before a detachment of the 6th Foot had been sent for. Some young practical jokers at Presteigne dressed as Rebeccas converged on a toll-house where the keeper, a tall, well-built man, promptly took refuge under his bed. The pranksters then went on to the lower gate near the gaol where an old woman was in charge. To their surprise, she sallied forth, stick in hand, knocked down and apprehended one man, while putting the rest to flight. Five more were later arrested, and Martha the Turnpike became something of a local by-word.

After an investigation by a commission of enquiry the new Turnpike Act of 1844, known as Lord Cawdor's Act, reduced and rationalised tolls. A distinguished magistrate, T.F. Lewis of Harpton, described the riots as 'a very creditable portion of Welsh history', and explained: 'The people saw that their only remedy was to take the law into their own hands. The Rebecca conspiracy was organised with much skill, and carried through with much fidelity'. He congratulated the participants on standing down as soon as their objectives were attained; but within a few years the mantle of Rebecca passed to others.

In certain rivers, including the Claerwen, Elan, Edw and Wye, there was a tradition of catching salmon in the shallows when they swam upstream to spawn. The fish, smoke-dried, provided an invaluable stock of food for the winter. When new laws took away their perceived rights in the cause of fishery protection people invoked Rebecca. In his book, *The Tale of a Wye Fisherman*, H.A. Gilbert reproduces this account from the *Hereford Times* of 6 December 1856:

> Rebecca made her appearance in Cwmtoyddwr and from thence proceeded over the bridge to Rhayader, accompanied by about eighty of her daughters, forming a procession of four abreast. First went Rebecca carrying a gun, supported by two sword-bearers, right and left, with their faces blackened and their shirts worn over their clothes after the fashion of smock frocks, with a handkerchief tied around their heads. These were followed by five ranks, four abreast, each outside man carrying a cutlass or sword and the inside men spears or poles. Then followed four men carrying a carriage (similar to a stretcher) with a large quantity of straw tied up in bundles. These were succeeded by a long train, four abreast, carrying guns, spears, pitchforks and other weapons. They proceeded to opposite the Lion Hotel, where they fired two guns, and from thence

marched round the market place, where they fired again. Thence they proceeded to Cwmtoyddwr Bridge, where they were joined by a reserve army of forty or fifty more, all with their faces blackened, and in the same kind of dress.

The careful ritual was clearly important to those taking part, and after it they went down to the Wye to spear salmon by the light of torches. Despite the arrest of Old Rebecca, the poachers' leader, in 1861 — he was fined £7 — similar actions continued for decades, with particularly severe outbreaks between 1877 and 1881. In November 1878 Kilvert noted in his diary: 'Went down to the drill hall at 7.30 to see the Rhayader volunteers drill, but the hall was deserted and the volunteers had gone to see or take part in the Rebecca riots, a large party of Rebeccaites being out spearing salmon below Rhayader Bridge. We [he was accompanied by Rev. Langhame, the vicar] watched the spearing from the Bridge, a most picturesque sight'.

These occasions were sometimes far from picturesque and involved pitched battles between gangs of up to a hundred men armed with guns and bludgeons, and police and waterbailiffs. In 1880, when a large number of men besieged the police station at Llanbadarn Fynydd shots were fired at a door and window, and a constable's arm was broken.

Mrs Hetty Price remembered Cwmdauddwr at the same period:

The Claerwen and the Elan were noted for trout fishing, also for salmon in season. Out of season there were great times when a crowd of sporting young men used to disguise themselves and go out every night, with torch lights and spears, and fish every ford. It was against the law, and there were river watchers kept. But they were afraid to go too near these 'Rebeccas', so the salmon were caught, and very many homes in the valley used to salt and dry these great fish hung up the great old open chimneys — and very appetising too indeed they tasted.

The farmworker called simply 'Emrys' in Elizabeth Clarke's book, *The Valley*, both took part in poaching himself and remembered his father's stories of seeing tollgates burnt to the ground by earlier Rebeccas.

Tollgate breakers, like salmon poachers, drew on a deeply-rooted tradition of communal enforcement of rights and codes of conduct which included the *ceffyl pren* [wooden horse] ceremony, called in England

Salmon poachers said to be on the Wye at Rhayader

riding the stang. Under this procedure a person perceived to be contravening acceptable morality was given a mock trial before being paraded in person or in effigy on a wooden pole, to the accompaniment of a great deal of discordant noise known as rough music. In the 1880s or 90s at Presteigne a torchlit procession with band playing escorted the effigy of an unpopular person to Broad Street, where it was ceremonially burned. On another occasion a similar ritual ended on the football field with the burning of the effigy of a much-disliked church organist. A newspaper account of 1898 describes an event of this kind at Llanbister, when a Rebecca gang with blackened faces descended on the (separate) homes of a man and a woman accused of 'a breach or morality'. They were forced in a nearly naked state—this was in January—to walk backwards and forwards in a stream for 20 minutes and then to run up and down in a field while they were beaten with straps and sticks. They were then taken to the man's house, where Rebecca sat in judgment. They were sentenced to receive further flogging and to be marched up and down, hand in hand. Their hair was then cropped, and they were threatened with being tarred and feathered should their aberrant behaviour persist.

Oral tradition from Llanbister provides variations. According to one account, two young couples living in houses on the edge of Maelienydd Common in the south-east of Llanbister parish were on friendly terms. When one of the men died the other helped his widow but his neighbourly

SIGNS OF STRIFE

ministrations led to a warmer relationship. In the hope of regaining his affections his wife called in the Rebecca band, which mainly consisted of her relatives, members of the nonconformist chapel at Heartsease. The vigilante action proved to be counter-productive, since the errant husband and the young widow simply went off together after their ordeal and set up house elsewhere. A further narrative concerns a man and his wife living, still at Llanbister, on a small rocky holding. My informant has requested me to withhold their name since their relatives may still be residing in the parish. The man's unmarried sister went to live with the couple, and after a time rumours began to circulate that all three were sleeping together. Late one night a Rebecca commando turned up, went into the house (of which, as usual for the time, the door was not locked), and marched up the stairs into the bedroom. They roused the sleepers, turned them out in their night attire, and made then parade up and down the adjacent field, thistle stumps and cowpats notwithstanding. The night was frosty and also moonlit, but not enough for the vigilantes' black faces to be identified.

Eventually one of the women felt she could walk no more. In the words of a local poet, David Roberts:

> 'Oh dear', she said, 'I cannot run',
> For she was fat as any bun;
> But when she thought the race was run
> She felt the birch behind her.

To conclude the ordeal, the women's heads were cropped; the man had one side of his head shaved and the other of his moustache. Next morning he complained to the police constable at Llanbister whose subsequent exhaustive enquiries proved fruitless. No wonder, said local people, it was he who had wielded the razor.

Meanwhile, poaching incidents continued. Irish navvies engaged in building the Elan Valley dams happily joined in. Don Gardner, whose father was the schoolmaster at New Radnor, remembered the tales of the village police sergeant who had served at Rhayader as a young constable:

> In our schoolhouse kitchen, I would sit open-mouthed as a boy listening to this magnificent sergeant resplendent in his tightfitting uniform and silver buttons as he related stories of his encounters with the Irish poaching gangs. Stationed in Rhayader, he was called out night after night to do battle with his truncheon against the

219

sticks and cudgels of the wild Irish. The fights were wholehearted and no quarter given and the victory was not always with the police. A twenty-pound salmon hanging from a policeman's door-knob the next morning was the token of undefeated defiance.

In 1904 200 fish were taken, and a further outbreak took place in 1907. In December 1931 headlines in the *Daily Express* ran: 'Salmon Beds Menaced by Poaching gang. Havoc of Spawning Season Raids. Cruel Weapons'. Robert Gibbings wrote: 'In some parts of the British Isles the vocation of poacher is not held in high esteem, but in many parts of Wales it is regarded as a most honourable calling'. He describes the occasion in December 1932 when Rebecca descended on the River Edw after a dispute over fishing rights:

> In one night at least eighteen salmon were killed, and then flashlight photos were taken of the fish and their captors armed with gaffs. The men had disguised their features with burnt cork and cotton wool, for they intended the records to be seen not only by their friends, but by those against whom they had a grudge. They were exhibited in local shops, and even appeared in the newspapers. Proceedings took place before the local bench, but the magistrates considered that the photos did not provide sufficient evidence of identification, and they were compelled to dismiss the case.

The rector of Aberedw, Rev. Alan Charters, remarks that copies of the photographs are still treasured in local farmhouses and that the rumoured leader of the poachers, Marmaduke Morris, now lies in the churchyard, 'safely beyond the reach of the River Authority'.

Many people still have poaching stories—and even experiences to relate. For example, in the 1960s when a Rhayader man was booked for poaching a crowd of some 80 men gathered outside the police station and started scuffling. The police sergeant came out and intervened. The crowd moved some distance away, then the trouble began again. Once more the sergeant stepped in. The exercise—for such it—was continued until the policeman, having been lured farther and farther from the station, was grabbed and hung over the parapet of the Wye Bridge. There the crowd threatened to drop him into the water unless he swore never to book a poacher again. He complied, and stuck to his bargain. 'They'd a-dropped 'im in, too', said my informant.

CHAPTER 9

Full Circle

Calendar observances and rituals now follow an increasingly stereotyped, national pattern. Commercial considerations and mass communications dominate, leaving little scope for local events and home-made celebrations. Much of this account of seasonal customs in Radnorshire is therefore, unfortunately, written in the past tense. There are welcome signs, though, of people swimming against the stream. The advent of the year 2000 was marked at Hundred House by a torchlight procession and a bonfire. Those taking part were fortified with tea and hot soup, and cheered by a millennium medley song sheet. Another example comes from Newbridge-on-Wye, where the same occasion saw carols on the green, accompanied by the accordion of Donald Jones, followed by songs from a local group, the Wassailers, in the New Inn. The occasion was completed by the Newbridge Players' performance of a traditional mumming play, which, wrote the *Brecon and Radnor Express*, 'with its origins in the conquest of evil forces and its message of hope and plenty for the coming year, still has a place in the modern world'.

Spring
Devolution in Wales has led to a campaign for St David's Day (1 March) to be made a public holiday. 'The celebration of our patron saint's day', wrote Tarian Cwmru's secretary, 'is important as an expression of our identity as a nation, and it should be accorded the recognition and dignity it and Wales deserve'. In the past Disserth's sick and benefit club held its annual parade and dinner on St David's Day. So did the Oddfellows at Presteigne, though later they moved to the August Bank Holiday (which was instituted in 1871).

221

Shrove Tuesday, depending on the date of Easter, can fall at any time between early February and early March. Pancakes are still cooked, but not for a century in Radnorshire have church bells rung at midday as a reminder to put the pans on. It was once customary for mistletoe taken down on Twelfth Night to be saved and used to help kindle a fire under the pancakes.

A tug of war in the streets of Presteigne survived until the end of the nineteenth century. From an upper window of the Old King's Head (now a private house at 44 High Street) a rope some 60 or 70 feet long was dropped to waiting contestants, two teams of 12 men. One side's objective was the Lugg Bridge, where dipping an end of the rope in the river would signal victory. Their opponents sought to pull the rope down Pound Lane and into the Lugg by West Wall. A win for the former team predicted a fall in the price of bread; the converse for the latter. Alternatively, according to a report on the event in the *Hereford Times* in 1881, the custom 'in former times freed the tolls'. Similar contests took place in Builth and in Ludlow.

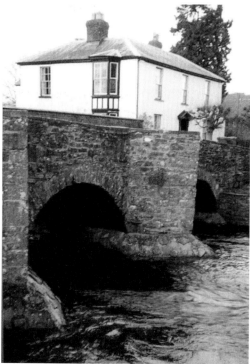

The Lugg bridge, Presteigne, one objective of a tug of war

Shrove Tuesday is the last day before Lent. On Mid-Lent Sunday, also known as Mothering Sunday, grown up children returned to their parental home with gifts such as simnel cakes. In a pleasant sequel to this practice, which died out early in the last century, adult children now often take mothers for a pub lunch, as well as sending a card.

Palm Sunday, the last before Easter, was also called Flowering Sunday because of the custom of dressing family graves with flowers. Parts of Radnorshire preferred Easter Saturday, on which day in 1870 (16 April) Kilvert noted: 'The roads were lively with people coming and going and the churchyard a busy scene with women and children and a few men moving about among the tombstones and kneeling down beside the green mounds flowering the graves'. The work went on well after nightfall, by moonlight, and next day Kilvert saw graves decked with primroses, daffodils, flowering currant, laurel and box.

Kilvert also mentioned (in 1874) 'holy bread'—buns or bread baked on Good Friday, kept for a year, then grated to be given as a remedy for illness. At Cascob housewives—who believed that bread set to rise before 7 on Good Friday and baked before 11 would never go mouldy—made black bread, known as hog bread, on this last day of Lent and stored some of it in the roofs of their houses as a sort of insurance against ill hap. A parallel practice simply preserved a hot-cross bun from one Good Friday to the next.

On Easter Sunday as late as the 1950s one 14 year-old girl at Knighton followed the tradition of giving daffodils to her mother and saying:

> Daffodillies yellow, daffodillies gay,
> To put upon the table on Easter Day.

A boy of the same age in the same town preferred a different ritual, not at Easter but on 1 April:

> It is a day when you hoax friends of yours with jokes like sending them to the shop for some pigeon's milk, or telling them to dig a hole because the dog has died; when they come back and ask where the dead dog is you say 'April fool' and laugh at them. There are some when you just say 'Your shoe-lace is undone' or 'Your belt is hanging' or 'Go and fetch that plate off the table', and of course their shoe-lace is tied up tight, and their belt is not hanging, and there is no plate on the table, so you say 'Ever been had, April fool'.

As with some other traditional observances (see below), the fooling had to stop at noon.

On Easter Sunday, Hannah Whitney of Clyro told Kilvert, people went early to Wild Duck Pool above Newbuilding 'to see the sun dance and play in the water and the angels who were at the Resurrection playing backwards and forwards before the sun'. Moved by a similar belief, Llaethdy residents walked up Pegwm Pole to see the sun rising and then dancing in the sky. One wonders whether there are still any family stories relating to such practices.

A custom widely reported at Easter in both England and Wales was known as lifting or heaving. The only report from Radnorshire dates from 1839 and is supplied by a rather tetchy—or, to use local dialect, 'crowsty'—observer in Rhayader:

> A number of the mobility collect together at an early hour and parade the streets, decorated with an extravagant train of ribbons, and accompanied with a band of music suitable to the occasion and a *curale chair*, in search of the softer sex; and if any unfortunate crosses their path she is placed in the chair and her tormentors dance round her, sometimes ravishing a kiss from the unwilling object of their ungallant attentions. Whenever they fail by the rapid retreat of any damsel whom they may fancy for their Queen, they besiege the house and even enter through the windows in spite of the inmates; sometimes they resort to measures more violent, by breaking the locks of doors, in pursuit of their retiring object, to make her pay, as

'Heaving'

it were, her final debt. On the subsequent day [Easter Tuesday] certain damsels, in order to take revenge upon their ignoble tormentors, parade the streets at an early hour and act precisely in the same manner as the males, with this distinction, that their soft attentions are given equally to benedicts [newly-married men] and bachelors, to the annoyance of both.

Summer

The arrival of the month of May was once thought likely to bring the attentions of witches and fairies. Sprigs of birch or mountain ash were hung over doorways to keep adverse influence at bay (see also chapter 5). Of maypoles there seem to be no early records in Radnorshire but in 1849 a valiant attempt to introduce one at Presteigne was reported in the *Hereford Times*:

> The town's-people were early awaked on the 1st inst., by the joyous sound of the Presteigne Juvenile Band wending through the streets. The youthful population was soon on the move towards the pleasant Warden Garden, where the merry dance was kept up for upwards of two hours. In the meantime other parties were dressing a splendid May-pole, which was erected at the cross at the top of High-street, and had a pleasing and pretty effect, being, I believe (says our correspondent), the first ever erected in the town, or perhaps in the county of Radnor. Several hundreds of well-dressed and respectable parties enlivened the rusticity of the scene, and by seven o'clock the tall, aspiring pole was firmly erected. The parties then adjourned from Warden Green, preceded by the band of music, and the rural dance was resumed round the novel and beautiful May-pole. ... Harmless recreation and merriment were carried on throughout the entire day.

Such entertainment may have seemed insipid, and the event does not seem to have been repeated. No doubt it contrasted unfavourably with the heady lure of the May Fairs (see also chapters 2 and 7), of which a pale shadow still lingers at Presteigne, Rhayader and Knighton.

Oak Apple Day (29 May) is now barely noticed, but until early in the twentieth century houses might be decorated with sprigs of oak, and people wore little sprays of leaves or oak-apples. Another of the benefit clubs at Presteigne, the Foresters (founded in 1865) held a procession with banners flying and band playing, headed by Robin Hood and his merry men.

After a service in the church came a pub dinner, followed by sports and dancing in a field near the Grove, beyond Ford Bridge. Other friendly societies at Presteigne, Rhayader and Knighton (see below) celebrated on different occasions. After the Old Age Pensions and National Insurance Acts of 1908 and 1911 benefit clubs declined, though some continue to exist as charitable bodies, their main functions having been assumed by the Welfare State.

During June and July various towns and villages held wakes (see chapter 7). Presteigne's Warden's Wake on 20 June shared the day with the New Club's procession. On Midsummer Day (24 June), there survived at Rhayader what Jonathan Williams saw as a relic of druidism:

> On the summit of Maes-mawr, near the town, a very ancient custom prevailed of lighting up on Midsummer Day annually a large fire, around which the assembled populace carrying flambeaux in their hands, danced and sang.

It seems more likely that this was a fire in honour of St John the Baptist, the feast of whose nativity coincides with Midsummer Day, and is still celebrated in parts of Europe with bonfires. However, these may be connected with pre-christian celebrations, including the burning in Wales of *y fedwen haf*, the summer birch. It is unlikely, though, that the people of Rhayader in the late 18th century gave any thought to pagan resonances.

Even so, their celebration must have been a colourful happening, a contrast with the more prosaic landmarks in the turning year which are characteristic of the early twenty-first century. Elaborate, highly-organised events such as the annual Royal Welsh Show at Llanelwedd, impressive though they are, lack the raw feeling of people, flaming torches in hand, dancing and singing round a fire as it blazes in the darkness of a summer night.

Autumn

In October, after harvest, walks, fairs and feasts continued. The Crown Club at Knighton (founded in 1770), one of several such bodies in the town, held its celebration on the first day of the month. This is a description of the event in 1876:

> The Crown Friendly Society held their 105th anniversary ... After meeting at the Crown Hotel and calling over the roll, the members walked in procession to the National School, headed by their beau-

tiful new silk banner and the Knighton brass band under the leadership of Mr Charles Lloyd. The Rev. J.B. Brown officiated at the
schoolroom. At the close of the service the procession re-formed
and paraded the town till 2 o'clock, when all adjourned to the
Crown Inn, where an excellent dinner was provided by Mr and Mrs
Haines. ... Upwards of 100 sat down to dinner. After the repast, the
usual toasts were given and duly responded to. From the statement
read by Mr I.P. Davies, the secretary, it appeared that the club is in
a prosperous state, the funds having increased and several new
members joined during the year.

At the end of the month, Hallowe'en (31 October), better known in
Radnorshire as Llan Hallantide, was marked by the baking of a special
Llanhallant Cake and by various rituals for divination (see chapter 5). D.E.
Owen, who included the occasion with the pre-Reformation survivals
which he detected in the county, wrote in 1911:

> the homesteads of Radnorshire were illuminated with rush candles
> to welcome the young people to indulge in games peculiar to the
> occasion and the old people to narrate the folk-lore of the neigh-
> bourhood. The memory of those happy meetings is still green.

He does not specify the games but one assumes that they would have
included apple-bobbing and ducking for pennies. Thanks to commercial
pressures, Hallowe'en is now inundated with plastic facemasks, witches'
cloaks and satanic tridents, supplemented by horror films.

Among various sales and events held in October is the Hundred House
Stock and Agricultural Show, a very good example of a small community's
determination to hold to its own traditions in its own way.

Winter
One of the times when the poor had licence to ask for help from the
better-off was on St Thomas's Day (21 December). They went round
farms and big houses asking for gifts of wheat, which millers then ground
into flour free of charge. The custom, known as thomasing or gooding,
delivered a useful supplement to poor families' Christmas fare. A local
jingle ran: 'A-gooding, a-gooding, to make we a pudding'. At Disserth
the process was slightly abbreviated because flour rather than wheat was
usually donated.

Even in modestly well-off farming families, children did not expect or receive lavish presents at Christmas. A bar of chocolate, an orange and a few pennies made up a typical gift. Mona Morgan remembers such things as an apple, an orange, a sugar mouse, a packet of sweets or a handkerchief in her Christmas stocking. Beside the bed there might be a Noah's Ark, a box of jigsaw bricks or a pencil box.

Decorations, including holly and mistletoe were not put up until Christmas Eve, or even Christmas Day. Church bells rang in the day, as they also rang it out. Chapel and church-goers went to the very early *plygain* (see chapter 6) or the more conventional morning service.

Rev. J.T. Evans wrote of a 90 year-old Cascob woman (born in 1820) who told him that fragments of the Christmas Log were carefully saved from the burning and kept to put on the following year's fire, so preserving the house from accidental ignition. She unwittingly echoed the lines from a poem of 1648 by Robert Herrick:

> Part must be kept wherewith to teend
> The Christmas Log next yeare;
> And where 'tis safely kept, the Fiend
> Can do no mischiefe there.

Until about 1900 a football match was played every year on Christmas Day between Glascwm and Bettws. The respective goals were the two church doorways four miles apart. The teams comprised some 40 men each, and there were very few rules. A similar contest took place on the same day at Dolefawr, near Rhayader, between teams from the Claerwen and Elan valleys.

Meanwhile, handbell ringers went round in Howey; the town band played in Presteigne, and no doubt elsewhere. Carol singers at Knighton ended their performance with this pointed request as they knocked at the door:

> Little robin redbreast sat upon a tree:
> I wish you a merry Christmas, it's a greeting from me.
> With apples to eat, nuts to crack,
> I wish you a merry Christmas with a big rat-tat.

Mona Morgan recalls singers who 'disguised themselves by blackening faces and wearing false beards and moustaches, thus providing a good deal of fun for those working out who they were'.

A different company going round during the 12 days of Christmas was described by Kilvert. The passage does not appear in his published diaries, nor was it seen by William Plomer when he made the selection which appeared in 1938-40. We owe it to Kilvert's niece-by-marriage, Essex Hope. Somewhat confused, Kilvert considered the performance to be a jumble of three events from the bible; he called it 'The Feast of the Ass':

> It was between the Christmasses, and at eight o'clock I was sitting with some other people around the fire, when we heard tramping outside, and a loud knocking on the door, which was locked. There was the sound of a flute a moment later, and a man began singing - then a few minutes later another man, inside the room, went to the door and sang what was apparently an answer to the song without. Then the door was thrown open, and in walked about a dozen people, headed by a most extraordinary apparition, an animal covered by a flowing sheet, and surmounted by a horse's skull, to which a bridle was attached. This apparition, I saw a moment later, was really a man covered with a sheet; his head was bowed down, and a skull had been fastened to it. The people sang, collected some money, and then went off. They ought by rights, apparently, to have had an ass's skull, but then, dead donkeys are proverbially hard to come by.

This undated passage, perhaps relating to Clyro, is a confused account of the 'Mari Lwyd' (Grey Mare), a ritual performed during the 12 days of Christmas in many parts of Wales, which involved a luck-bringing mock horse with various attendants who exchanged partly-improvised song verses with householders before being invited in.

Only one other description from Radnorshire has so far come to light, in a *Wellington Journal* article of 1930 by Roger Williams, whose source was an unnamed 'old gentleman' born at Glascwm who recalled rural life in the 1860s. His invaluable narrative is reprinted here at some length:

> The 'Grey Lady Party' was so much enjoyed and so popular that even after many of the young men had left rural life and gone to work in the industrial districts of South Wales, they would come home in large numbers a fortnight or so before Christmas to prepare for, and join in, the Christmas fun.
>
> Now what was called the 'Grey Lady' was the figure of a horse's head which the party took with them, and a feature of the season's

The Mari Lwyd greeted at the door (David Davies)

amusement was the preparation of this effigy. This would be begun soon after Michaelmas, by obtaining a horse's head and boiling it until all the flesh came off, but great care was taken to preserve the teeth. The bones were then polished until they looked like ivory. Into the back of the skull a prop was fixed; a tongue of white material was cleverly inserted, and arrangements were made for working the jaw. This head was covered in white calico or linen, and the material fell loosely over the man who was to play a great part in the performance of the 'Grey Lady'. Two black ink bottles formed the eyes, and round the rim a white circle was painted. The ears were made from the material of an old felt hat, or a piece of shining leather, and these showed up well over the white cloth. A black leather riding bridle was well devised, and the reins were made of wide ribbons of some bright hue, and to them were fastened streamers of many colours. The finishing touch was putting on the mane, which was formed of plaited ribbons of brilliant hue, set off by the highly coloured rosettes made by the local dressmaker who gave the men-folk a helping hand.

The party responsible for making the 'Grey Lady' having finished their work, the next step was the training of the bearer ready for the event, as his antics had to be performed to order.

During the whole of the time that the party of some half dozen or so were meeting night after night to get the 'Grey Lady' ready, other farm and village lads met in the barns and at the store-rooms of the village mill; if the weather was very cold, the miller would allow the use of his room under the kiln, in front of a lovely fire. Here they practised songs, many of them composed by the lads themselves, and they committed to memory the opening and closing stanzas, which were written in triplet form.

It was not only those who took an active part in the performance of the 'Grey Lady' who were busy, for the farmers and their men were preparing to receive the party with triplet verses from within the house, and after a more or less lengthy combat of wits, the party would be admitted and regaled with home-brewed beer and cake, made in the good old Welsh style by the farmer's wife and daughters and others of the household.

The visit of the 'Grey Lady' was welcomed in every house in the district. On the night of an expected visit all the members of the homestead and a number of visitors would gather round the fire and the conversation would be entirely about the doings of the 'Grey Lady's' party on previous occasions.

My informant told me of a certain farmer who had been entertaining his gathering so well with some of the old verses that he seemed to become inspired and went on composing new triplets with such ease that his hearers were astonished. When it was near midnight on this occasion, the farmer's wife advised the party to disperse saying that the 'Grey Lady' company must have missed their way, but the farmer said he had never known the party to fail in carrying out its programme, and at that moment conversation was interrupted by the announcement that the 'Grey Lady' was at the door, surrounded by a score of the young wits of the district.

The 'Grey Lady' began prancing with the young men shouting 'Whoa Mari fach!'. When at last the 'Grey Lady' consented to stand still, the singing began, the first verses explaining their mission and the difficulties of their journey. These ended with a challenge to those inside to reply to them in verse. The farmer was at once on his feet, answering the outsiders with his ready wit, and the battle of rhyming repartee was in full progress. The party outside sang triplet after triplet and were answered in the same measure from within.

These triplets, or 3-lined verses, were curious. They were composed on the spur of the moment and sung as a solo; the last line was then sung as a chorus, and afterwards the whole triplet as a chorus, concluding with some refrain such as 'Nos heno, nos heno!' which means in English 'To-night, to-night!'.

As the musical conversation proceeded, the voices of the various soloists would be identified, and then the verses might become rather personal. The old ones from within would tell the young men outside things they would have preferred unknown, but in good spirits they would reply by relating some pranks of long ago which the older ones had thought were quite forgotten.

This contest went on sometimes for several hours, but eventually the party outside was allowed to be triumphant, those inside being anxious to see the 'Lady'. The door was thrown open, and those in charge led 'her' in first, followed by the rest of the party, all dressed in novel costumes, with their faces masked or blacked. Now the merry time had arrived, although the children and girls were sometimes half-terrified at the prancing and snapping of 'Mari', and ran away upstairs to hide themselves.

The 'Grey Lady' would dance round the house, turning over chairs and snapping at the pictures on the wall. Then 'she' would take up position in the centre of the kitchen, and all the party would gather round 'her'. She would then take off the cap of one of the party with her teeth and pass it round to the company for contributions. Then the barrel was tapped and the cake cut, and the gathering which had begun with a combat of wits was thoroughly merry and jovial.

When the time for departure came the 'Mari Lwyd' party sang a farewell song, composed for that purpose, expressing what a joyous time they had had and thanking the family for their hospitality. The following is an example of one of the verses:-

And we do hope before we part to taste some of your beer,
Your beer, your beer, your Christmas beer, that seems to be so
    strong;
And we do wish that Christmastide was twenty times so long.
Then sing with voices cheerfully for Christ this time was born,
Who did from death deliver us when we were all forlorn.

On New Year's Day children went round 'gifting'. Minna Barron, writing of late Victorian times at Presteigne, quotes a rhyme they chanted:

The cock flew up the yew tree, the hen went cackling by.
If you haven't got a penny please to gimme a mincepie.

A supply of apples, oranges, pennies and ha'pennies was kept ready for the expected young callers. Mona Morgan remembers a fuller version of the rhyme:

> New Year's gift! New Year's gift!
> We wish you a merry Christmas and a happy New Year,
> A pocket full of money and a cellar full of beer,
> A good fat pig to last you all the year.
> So please give us a New Year's gift this new year.
> The roads are very dirty, our boots are very thin,
> We have a little pocket to pop a penny in.
> The cock was in the roosting-house, the hen came chuckling by,
> Please give us a penny or a mince pie.
> If you haven't a penny a ha'penny will do,
> If you haven't a ha'penny God bless you.
> New Year's gift! New Year's gift!
> Please give us a New Year's gift this new year.

She suggests that gifting had more or less died out by the time of the First World War but in the 1950s Iona and Peter Opie found from a 13 year-old Radnorshire schoolgirl that the custom was still very much alive: 'On January 1st I always go New Year's gifting with my sister and friends, about four of us. I get up about 7 o'clock and call for my friends and go round the houses and farms', she said. The words sung were very similar to Morgan's lines two to six, with the same incongruous mention of Christmas which by then was seven days past. Perhaps Christmas here refers to the 12 days.

The girl added that they collected nine or ten shillings every year, though people sometimes gave apples or mincepies instead of money. An important guideline was: 'You must be gone before twelve o'clock or they will call you a fool and the people won't give you anything, and when the people see you next time they will shout fool at you'. Some of the girls in villages such as Bleddfa or Llangynllo added their gifting money to the proceeds of their earlier carol singing to pay for a special outing to Knighton.

Soon after midnight on New Year's Eve women visited certain wells such as one at Disserth (see chapter 1) to draw water which was thus the first of the new year. The cream of the well, as it was called, had medicinal properties, or so participants believed. At the same time farm labourers were setting off for the fields to 'burn the bush' — though the ceremony involved neither a bush nor its complete burning. A hollow globe made of hawthorn shoots was singed in turn in a series of small fires of brushwood and wheat straw lit in each of a farm's wheat fields. The men, fortified during their task by plenty of beer or cider, took the 'bush' back to the farmhouse, where it would be carefully preserved until the same day in the following year. At Cascob, and undoubtedly elsewhere, the ritual was thought to preserve the wheat from a disease called 'smuts'.

'From Chapel Farm at Bettws, at three o'clock on the morning of New Year's Day', wrote Kilvert, 'I have seen the valley of the Wye alight and twinkling with fires, "burning, the bush" at almost every point'. He went on to describe a variation on the ceremony: 'On Twelfth Night (old Christmas Eve) [5 January] twelve fires were lighted in wheatfields on many farms; they were believed to represent the Twelve Apostles, and to prevent the wheat from becoming "blue-ended"'.

In the absence of a detailed account from Radnorshire it seems useful to give details of the custom just a mile over the Herefordshire border near Gladestry. A letter, signed J.W., in the 1820 *Gentleman's Magazine*, says that at Mr Tully's farm in Huntington the men walked into the wheatfields and at 6 pm lit one large and twelve smaller fires on high ground. They shouted toasts, drank cider, and returned to the farmhouse for supper, followed by songs. At 9 or 10 in the evening a second procession went into the byres, drank to each of the 24 oxen in turn, and sang an appropriate verse such as:

> Here's to thee, Benbow, and to thy white horn.
> God send thy master a good crop of corn,
> Of wheat, rye and barley and all sorts of grain.
> You eat your oats and I'll drink my beer:
> May the Lord send us all a happy New Year.

Next a cake was fixed on one of the horns of the leading ox. A boy then touched the animal with a goad, causing it to toss its head and dislodge the cake, which the bailiff then divided amongst the company. Back in the farmhouse more eating, drinking and merrymaking followed, going on until the early hours of Twelfth Day.

There was a persistent belief that at cock-crow on the same day (Old Christmas Day), cattle knelt in their byres. (Some apparently thought that only animals of seven years old and upwards were involved, which would mean few indeed). Rev. W.E.T. Morgan passed on a story told to him by a Llanigon woman who in turn acquired it from a young man when she was in service at Michaelchurch-on-Arrow:

> On the night of the 12th Eve, Old Christmas, all the oxen that reached the age of five years (oxen were then used for ploughing and were allowed to live to that age) fell on their knees as the hour of 12 struck, and remained kneeling for some time. The man told her that he had once seen the sight, the oxen falling on their knees, sighing and groaning piteously, with tears rolling from their eyes in torrents, a sight he never wished to see again, so painful was it.

The same day saw the flowering of Glastonbury thorns believed to be scions of the tree which had grown from Joseph of Arimathea's staff when he planted it in the ground of Glastonbury Tor in Somerset. Two of these were thought to bloom in Radnorshire on opposite sides of the county at Newbridge-on-Wye and Norton respectively, but there seem to be no recent reports of the phenomenon.

Soon after Old Christmas comes St Hilary's Day (13 January). On the following Monday at Llanbister a curious ceremony known as Knife Money or Clwt-y-Cyllell (literally the Welsh for 'knife rag') takes place. Essentially it involves bidding to decide who should collect rents on Crown land in the area during the ensuing year.

Norton church, where a scion of the Glastonbury thorn was reported, in years past, to flower on Old Christmas Day

235

The proceedings end at noon, and the lowest bidder obtains the appointment. Those concerned meet in King's Rent Hole Field on Tyn-yr-ynn Farm, and to register a bid a person (who must be resident within the manor) enters a hole cut in a bank and repeats this time-honoured formula: 'I have come here to take the collection of the Chief's Rent for one year, the year ---- to ---- on all married occupiers, at one-half on single occupiers, widows and all bytakes, the occupier living inside the Manor, the full amount on the occupier living outside the Manor'.

The ceremony has been known for 200 years but must go back much further than that because the rents are expressed in multiples of a groat (4d.) and range between 4d. and 13s. 4d. It might be said that in this way the ritual year in Radnorshire ends—or begins—not with a bang but a whimper.

Bibliography

Abbreviations
HJ: *Hereford Journal*
HT: *Hereford Times*
TRS: *Transactions of the Radnorshire Society*
TWN: *Transactions of the Woolhope Naturalists' Field Club*

Books are published in London unless otherwise shown

Anonymous, 'Dr John Dee', TRS, 3 (1933), 10-14
    A Journey to Llandrindod Wells ... by a Countryman (1746)
    'A New Election Song', ed. R.C.B. Oliver, TRS, 57 (1987), 80-3
    Radnorshire County Handbook, Cheltenham (nd)
    'Summer Rambles in Wales', *Cambrian Quarterly Magazine*, 1 (1829),
        121-132
    Tales of Old Inns, 2nd ed. (1929)
Aubrey, John (1626-97), *Brief Lives*, ed. J. Buchanan-Brown (2000)
    Remaines of Gentilisme and Judaisme, in *Three Prose Works*, ed.
        J. Buchanan-Brown, Fontwell (1972)
Avery, Gillian, *Call of the Valley* (1966)
Bannister, A.T., 'The Hereford Miracles', TWN (1905), 377-83
Barber, Chris, *Mysterious Wales* (1983)
Baring-Gould, Sabine (1834-1924), *A Book of South Wales* (1905)
Barrell, John, 'The Australian Convicts of Radnorshire', TRS, 60 (1990), 27-31
Barron, Minna A., 'Presteigne in Late Victorian Days', TRS, 25 (1955), 4-7
Bidgood, Ruth, 'Cattle and sheep-droving in the Abergwesyn area', *Signposts*,
    no. 21 (Mar. 2000), 4
Biggerton-Evans, Kathleen A., *History and Description of Gladestry Church and
    Parish*, Gladestry (1922)
Black, Jeremy, *A New History of Wales*, Stroud (1922)
Black, W.G., 'On Colour in Folk Medicine', *The Antiquary*, 1 (1880), 110-113
Bonser, K.J., *The Drovers* (1970)
Booth, R. (comp.), *Rhayader Guide*, np (1981)
Bord, Janet and Colin, *The Secret Country* (1976)
Bradley, A.G., *Highways and Byways in South Wales* (1903)
    The Romance of Wales (1929)
Bradney, Joseph A., 'Pilleth, Nant-y-groes, and Monaughty', TWN (1925),
    185-92
Bright, Geoffrey (ed.), *A Short History of the Radnorshire and West
    Herefordshire Hunt*, Hereford (1961)

Brown, Roper L., 'St Harmon: Before and After Kilvert', TRS, 63 (1993), 61-68
Bryans, W.S., 'Place Names in the Llangunllo District', TRS, 3 (1933), 57
Bufton, W.J. (1872-96), revised J.O. Bufton, *Illustrated Guide to Llandrindod Wells* (1906; orig. 1897)
Cannadine, David, *History in Our Time* (1998)
Charters, Alan, *Aspects of Aberedw*, Aberedw (1993)
Cheese, Edmund H., 'Painscastle-in-Elfael, Radnorshire, TWN (1887)
Clarke, Elizabeth (1910- ?), *The Valley* (1969)
Cole, E.J., 'Schedule of Radnorshire Place Names. Parish of Llowes', TRS, 5 (1935), 68-75
　　'Parish of Bryngwyn', TRS, 7 (1937), 71-76
　　'Parish of Llanstephan', TRS, 8 (1938), 18-22
Cole, E.J.L., 'Thieves, Robbers and Gaol-breakers', TRS, 35 (1965), 30-2
　　'William Henry Howse', TRS, 35 (1965), 8-9
Cooke, David, and Grant, John, *Grant's Guide to Hay-on-Wye, Talgarth and the Black Mountains*, Hay (nd.)
Crystal, David, 'Death Sentence', *Guardian*, 2nd section (25 Oct. 1999), 2-3
Cyngor Sir Powys/Powys County Council, *Cynllun Iaith Gymraeg/ Welsh Language Scheme*, Llandrindod Wells (1995)
Davies, David (1849-1926), *John Vaughan and his Friends*, np (1897)
Davies, David Rees (incumbent at Nantmel, 1936-50), articles in *Radnor Times* (1 Nov. 1952, 8 Nov. 1952, 17 Jan. 1953, 13 Jun. 1953, 18 Jul. 1953, 25 Jul. 1953, 8 Aug. 1953)
　　'St David and Radnorshire', TRS, 46 (1976), 73-77
Davies, D. Stedman, 'How old is this Church?', TRS, 20 (1945), 38-40
　　'Llangynllo', TRS, 12 (1942), 64-71
　　'Radnorshire Inns', TRS, 11 (1941), 3-19
　　'Yew Trees in the Churchyards', TRS, 15 (1945), 33-8
Davies, Edith Ellen, *The Health-Giving Wonders of Llandrindod Wells. How They Were First Discovered. The Legend of Pengrych of the Curly Head*, Haverfordwest (nd.)
Davies, Edward (1756-1831), *Celtic Researches* (1804)
Davies, Elwyn, *Rhestr o Enwan Lleoedd/A Gazetteer of Welsh Place-Names*, Cardiff (1967)
Davies, Owen, 'Charmers and Charming in England and Wales from the Eighteenth to the Twentieth Century', *Folklore*, 109 (1998). 41-53
　　'Cunning-Folk in England and Wales during the Eighteenth and Nineteenth Centuries', *Rural History*, 8, pt 1 (1997), 91-107
　　'Cunning-Folk in the Medical Market Place during the Nineteenth Century', *Medical History*, 43 (1999), 55-73
　　Witchcraft, Magic and Culture, 1736-1951, Manchester (1999)
Davies, T.P., 'Llandrindod Wells in the Eighteenth Century', TRS, 4 (1934), 10-16

BIBLIOGRAPHY

'Schedule of Radnorshire Place Names. Cefnllys Parish', TRS, 2 (1932), 31-38

'Parish of Llanfihangel Helygen', TRS, 10 (1940), 67-70

Davies, W. Ll., 'The Conjuror in Montgomeryshire', *Montgomeryshire Collections* (1937-40), 45-6; 158-70

Dawson, M.L., 'Notes on the History of Glasbury', *Archaeologia Cambrensis*, 6th ser., 18 (1918), 6-34; and 7th ser., 3 (1923), 279-319

'Painscastle and its Story', *Archaeologia Cambrensis*, 7th ser., 3 (1923), 28-52

Draper, Brian, *The River Teme from its Source to the River Severn*, Martley (nd)

Drayton, Michael (1563-1631), *Polyolbion* (1612-22)

Dunn, Elizabeth, 'Owain Glyndŵr and Radnorshire', TRS, 27 (1967), 27-35

Edwards, Anthony, *Appointment in Aberedwy*, Tregarth (1992)

The Massacre at Aberedw, Tregarth (1999)

Fairs, Geoffrey L., *A History of the Hay. The Story of Hay-on-Wye*, London and Chichester (1972)

Farmer, David Hugh, *The Oxford Dictionary of Saints*, Oxford, (1988; orig. 1978)

Fenn, R.W.D., 'The Cult of Thomas Becket and the Welsh Marches', TRS, 54 (1984), 17-29

Sanctuaries and Saints. An Essay on the Churches and Saints of Brecon and Radnor, np (1964)

and J.B. Sinclair, 'Old Radnor Parish Church', TRS, 58 (1988), 78-91

Fisher, J., 'Welsh Church Dedications', *Transactions of the Honourable Society of Cymmrodorion* (1908), 76-108

Fisk, Eugene, *Clyro*, Clyro (1988)

Florence of Worcester, *A History of the Kings of England*, trans. J. Stevenson, Felinfach (1988)

Frankenburg, Ronald, *Communities in Britain. Social Life in Town and Country*, Harmondsworth (1966)

Fraser, Maxwell, *West of Offa's Dyke. South Wales* (1958)

Frere, Sheppard, *Britannia. A History of Roman Britain* (1978; orig. 1967)

Friar, Stephen, *A Companion to the English Parish Church*, Stroud (1996)

G., E., 'Nature's Pharmacopoeium. A Description of Llandrindod Wells, in Rhadnorshire [*sic*], in 1748', *Gentleman's Magazine*, 18 (1748), 469

Gardner, Don, *Discovering Mid-Wales*, Cardiff (1978)

Geoffrey of Monmouth, *The History of the Kings of Britain*, trans. L.Thorpe, Harmondsworth (1968)

Gerald of Wales, *The Journey through Wales*, trans. L. Thorpe, Harmondsworth (1978)

Gibbings, Robert, *Coming down the Wye* (1942)

Gilbert, H.A., *The Tale of a Wye Fisherman* (1928)

Godwin, Fay, and Shirley Toulson, *The Drovers' Roads of Wales* (1977)
Gregory, Donald, *Radnorshire: A Historical Guide*, Llanrwst (1994)
Green, Jennifer, *The Morning of her Day. The Story of Mary Morgan* (1987)
Grice, Frederick, *Francis Kilvert and his World* (nd)
    'Kilvert and Folklore', *Folklore*, 85 (1974), 199-201
Griffiths, Ralph, 'Some secret supporters of Owain Glyn Dŵr?', *Bulletin of the Institute of Historical Research*, 37 (1964), 77-100
Grigson, Geoffrey, *The Englishman's Flora* (1958)
Gwyndaf, Robin, 'The Past in the Present: Folk Beliefs in Welsh Oral Tradition', *Fabula*, 15 (1994), 226-60
Hamer, W. Bowen ('Elan') (died 1948), 'Notes on the Antiquities of Radnorshire', HJ (Nov. 1907 - Oot. 1909)
    Radnorshire in History, Topography and Romance, Llandrindod Wells (1914)
Hatfield, William, *Knighton and District*, Hereford (1947)
Haycock, Marged, 'Lewys Glyn Cothi and Radnorshire', TRS, 64 (1994), 25-35
Heuken, Elissa P., *National Redeemer. Owain Glyndŵr in Welsh Tradition,* Cardiff (1996)
Hereford, John, *The May Fair* (1948)
Hodges, Geoffrey, *Owain Glyn Dŵr*, Almeley (1995)
Holmes, Richard, *Shelley. The Pursuit* (1974)
[Horsey, George], *The Trail of the Black Ox*, [Builth Wells] (nd)
Houlder, Christopher, *Wales: an Archaeological Guide* (1974)
Howells, W., *Cambrian Superstitions*, Tipton (1831); repr. Felinfach (1991)
Howse, W.H. (1884-1966), *Disserth, Radnorshire: Its Church and its History and Folk-lore*, Llandrindod Wells (1952)
    The History and Legend of Stapleton Castle, Leominster [1946]
    'Knighton and Rebecca', TRS, 13 (1943), 54-5
    'Llanbister Church', TWN (1958), 165-6
    Norton, Radnorshire. The Story of a Country Parish, Presteigne [1952]
    'Notes on Glascwm', TRS, 21 (1951), 24-34
    'Notes on the History of Glasbury', TRS, 18 (1948), 30-1
    Old-Time Rhayader, Llandrindod Wells [1951]
    Place Names and Charities of Presteigne, Leominster (1946)
    'The Practice of Witchcraft', HT (1 Dec. 1961)
    'Radnor Miseellany', TRS, 22 (1952), 72-7; and 23 (1953), 69-77
    Radnor Old and New, Hereford (1944)
    Radnorshire, Hereford (1949)
    '*Radnorshire*. Some Corrections and Additions', TRS, 29 (1949), 3-11
    'Radnorshire Dialect', TRS, 30 (1960), 41; and 32 (1962), 68
    'Ranorshire Inns', TRS 15 (1945)' 54-7
    'The Speech of Radnorshire', TRS, 22 (1952)' 58-63

BIBLIOGRAPHY

Welsh Border Town. Presteigne: Its Story, Romance, and Pleasures for Travellers, Presteigne [1956]

Hughes, Colin, 'A Very Creditable Portion of Welsh History? The Rebecca Riots in Radnorshire', TRS, 67 (1997), 101-116

Hultin, Neil C. 'The Songs and Ballads of R.F. Kilvert', *Folklore*, 92, pt 2 (1981), 174-189

Hutchinson, John, 'Charles I in Breconshire and Radnorshire', TWN (1914), 217-220

James, J. Luther, 'Schedule of Radnorshire Place Names. Glascwm', TRS, 9 (1930), 29-40

Jervoise, E., *The Ancient Bridges of Wales and Western England* (1936)

Jones, Anne E., 'Folk Medicine in Living Memory in Wales', *Folk Life*, 18 (1980), 58-68

Jones, David, 'Schedule of Radnorshire Place Names. The Parish of Disserth and the Township of Trecoed', TRS, 2 (1932), 26-30

Jones, John, *The Colva Legend. The Giant's Grave of Red Wolf Gethin*, Kington (1942)

Jones, John, *History of the Baptists in Radnorshire* (1895)

Jones, John B., *Offa's Dyke Path* (1976)

Jones, P. Thoresby, *Welsh Border Country* (1949; orig. 1938)

Jones, T. Thornley, 'The Giants' Graves', TRS, 21 (1951), 49-52

Jones, Theophilus, *A History of the County of Brecknock*, Brecknock (1898; orig. 1805)

Jordan, Albert, *History of the Church and Parish of Llanbadarn-Fawr, Radnorshire*, Brecon (1926)

Kightly, Charles, *Country Voices* (1984)

Kilvert, Robert Francis (1840-79), *The Diary of Francis Kilvert, April-June 1870*, ed. K. Hughes and D. Ifans, Aberystwyth (1982)

   Kilvert's Diary, ed. W. Plomer (3 vols, 1938-40)

   'Radnorshire Legends and Superstitions', ed. E. Hope, *Occult Review* (1921), 152-160; repr. TRS, 24 (1954), 4-12

Lawrence, Bryan, 'Llaithddu, David's Well, and New Well', TRS, 62 (1992), 66-72

Leather, E.M., *The Folk-lore of Herefordshire*, Hereford (1912)

   'Herefordshire Folk Tales: Black Vaughan of Hergest', *Herefordshire Magazine*, 1 (1907), 26-30

   'Scraps of English [*sic*] Folklore: Monmouthshire and Radnorshire', *Folklore*, 24 (1913), 110

Leversedge, Cherry, (comp.), *Pictorial Radnorshire of Bygone Days*, np (1989)

Lewis, George F., *Haber Nant Llan Nerch Freit. An Upbringing on a Radnorshire Hill Farm*, Almeley (1998)

Lewis, M. Gwyneth, *Printed Maps of Radnorshire, 1578-1900*, Aberystwyth (1977)

Lewis, R. Stedman, 'The Cupboard is not bare', TRS, 35 (1965), 51-4

Lias, Anthony, *Place Names of the Welsh Borderlands*, Ludlow (1991)

Lipscomb, G., *Journey into South Wales ... in the Year 1799* (1802)

Lloyd, Allun R., 'The Anglicisation of Welsh Place Names in the New Radnor Area', TRS, 29 (1949), 55-8

Lockwood, David, 'Francis Kilvert and Radnorshire', TRS, 63 (1993), 55-60

Maddox, Wilfred. C., 'Disserth Church: A Pastoral Dissertation on a Venerable Edifice', unpublished typescript (1965)

    'A Presteigne Tragedy in the Year 1805', unpublished typescript (1965)

    'Radnorshire Customs and Superstitions', unpublished typescript (1965)

    'Some Radnorshire Epitaphs', TRS, 35 (1965), 58-65

    'Welsh Folk-lore, Customs and Superstitions', unpublished typescript (1965)

Malkin, Benjamin Heath (1769-1842), *The Scenery, Antiquities, and Biography of South Wales* (2 vols, 1804)

Marshall, George, 'The Fedw Stone Circle in the Parish of Glascwm, Radnorshire', TWN (1930), 119-22

Massingham, H.J., *The Southern Marches* (1950)

Mayhew, A.L., 'Some Radnorshire Words', *Notes & Queries*, 5th ser., 10 (10 Aug. 1878), 105

Minhinnick, Robert, *Selected Poems*, Manchester (1999)

Moore, H. Cecil, 'Water-break-its-neck', TWN (1893-4), 47-55

Morgan, Mona M. (1916-), *Growing Up in Kilvert Country. Recollections of a Radnorshire Childhood*, Llandysul (1990)

Morgan, W.E.T., 'A Few Folk- and Other Stories', TWN (1928), 96-103

    Hay and Neighbourhood, Hay (1932)

    'Llowes', TWN (1925), 221-3

    'Radnorshire Words', manuscript held by the Radnorshire Society

    'Rhosgoch and Painscastle', TWN (1911), 212-17

Moseley, A.J., 'Parish of Llanbister', TR3, 3 (1933), 41-5

    and T.P. Davies, 'Place-names in the Parish of Llanbister', TRS, 3 (1933), 46-56

Murray, Nicholas, 'Bruce Chatwin's Radnorshire', TRS, 62 (1992), 13-16

Newbery, Esylt (1881- ?), *Parson's Daughter Again* (1960)

Newbury, Robert, *St David's Church, Cregrina, Radnorshire. Some Notes on the History of the Church and Parish*, Cregrina (1958)

Norman, Robert E.P., 'Fair Rosamond', *Herefordshire Magazine*, 1 (1907), 222-9

Oliver, R.C.B., 'The Complaint of New Radnor Church', TRS, 48 (1978), 40-7

    'Jonathan Williams and his *History of Radnorshire*', TRS, 40 (1970), 11-20

    'The Gwardole Letters of 1843', TRS, 62 (1992), 17-37

    'The Shelleys of Radnorshire', TRS, 41 (1971), 8-21

BIBLIOGRAPHY

Opie, Iona and Peter, *The Lore and Language of Schoolchildren* (1959)

Opie, Iona, and Moira Tatem (eds), *A Dictionary of Superstitions*, Oxford (1989)

Owen, David Edmondes (1866-1922), 'Notes on the Antiquities of the Parish of Llanelwedd', TRS, 18 (1948), 3-20

    'Pre-Reformation Survivals in Radnorshire', *Transactions of the Honourable Society of Cymmrodorion*, (1910-11), 92-114

Owen, Elias, 'Folk-lore, Superstition, or what-not, in Montgomeryshire', *Montgomeryshire Collections*, 15 (1882), 121-154

Owen, Trefor M., *Welsh Folk Customs*, Cardiff (1959)

Palmer, Roy, *The Folklore of (old) Monmouthshire*, Almeley (1998)

Palmer, William T., *The Verge of Wales* (1942)

Parker, Keith, *A History of Presteigne*, Almeley (1997)

    Radnorshire from Civil War to Restoration, Almeley (2000)

Parris, Patricia, 'Mary Morgan: Contemporary Sources', TRS, 53 (1983), 57-64

Parry, Edward, *Royal Visits and Progresses in Wales*, Chester (1850)

Parry, Richard, *The Further Recordings of Richard Parry, the Kington Historian*, ed. J. Southwood, Kington (1984)

Parry-Jones, Daniel (1891-1981), *A Welsh Country Parson* (1975)

Payne, Fransis G., *Crwydro Sir Faesyfed*, Llandebïe (2 vols, 1966-8)

Peate, Iorwerth C., *The Denbigh Cockpit and Cockfighting in Wales*, Cardiff (1970)

Pettigrew, Thomas Joseph, *On Superstitions Concerned with the History and Practice of Medicine and Surgery* (1844)

Portman, C.G., *The Sacred Stones, Sacred Trees, and Holy Wells of Hay and the Neighbourhood*, Hay (1907)

Potts, W.H., *Roaming down the Wye* (1949)

Powys County Record Office, *The Archive Photographs Series: Radnorshire*, Stroud (1997)

Pretty, David, *The Rural Revolt that Failed - Farm Workers' Trade Unions in Wales, 1889-1950*, Cardiff (1989)

Price, Hetty (1874 - ?), 'Cwmdauddwr Memories', with foreword. by T.P. Vaughan Prichard, TRS, 18 (1948), 46-51

Prothero, Taffy (1901-96), *Dear Pamela. Letters from a Radnorshire Farm*, Almeley (1997)

Prys-Jones, A.G., 'On Radnor Forest', TRS, 4 (1934), 17-18

Pugh, Jonathan Argoed, 'The Parish and Place Names of St Harmon', TRS, 4 (1934), 33-54

Ralph-Bowman, Peter (1913-97), *Ah-Yes. An Introspective Retrospect*, Leominster (1999)

Rees, Alwyn and Brinley, *Celtic Heritage. Ancient Tradition in Ireland and Wales* (1961)

Rees, G.N., *The Mother Church of North Radnor. St Cynllo's Church, Llanbister*, [Llanbister] (1995; orig. 1972)

Rees, William Jenkins, *Lives of the Cambro-British Saints*, Llandovery (1853)
Remfrey, Paul Martin, *Castles of Radnorshire*, Almeley (1996)
Rossetti, William M., 'Shelley at Cwm Elan and Nantgwilt', in Tickell, 17-35
Scandrett, William, 'Llandrindod Wells. A Poem', ed. R.C.B. Oliver, TRS, 57 (1987), 74-9
Sharpe, Frederick, *The Church Bells of Radnorshire*, Brackley (1947)
Sibley, F.W., 'Schedule of Radnorshire Place Names. Parish of Llanbadarn-Fynydd', TRS, 2 (1932), 39-44
Sikes, Wirt, *British Goblins: Welsh Folk-lore, Fairy Mythology, Legends and Traditions* (1880)
   Rambles and Studies in Old South Wales (1881)
Simpson, Jacqueline, 'Fifty British Dragon Tales: an Analysis', *Folklore*, 89, pt 1 (1978), 79-93
   The Folklore of the Welsh Border (1976)
   and Steve Roud, *A Dictionary of English Folklore*, Oxford (2000)
Sinclair, J.B., and R.W.D. Fenn, *Old Radnor Parish Church. A Short History*, np (1991; orig. 1988)
Snell, P.J., *The Celtic Borderland* (nd)
Stephens, Meic (comp. and ed.), *The Oxford Companion to the Literature of Wales*, Oxford (1986)
Stone, Moira K., *Mid Wales Companion*, Oswestry (1989)
Suggett, Richard, 'Festivals and Social Structures in Early Modern Wales', *Past and Present*, no. 152 (Aug. 1996), 79-112
Thomas, E. Aubrey, 'Shearing in a North Radnorshire Farm', TRS, 14 (1944), 66-8
Thomas, E.B., 'Breconshire Village Folklore', *Folk Lore* (1913), 505-17
Thomas, Keith, *Religion and the Decline of Magic* (1971)
Thomas, S.P., 'Twelve Miles a Day: Some Thoughts on the Drovers', TRS, 54 (1984), 58-66
Thompson, E.P., *Customs in Common* (1991)
Tickell, R. Eustace, *The Vale of Nantgwilt* (1894)
Toulson, Shirley, *see* Godwin
Trevelyan, Marie, *Folk-Lore and Folk-Stories of Wales* (1909)
Turner, Thomas, *Narrative of a Journey, Associated with a Fly, from Gloucester to Aberystwyth, July 31 - September 8, 1837* (1840)
Tudor, O.Ll.R. and J.H. Lloyd, *Some Notes Historical and Descriptive of the Churches and Parishes of Aberedw and Llanfaredd*, Cardiff (1917)
Vaughan-Thomas, Wynford, and Alun Llewellyn, *The Shell Guide to Wales* (1973)
Venables-Llewelyn, C.L.D., 'Schedule of Radnorshire Place Names. Parish of Llanyre', TRS, 1 (1931), 17-31
Watkins, Alfred, *The Old Straight Track* (1925)

Watkins, W., 'Llanfihangel Rhydithon Seventy Years Ago', TRS, 4 (1934), 24-9;
    5 (1935), 40-9
    'Radnorshire Musings', TRS, 10 (1940), 27-34
Watkins, W.J.H., 'A Cycle of Stories Current in Radnorshire', *Folklore*, 43
    (1932), 424-7; also in TRS, 2 (1932), 4-6
Weale, W.A.J., 'Some Radnorshire Place-names', TRS, 8 (1938), 30-7
Webb, John and T.W., *Memorials of the Civil War between King Charles I and
    the Parliament of England* (2 vols, 1879)
Westwood, Jennifer, *Albion. A Guide to Legendary Britain* (1987; orig.1985)
W.I. Members (principally Mrs J.A.P. Thomas), 'Field Names of Radnorshire',
    unpublished typescript (8 vols, 1988) in Llandrindod Wells Library
Williams, Jonathan (1754-1929), *The History of Radnorshire*, Tenby (1859);
    repr. Brecon (1905) and Rhayader (1999)
Williams, Roger, 'Aberedw and District', TWN (1940), 88-93
    as W.R., 'The Grey Lady - an old Radnorshire Custom', *Wellington
        Journal* (27 Dec. 1930)
    'Schedule of Radnorshire Place Names. Parish of Llanfaredd', TRS, 1
        (1931), 37-41
    '... Aberedw', *id.*, 42-6
    '... Llandrindod', *id.*, 47-8
    '... Knighton', *id.*, 49-52
Williams, Sylvia, *Llyswen & Boughrood. A Visitor's Guide to the Area*, np
    (1994, 2nd ed.)
Wood, James G., 'Radnor as a Place Name', TWN (1911)
Wright, Sid[ney Arthur], *Silver John*, Hereford [1943]
    Up the Claerwen, Birmingham (1948)
Wynn-Jones, Walford, *A Guide to the Church of Our Lady of Pilleth*, np (1989)
Young, Francis Brett (1884-1954), *The House Under the Water* (1932)

Index

Place names are given in the version commonly used, with correct Welsh forms added where appropriate in brackets. Variant spellings may be found in passages quoted in the text, where authors' preferences have been respected. Numbers in italics (except reference to prelim pages) refer to illustrations.

INDEX

Also from Logaston Press

Churches of Herefordshire & their Treasures
by John Leonard   ISBN 1 873827 91 1   £12.95

This book is an exploration of Herefordshire's churches. It is not a straight gazetteer, for the author is concerned to place the churches in context, to tell the story of their evolution over a thousand years, and to indicate those buildings which are most rewarding to visit because of their architectural, artistic or religious interest.

Introductory chapters tell of the origins of the churches, of the influence of the Welsh, Anglo-Saxons and the Normans; there then follows a description of the treasures of the churches—the Herefordshire School of Romanesque Sculpture; the fonts; roofs; screens; stained glass; memorials and effigies which enrich the great majority of our churches.

The book then divides the county into areas in which the author indicates his personal choice of the medieval churches that he considers to be the most interesting to visit. All the medieval churches appear in the gazetteer of each area, often with reference back to the earlier chapters. Finally, the post-medieval churches, from the 17th to the 20th centuries, are considered across the county as a whole.

This book is richly endowed with illustrations, containing over 290 photos and plans, some of them dating from the 1800s.

Also from Logaston Press
Monuments in the Landscape Series

Vol. III Castles of Radnorshire
by Paul Remfry ISBN 1 873827 54 7   £7.95

Paul Remfry, who studied the history of the Welsh Princes of Central Wales in some depth whilst undertaking his M.A., is also a keen explorer and interpreter of castles.

The history of Radnorshire from the time of the Norman conquest up until the end of the 13th century is covered in detail, providing the background for the period when most of the castles were built and in use. In a separate gazetteer Paul then weaves this information together with that specific to each site and examination of what lies on the ground, to create a picture of each castle, its owners, its use and eventual demise.

Vol. III Castles of Breconshire
by Paul Remfry ISBN 1 873827 80 6   £8.95

It was not long after the Norman kings had completed their great tax survey, The Domesday Book, that a series of attacks was launched on Wales. in Breconshire during 1093 the forces led by Bernard Neufmarché were establishing a walled town, priory and castle on the river Honddu at Brecon, the castle proving capable of defence in almost all the subsequent conflicts.

The first part of the book details the campaigns which led to the building, capture, destruction and possible rebuilding of the castles of Breconshire. It relates the various allegiances between Normans, English and Welsh, with marriage often used to strengthen title, or expand territorial gains. The second part takes each castle in turn, giving its history, and describing what is left or is likely to be beneath the vegetated mounds and hollows.

Also from Logaston Press

Radnorshire from Civil War to Restoration
A study of the county and its environs 1640-60
in a regional setting
by Keith Parker   ISBN 1 973827 86 5 (Pbk) £12.95
ISBN 1 873827 96 2 (Hbk) £18.95

Whilst this book is a record of the social, political, religious and military state of affairs in Radnorshire from before the Civil War to the Restoration, by its nature much reference is made to events in neighbouring counties and further afield. Many of those affecting Radnorshire had a base elsewhere, and the military almost universally operated from outside the county.

Keith Parker has made much use of primary sources of information to confound the generally held view that Radnorshire was both a poor county at the time of the Civil War and essentially Royalist in outlook. A more confusing picture emerges of strongly held views by a few on each side, though most notably the pro-Parliamentarians, in a sea of neutrality, bewilderment and opportunism.

This is a story of Radnorshire gentry, farmers and clergymen caught up in an age of both danger and vibrant political and religious debate, when many had a rare chance to shape the future.

Keith Parker, a native of Kington and graduate of Birmingham and London Universities, lives in Presteigne where he was formerly deputy head of John Beddoes School. For many years he has lectured on local history for the Extra-mural Department of the University of Wales, Aberystwyth, and for the Workers' Educational Association. 1997 saw the publication of his popularly acclaimed *A History of Presteigne*, also published by Logaston Press.